The parish registers of
England

J. Charles Cox

Alpha Editions

This edition published in 2019

ISBN : 9789353869595

Design and Setting By
Alpha Editions
email - alphaedis@gmail.com

THE
PARISH REGISTERS
OF ENGLAND

BY

J. CHARLES COX, LL.D., F.S.A.

"EVERY PARISH MUST HAVE A HISTORY, EVERY PARISH
HAS A REGISTER, EVERY PERSON HAS A PARISH."
BISHOP STUBBS

WITH TWENTY-FOUR ILLUSTRATIONS

METHUEN & CO. LTD.
36 ESSEX STREET W.C.
LONDON

IT IS A GRATIFICATION

TO INSCRIBE THESE PAGES

TO MY OLD FRIEND

ROBERT MEYRICKE SERJEANTSON, M.A., F.S.A.

RECTOR OF ST. PETER'S, NORTHAMPTON

AS A SMALL TOKEN OF MY GRATITUDE

FOR THE VERY CONSIDERABLE ASSISTANCE

HE HAS SO FREELY RENDERED

TOWARDS THEIR PRODUCTION

PREFACE

IT is just half a century since I began, in the year 1860, making extracts from parish registers in West Somerset, where my father was beneficed, a pursuit followed up with some success a few years later in my own county of Derbyshire. At that time the only work on the subject was *The History of Parish Registers in England*, by Mr. J. S. Burn, published in 1829. A second edition, considerably extended, was issued in 1862. With the latter were incorporated the salient points of the same writer's brief book entitled *History of the Fleet Registers*. Mr. Burn's book, long since out of print, is still of value, and contains a variety of legal information, but it is ill digested throughout and confusedly arranged.

In 1870 Mr. R. E. Chester Waters reprinted a pamphlet on parish registers from the pages of *The Home and Foreign Review*. A few years later, I learnt, through a friend, of Mr. Waters' intention to extend and reprint his treatise, and, knowing how he was crippled by infirmities, I put a variety of extracts at his disposal and gave some assistance in other ways. The book issued by Mr. Chester Waters in 1882, under the title of *Parish Registers in England, their History and Contents*, had become expanded from a pamphlet of three sheets into a compact little volume of 122 pages. This work, a great improvement upon the straggling chapters of Burn's bigger book, was much appreciated, especially by the clergy; but it has been long out of print, and difficult to procure through second-hand agencies.

Meanwhile, I kept steadily before my mind the hope of producing a book which, whilst based upon the labours of my predecessors, Burn and Waters, should strike out a wider line of its own, and aim at a better arrangement and at a fuller explanation of unusual points. At last, after many interruptions, literary and otherwise, the idea has matured, and these pages are put forth with a fair amount of hope that they may prove useful and helpful to those who desire to have a better understanding of parochial registers.

Another book on this subject was produced in 1908, of the highest value and yet in no sense clashing with this work or causing me to falter in my task, which had then made considerable advance. I allude to Mr. Arthur Meredyth Burke's volume called *A Key to the Ancient Parish Registers of England and Wales.* In the following year a supplement of addenda and corrigenda was also issued. The object of this laborious work is to provide those who have reason to consult parish registers with an easy and reliable guide as to the period covered by each of them, and also with information as to their having been printed, if such has been the case. It is only those who have had occasion to consult such registers who are aware how common are the blunders as to their dates in the usual local works of reference.

In conjunction with Mr. Burke, a particular endeavour has for the first time been made to definitely settle the long vexed question as to the existence of parochial registers prior to the year (1538) when Thomas Cromwell first ordered them to be kept. The number of these early examples has hitherto always been exaggerated. Each instance is discussed in the last chapter, and they prove to be under a score, instead of upwards of forty. Of the two which are the oldest—Tipton, 1513, and Altham, 1518—full details are given.

It is foreign to my purpose to discuss the advisability or methods of changing the custody of the parish registers in these pages, but no one can be more impressed than myself with the culpable carelessness shown, and continued to be shown, by a minority of the beneficed clergy as to their safe keeping. In three instances, early registers from which I took various extracts within the last thirty years have hopelessly disappeared. The large number of registers lost since the Blue Book of 1833 is discussed with some detail in the last chapter.

As to Bishops' Transcripts, no words can be too strong as to the scandal of their condition. Mr. Waters' statement of 1882 is amply warranted: "They present a lamentable picture of episcopal negligence, parochial parsimony, and official rapacity." It would be useful if some genealogist would undertake a systematic work on their often pitiful remains.

To comply with the requirements of my long-suffering publishers, and a generally expressed wish that this book should be of modest dimensions, severe excision has been used.   Less than half of the original number of selected extracts have survived the process of sifting.

No reference will be found to Briefs in these pages, though long lists appear on the fly-sheets of some registers.   Those desirous of following up this subject are referred to an excellent and exhaustive volume issued by Mr. W. A. Bewes in 1896, entitled *Church Briefs.*

The details as to visitations of the plague, set forth at some length from the registers in Chapter IX, will be found to correct some of the exaggerations and misstatements of local historians, notably in the case of Derby.

With regard to assistance in bringing out this book, my gratitude is in the first place due to the Rev. R. M. Serjeantson, who has not only supplied a large number of Northamptonshire register extracts, but has also carefully read the proofs.   In the next place it is a pleasure to thank Mr. Burke for his generous kindness and help; without the aid of his *Key*, and his personal supervision, the appendixes could not have been produced.   Many of the clergy have been most courteously prompt in their replies to troublesome queries.   Among them I should like to mention the Rev. J. F. Monckton, vicar of Sinnington; the Rev. T. S. Lea, rector of Penkevil; the Rev. G. B. R. de Jersey, vicar of Kingsbury; the Rev. S. G. H. Sargeant, vicar of Nonington; the Rev. C. Swatridge, rector of Thurlton; the Rev. G. S. Biddulph, vicar of Stretton Grandison; and more especially the Rev. H. H. Whitaker, the vicar of Altham.

I am hopeful ere long of producing a companion volume on Churchwardens' Accounts, of which a large number of pre-Reformation examples (many quite unknown) remain, including also Constables' and Poor Accounts. Towards this book considerable preparations have been made. I shall be particularly obliged for a post-card note as to any pre-Reformation instances, as some may have been overlooked.

Corrections of these pages will also be welcomed.

J. CHARLES COX

13 LONGTON AVENUE, SYDENHAM
February 1910

CONTENTS

CHAPTER I

'ACTS OF PARLIAMENT AND CANONS

CHAPTER II

THE STORY OF THE REGISTERS

CHAPTER III

CHANGES IN RELIGIOUS FORMULARIES

CHAPTER IV

BAPTISMS

CHAPTER V

CHRISOM CHILDREN, FOUNDLINGS, ETC.

CHAPTER VI

MARRIAGES

CHAPTER VII

BURIALS

CHAPTER VIII

ACCIDENTS

CONTENTS

CHAPTER IX

THE PLAGUE AND OTHER SICKNESS

CHAPTER X

HISTORICAL

CHAPTER XI

STORMS, FROSTS, AND FIRES

LIST OF ILLUSTRATIONS
IN THE TEXT

LIST OF PLATES

xviii

These all are gone, their little day is o'er,
They laugh, they weep, they sport, they toil no more ;
Their feet are still, and others in their room
With busy step are hurrying to the tomb.
We, in our turn, to others shall give place,
And others yet come forth to run the race ;
And yet that race by others shall be run
Till time is over and the world is done.

From the Burton Latimer Registers, 1823–24

PARISH REGISTERS

CHAPTER I

ACTS OF PARLIAMENT AND CANONS

Cromwell's order of 1538—Popular dislike—Action of 1547, 1555, and 1558—Bills of 1563 and 1590—Convocation in 1597 and 1603—Action of Parliament in 1644 and 1653—Registration Acts of William III—Lord Hardwicke's Act of 1753—The Stamp Act of 1783—Rose's Act of 1812

IN July 1535, Henry VIII, by virtue of the Act of Supremacy, appointed Thomas Cromwell, who was at that time Lord Privy Seal, to be his Vicar-General. Cromwell in his early life had been a resident in the Low Countries, and would therefore have knowledge of the baptismal registers introduced there by the Spanish clergy. His much improved scheme for securing the registration in his own country of births, deaths, and marriages, at little or no expense, is the one commendable action in the public life of this marvellously shrewd but absolutely unscrupulous man. There can be no doubt that Cromwell's registration project must have been planned and discussed during the first year of his ecclesiastical administration. The rumour spread far and wide to the effect that this strange new power, which had sprung up within the Church of England, was about to levy a tax for his master's coffers on the administration of the Sacraments. This rumour, in which there was quite possibly some truth, naturally aroused the

I

keenest resentment among the masses. The very first of
the list of popular grievances put forth by the insurgents of
the Pilgrimage of Grace in 1536 was " That no infant shall
receive the blessed Sacrament of Baptisme bott onlesse an
trybette be payd to the king." A pamphlet printed in 1537
states that the Yorkshire insurgents gave out that the people
were ordered henceforth to pay the crown for christenings,
marriages, and burials.

Cromwell, however, who must have been thoroughly
aware of the extent and gravity of the great popular risings
against his initial steps in the suppression of the monasteries,
was clever enough to withdraw for a time, and probably to
modify his original registration project.

It was not until three years later that Cromwell issued
injunctions to every parish in England and Wales, ordering
the parson to enter every Sunday in the presence of the
wardens, or one of them, all the baptisms, marriages, and
burials of the previous week, in a book which was to be kept
in a two-locked coffer, under pain of a fine of 3s. 4d., to be
applied to the repair of the Church. The following is the
exact phraseology of this order, which is dated 5th September
1538, as set forth in the State Papers, save that the contracted words are extended :—

"In the name of God Amen. By the authorite and comission
of the most excellent Prince Henry by the Grace of God Kynge of
Englande and of France, defensor of the faithe Lorde of Irelande,
and in erthe supreme hedd undre Christ of the Church of Englande,
I Thomas lorde Cromwell, lorde privie seall, Vicegerent within this
realme, do for the avancement of the trewe honor of almighty God,
encrease of vertu and discharge of the kynges majestie, give and
exhibite unto you theise injunctions folowing, to be kept observed
and fulfilled upon the paynes hereafter declared. . . .

"That you and every parson vicare or curate within this diocese
shall for every churche kepe one boke or registere wherein ye shall
write the day and yere of every weddyng christenyng and buryeng
made within yor parishe for your tyme, and so every man succeed-

yng you lykewise. And shall there insert every persons name that shalbe so weddid christened or buried. And for the sauff kepinge of the same boke the parishe shalbe bonde to provide of these comen charges one sure coffer with twoo lockes and keys wherof the one to remayne with you, and the other with the said wardens, wherein the saide boke shalbe laide upp. Whiche boke ye shall every Sonday take furthe and in the presence of the said wardens or one of them write and recorde in the same all the weddinges christenynges and buryenges made the hole weke before. And that done to lay upp the boke in the said coffer as afore. And for every tyme that the same shalbe omytted the partie that shalbe in the faulte therof shall forfett to the saide churche iiis iiiid to be emploied on the reparation of the same churche. . . .

"THOMAS CRUMWELL"

Although the very whisper of disapproval of the king's ecclesiastical or general policy had by this time been converted into an act of high treason, and any hint or form of active opposition suppressed with brutal ferocity—such as one of the fairest of our historians terms a veritable "reign of terror"—there was no small resentment up and down the country to this registration order. It is but fair to state that this resentment was mainly due to popular misconceptions as to the details of the scheme, which, as has been shown, imposed no kind of fee on any one, save the purchase by the parish of a book, and simply added to the duties and responsibilities of the beneficed clergy and the churchwardens.

There are three extant communications at the Public Record Office addressed to Cromwell in the early part of 1539, which reflect this current distrust.[1] The first of these, dated 15th February, is from John Marshall, of South Carlton, Notts, stating, *inter alia*, that in those parts of Nottinghamshire and Lincolnshire around Newark there was much resentment as to the various new "fashions," and no little fear that some "paymentes shuld or myght grow

[1] Dom. State Papers, Henry VIII, vol. xiv. pt. 1, Nos. 295, 507, 815.

uppon them at lengthe to the kyngs hyghnes." On 12th
March, Richard Covert and John Michel wrote to Cromwell
and the privy council as to words used by one William Hole,
a smith of Horsham, to the effect that there "wasse come
downe comyssion or comandement that a writen tribute or
some of monye shuld be payd to the Kynges highnes for
weddynges crystenyngs and buryalls, and that ther shuld
be payd to the Kyng for every one of these v*d* or more
and to the lorde of the Franches as moch." The alleged
offender was sent up to London to appear before the council.
The third letter is one, which has been several times cited,
from Sir Piers Edgcumbe as to the alarm felt in sundry
parts of Devonshire and Cornwall; it is dated 20th April,
and expresses a hope that these misgivings will be officially
set at rest:—" Ther mystrust is that somme charges more
than hath byn in tymes past shall growe to theym by this
occacyon off regesstrynge of thes thynges; wher in yff hyt
shall please the Kynge's majiste to put them yowte off dowte
in my poor mynde shall encresse moche harty loff."

The council of the boy-king, Edward VI, reissued in 1547
the registration injunctions of Cromwell almost word for
word, with the exception that the fine of 3s. 4d. for neglect,
was to be assigned to the " poore mens box of that parishe."
In the same year one of the visitation articles of the diocese
of Canterbury was—

"Whether they have one Book or Register safely kept, wherein
they write the day of every Wedding, Christening, and Burying."

Under Philip and Mary, in 1555, Cardinal Pole directed
that the Bishops in their visitations were to inquire—

"If the parish priest had a Register with the names of those
who were baptized, of the sponsors, of the married, and the dead."

Two years later, among the Cardinal's articles touching
the clergy was one—

"Whether they do keep the Book or Register of Christenings, Buryings, and Marriages, with the name of the Godfather and Godmother."

The question of registering the god-parents is discussed in a subsequent section.

In the first years of Queen Elizabeth, the registration injunctions were again reissued in almost the identical phraseology used under Henry VIII and Edward VI, with the slight alteration that the defaulting penalty was to be divided equally between the poor and the repair of the church.

The first interference of Parliament with matters of registration occurred in 1563. On 9th March a bill was read for the first time in the House of Commons to authorise every archbishop and bishop " to erect one Office of Registership of all the Church Books to be kept in every diocese." This bill was of an elaborate character: transcripts were to be sent of all parochial registers to the diocesan centre, and copies were to be executed of "all former church books of 24 yeeres continuance already passed or thereabouts" into " great deacent books of parchment." To cover expenses, the Bill provided that the parents of every child not baptized having lands to the value of £40, or goods to the value of £5, should pay at the christening 1d.; that every man of like possessions should pay 1d. on his marriage, and 2d. on the burial of his wife; that every woman of like possessions should pay 1d. at the burial of her husband; and that every such man or woman should pay 1d. at the burial of their son or daughter or household servant. These fees were to be paid to the churchwardens, and to be by these once a year transmitted to the diocesan register. The clergy, however, opposed the scheme, and the measure was dropped. The like fate befel another scheme for a general registry, arranged under counties, which was propounded in 1590 by Lord Treasurer Burghley.

Though these two schemes failed, they prepared the way for a genuine plan of general registration which was adopted in 1597. On 25th October of that year, a constitution issued by the convocation of the archbishop, bishops, and clergy of the province of Canterbury, and approved by the Queen under the great seal of Great Britain, directed the more careful keeping of parochial registers, which were pronounced to be of the greatest utility (*permagnus usus*). The registers were for the future to be kept on parchment, and parchment copies were to be made of those old registers which were on paper. For the prevention of guile or negligence in the keeping of the registers, it was enacted that the whole of the entries of the previous week were to be read out openly and distinctly by the minister on Sunday, at the conclusion of either mattins or evensong. The names of the minister and wardens were to be appended to every page of the register on its completion. Lastly it was ordained that a copy of the parish register was to be sent by the warden annually within a month after Easter, without any fee, to the diocesan register, and there to be kept faithfully among the episcopal archives. These copies, known as " Bishops' Transcripts," have, however, been most fitfully and slovenly kept, as is subsequently noticed.

A somewhat similar ecclesiastical mandate was issued in 1603, at the opening of the reign of James I, whereby it was enacted that a parchment book was to be provided at the expense of the parish, wherein were to be copied former paper registers, "so far as the ancient books thereof can be procured, but especially since the beginning of the reign of the late Queen." The safe keeping of the register was to be entrusted to "one sure Coffer with three Locks and Keys," to be in the several respective custody of the minister and the two wardens. The provision for the public weekly reading of the register was not repeated. This curious and generally forgotten order was only in operation for six years, and we are not aware that any memorandum exists as to its execution. The Sunday register entries of the past week by the minister, in the presence of the wardens, was, however, again enjoined, and so too was the order for the annual transmission of the bishops' transcripts, though the exact date was changed to within a month after 25th March.

The widespread disturbances during the Civil War, and the ejection of so large a number of the Episcopal clergy from their benefices naturally brought about considerable irregularity in the keeping of the register in not a few parishes, and occasionally resulted in their entire cessation The attention of Parliament was called to these irregularities, and on 6th December 1644, it was ordered that "it be referred to the committee for bringing in the ordinance for the establishing the Directory, to bring in a clause in that ordinance for registering the time of baptising of children, and their parents' names, and for registering of burials." In the same year it was further ordained that "there shall be provided at the charge of every parish or chapelry, a fair Register Book of velim to be kept by the minister and other officers of the church, and that the names of all children baptized, and of their parents, and of the time of their birth and baptising, shall be written and set down by the minister therein, and also the names of all persons married there, and the time of their marriage; and also the names of all persons buried in that parish, and the time of their death and burial; and that the said book shall be shewed by such as keep the same to all persons reasonably desiring to search for the birth, baptising, marriage, or burial of any person therein registered, and to take a copy or procure a certificate thereof."

Notwithstanding these regulations, it was found that during this transition state of matters religious, when

endeavours were being made to suppress Episcopal Church
government, and even the possession of a Book of Common
Prayer was visited with the severest penalties, registration was
reduced to chaotic conditions. In consequence the hand of
Parliament was again evoked in 1653, when an Act was passed
on 24th August. By this Act the ministers were required to
give up their register books to laymen, who were to be
called "parish registers."[1] These new officials were to
enter all publications of banns, marriages, births, and burials.
For marriage entries they were empowered to charge a fee
of 12d., and 4d. for each entry of birth and burial. The
lay register was to be chosen by the householders of each
parish on or before 22nd September 1653, and as soon as he
had been sworn and approved by the local justice, his
appointment was to be entered in the register book. The
enactment by this same Act of civil marriage is subsequently
discussed. Here it may be remarked that this elaborate
Commonwealth legislation was ignored at the Restoration,
when the keeping of the registers reverted to the clergy.
The civil marriages before justices during 1653–1660 were,
however, legalised by Act of Parliament (12 Car. ii, c. 33)
during the latter year.

The whimsical Act of 1680 for burial in woollen, with
its enforced register entries, is also treated of in later pages.

The reign of William III saw several Registration Acts
passed, which were obviously designed to assist the ex-
chequer. Amongst other taxes designed "for carrying on
the war against France with vigour" was a graduated scale

---

[1] The comparatively modern word Registrar is not to be found in the Statutes,
nor in Johnson's Dictionary. "In the language of Roman jurisprudence," as
pointed out by Mr. Waters, "the archivist was *regerendarius* and the archives
were *regerta*, from which came in low-Latin *registrum* and *registrarius*. When
the *registrarius* signed Latin documents officially, he subscribed himself for
brevity *Registrar*, just as the *Prebendarius* signed himself *Prebendar*; and
the abbreviation of the Latin signature came to be mistaken, in a generation
ignorant of Latin, for the official designation in England."

AN ACT
ᴛoᴜᴄʜɪɴɢ
MARRIAGES
And the Regiſtring thereof;

And alſo touching

Births and Burials:

Wedneſday the 24ᵗʰ of *Auguſt*, 1653.

Ordered by the *Parliament*, *That this Act be forthwith Printed and Publiſhed.*

Hen: Scobell, Clerk of the Parliament.

London, Printed by *Iohn Field*, Printer to the Parliament of *England*. 1653.

FACSIMILE OF TITLE-PAGE OF 1653 REGISTRY ACT.

of duties imposed in 1694 (6 & 7 Wm. III, c. 6) on marriages, births, and burials; it also included a tax for five years upon bachelors and widowers. The tax collectors were allowed full access to the registers, and the penalty on the minister for neglect to register was £100. The following was the scale adopted :—

		£	s.	d.
For the burial of every person . . .		0	4	0
„ of a Duke (above the 4s.) . .		50	0	0
„ of a Marquis, etc., etc. in proportion				
„ of every person having a real estate of £50 per annum or upwards, or a personal estate of £600, or upwards . .		0	20	0
„ of the wife of such person having such estate . .		0	10	0
For and upon the birth of every person and child, except the children of those who receive alms		0	2	0
„ of the eldest son of a Duke .		30	0	0
„ of a marquis, and so forth.				
Upon the marriage of every person . . .		0	2	6
„ of a Duke . . .		50	0	0
„ of a Marquis .		40	0	0
„ of an earl . . .		30	0	0
and so forth.				
Bachelors, above 25 years old, yearly . .		0	1	0
Widowers „ „ .		0	1	0
A Duke, being Bachelor or Widower, yearly .		12	10	0
A Marquis „ „ .		10	0	0

In the following year it was enacted (7 & 8 Wm. III, c. 35) that a fine of 40s. was to be imposed on parents who omitted to give notice to the minister within five days of the birth of a child, and the minister was enjoined under a like penalty to keep a distinct reference of such so born and not christened, for doing which the parents were to pay sixpence to the clergy. This form, however, of registration was for the most part neglected, and in 1706 (4 Anne c. 12) an Act of Immunity was passed in respect to negligent clergy, wherein it was plainly stated that an enforcement of the heavy penalties would expose them and their families to ruin.

The year 1753 is memorable in the history of registration for the passing of "An Act for the preventing of Clandestine Marriages" (22 Geo. II, c. 33), which is generally known as Lord Hardwicke's Act. It prescribed a special form of entry for banns and marriages, and directed that all marriages were to be through either banns or licence, and were to be solemnised in some church or chapel which had been customarily used for such purpose. To this Act, and to the evils which it suppressed, further allusion is made in the section dealing with marriages.

The Stamp Act of 1783 (23 Geo. III, c. 71) imposed a duty of 3d. upon every entry in the parish register, and two years later was extended to Nonconformists. This invidious tax, which fell lightly on the rich, but was a distinct burden on the poor, placed the clergy in the unfortunate position of tax gatherers, and was a direct inducement to defective registration. This unpopular and obnoxious statute was repealed in 1794.

Rose's Act of 1812 "for the better regulating and preserving of Parish and other Register of Births, Baptisms, Marriages, and Burials in England" (52 Geo. III, c. 146), put the whole question of registration on a surer foundation. But the Act was loosely drafted; the only penalty imposed was transportation for fourteen years, whilst a subsequent clause provided that one half of all penalties shall go to the informer and the remainder to the poor of the parish! We have no concern in these pages with the further registration legislation of the nineteenth century.

CHAPTER II

THE STORY OF THE REGISTERS

The registers of 1538—Elizabethan registers—The transcripts from paper—Faulty registrations — Post - Restoration registers—The Stamp Act of 1783—Calendar changes—Large hand entries

A KNOWLEDGE of the history of the registration enactments of some three centuries, set forth in outline in the last chapter, is necessary to the due understanding of England's parochial registers.

The one fairly obvious fault of Cromwell's injunctions of 1538 was the neglect to specify the nature of "the one boke or registre" wherein the entries were to be made. Most of the first registers appear to have been written on paper, which was naturally used on the score of economy. This was the case even in an important parish, so near to the centre of court life, as St. Margaret's, Westminster.

The Churchwarden's accounts contain this entry :—

"1538. Paid for a book to registre in the names of buryals, weddings, and christ'nings, 2d."

It is not worth while to multiply instances of this, but we have noted seven similar entries in the churchwardens' accounts of other parishes ; in three of these cases it is specified that 2d. was the price of a quire of paper.

Although the use of parchment or vellum was not enjoined prior to the ordinances of Elizabeth and James I, just a few parishes were sufficiently enterprising to procure a thin folio book of parchment at the very dawn of registration. It is exceedingly rare to find an undoubted original register beginning in 1538; fully 95 per cent. of those that go back to that date are transcripts made towards the end of Elizabeth's reign or at the opening of that of James I. The first register book of Staplehurst, Kent, is one of the rare exceptions, where the original and the transcript exist side by side.

When parchment transcripts and current registers were ordered, various parishes not unnaturally followed the plan usually adopted with every class of official record, of procuring narrow strips or membranes and stitching them together to form a roll as occasion required. Such rolls have been noted in the Northamptonshire parishes of Burton Latimer (1538–1569), and Orlingbury (1564–1653); at Brenchley (1539) and Nursted (1561), Kent; at Appleby St. Michael (1582–1677), and Ambleside (1643), Westmoreland; and at Thormanby, Yorks (1658)..

The majority of the early registers are in Latin. During the Commonwealth, the use of Latin was generally abandoned, and but very occasionally resumed after the Restoration. The following sensible note occurs in the register of All Saints, Derby :—

"May 16, 1610. I see no reason why a Register for English people should be written in Latin. Richard Kilbie, Minister of All-Hallows in Derbie."

In the register of Clyst St. George, Devon, is an entry under 1735–36 to the effect that "the law now forbids ye keeping any records in Latin"; but in this statement the minister was mistaken, the Act of 1731 (4 Geo. II, c. 26) ordering that "all proceedings in Courts of Justice" were to be in the English language does not extend to parish registers. Miscellaneous memoranda, particularly those of a personal character, were frequently entered in Latin when the rest of the register was in English, and occasionally in Greek, French, and even short-hand.

The statement or heading at the beginning of the old registers is usually of a fairly simple character, as in the case of the register book of the long ago submerged church of

A regester booke of all the marriages Cryſtenin= ges & burialles that hath ben in the parriſhe of S^t peters in dunwich within the countie of Suff Sence the yeare of our lord God 1539

TITLE-PAGE OF REGISTER OF ST. PETER'S, DUNWICH.

St. Peter's, Dunwich. Occasionally the incumbent introduced extraneous or verbose matter, particularly if he was a controversialist. A good example of this occurs in the first register book of Newbottle, Northants :—

"October 1, 1538. Thys Boke, made by ye expresse commandment of our most Sovereygne Lorde Kynge Henry VIII, by ye grace of Gode Kynge of Englande and of France, Defender of ye fayth, Lord of Yreland, and ye supreme hede in earth of this hys church of England, for certain goodly usys, by his ryght excellent wyse and sage Counseul, divised and upon lyke consideracons instituted as by the divisyons of ye same in iii sundrie places here followynge may apere, begynninge in ye yere of hys prosperous and honorable reyne xxx, and in ye yere of our mayster Christ MDxxxviii, fyrst day of October, to be exercysed after ye forme as therafter ensueth. The Lord Thomas Comwell Lord privy seal and vicegerent to hys hyghnese of ye ecclesiastycal jurisdiction, exhibiting to us of ye clergy ye same with dyverse other at ye time lyke fraytful and laudable invention, meted to ye glory of God, to the King's honour and to ye great benefyts of ys hys realme and annilihatynge of ye bysshop of Rome hys very falsly pretendyd and usurped powres. I Edward Medley, beynge Vicar here, Robert Wyat and Thomas Harden churchwardens, statynge our lyke assyduouse prayer with all fidelyte and obsequence to ye accomplisshmet of ye contentes of ye same. Amen."

In larger parishes it was occasionally arranged, after the injunction of 1558, to keep two separate books for registration purposes, the one for baptisms, and the other for marriages and burials. Thus at St. Minver's, Cornwall, there are two registers, both of them beginning in the first year of Elizabeth. The first of these contains baptisms extending, with a few gaps, from 1558 to 1758; whilst the second volume records marriages from 1559 to 1754, and burials from 1558 to 1695. As a rule, however, the threefold entries of the parish registers were started in three different parts of the register book ; in the smaller parishes all the entries were not infrequently entered in one place in the exact order of their occurrence, whether baptisms, marriages, or funerals.

An exuberant admirer of Queen Elizabeth and her policy took the opportunity of beginning a new register book for St. Oswald's, Durham, to thus express his feelings :—

"The Register boke of the parysshe of St. Oswalds made the xxvth

day of Marche a.d. 1580 Ann. Elyzabethe xxii. wherein is contayned
the names of all suche persons as have been chrystened, maryed and
buryed within the sayd paryshe the yeares folowynge writen and
kepte accordinge to ye Quenes Injunctions by Charlys Moberlye
Vicar, James Lyddale, Thomas Haryson, Xpofer Rampshaw, James
Robynson, dated chosen and sworne churchwardens, accordinge to
the Quenes proceedinges, whose doinges god directe to hys glorye
and profette of the sayd parysshe, and to the mentaynyng of the
quenes Majesties godly proceedinges, whom god preserve to Reyne
over us, to the abolyshment of popery and strange and false
Religion, and to the Menteynge of the gospell, Graunt o lord yt
she may long continew a Mother in Israel with prosperwos healthe
honor and felycitie and after thys hyr gret governement in thys
lyffe, she may with Moyses, Josua, Debora, and other godlye
govnours, injoy a crowne of æternall glory, goed Reder say
Amen."

Now and again concern is expressed by the custodians
of registers as to their subsequent preservation.   One of the
quaintest of such interpolations is in the register book of
Rodmarton, Gloucestershire, under the year 1630, to the
following effect :—

> " If you will have this Book last, bee sure to aire it att the fier or
> in the Sunne three or foure times a yeare—els it will grow dankish
> and rott, therefore look to it.   It will not bee amisse when you finde
> it dankish to wipe over the leaves with a dry woolen cloath.   This
> Place is very much subject to dankishness, therefore I say looke to
> it."

Burn, in citing this entry, states that the situation of
Rodmarton is high and dry on a calcareous soil, and that the
" dankishness " complained of arose solely from the exuding
nature of the building-stone.

The second register book of Bishop Wearmouth, beginning
in 1653, has on its first page a commination against those
who should mutilate the pages or alter the entries :—

> "Signis hunc librum mutilare vel in ulla parte vel nomen aliquod
> delere, aut in falsum immutare audeat, pro sacrilego habeatur."

With regard to the Elizabethan and Jacobean transcripts of the older register, though care seems for the most part to have been taken to secure verbal accuracy with the names, there is no doubt whatever that, as a rule, the labour of transcribing was reduced to a minimum, and everything of an extraneous nature rigidly excluded. Hence the great majority of parchment registers beginning in 1538 or 1539 are uninteresting and almost valueless, save for genealogical purposes, right through the sixteenth century.

Thus when the register of Staplehurst, Kent, was recopied, the words printed between brackets were left out of the transcript.

"1543. December 31. There was buryed John Turner the elder [whose sowle Jesu pardon. Amen.]
"1545. June 6. buryed the soun of Thomas Roberts the younger, called Henry [upon whose soule I pray God have mercy].
"1548. September 11. buryed James Bragelomd an honest man and a good householder [whose soule Jesu pardon, and bring to eternal rest]."

An entry in the transcript of the register of St. Dunstan's West reads:—

"1560–1. February 17. Mr. Rithe buried."

But the old paper book adds:—

"A benchar of Lyncolnes Yne, buryed out of the newe brycke byldyngs, beynge in oure parishe, the nether syde of Lyncolnes Yne."

In obedience to the Elizabethan injunction, the transcripts are in many instances signed at the foot of every page, to ensure accuracy, by the minister and churchwardens of the year wherein the copy was executed. This fact gave rise to an ignorant and ridiculous blunder of past antiquaries and historians, who ought to have known better, as to the remarkable longevity assigned to clergy and their

2

wardens. A round dozen of such errors could be cited, made by the leading writers of the old-fashioned county histories; it must suffice to mention that Nichols, the very able historian of Leicestershire, gravely asserts that the vicar of Keigham held his benefice for ninety-two years, and had the same wardens for upwards of seventy years!

Usually, as is known from the handwriting, the copying of paper registers on to parchment was done by the incumbent; but in towns and larger parishes a paid lay copyist was occasionally employed. Thus at St. Peter's, Northampton :—

"A true and perfect extracte ' of all entries since 21 Elizabeth was' written and extracted by me Thomas Walsbey by or at the appointment of Master William Stocks, parson of the said church, and of Arthur Potter and Richard Rands, churchwardens, according to the true meaning of the constitution of the late convocation holden at London anno Elizabethæ Reginæ the fortyeth anno dni 1597."

At the beginning of the first register book of Beeston-next-Mileham, Norfolk, is the following entry, showing that the rector made the transcript from the original register :—

"Johannes Forby, Rector 1598, de integro ex antiquo exemplari scripsit hunc librum.

"Register booke for the parish church of Beeston-next-Mileham, to recorde all such their names as shall be within that parish either christened, maryed, or buried accordinge to the booke of constitutions and canons of the parliament in the yeere 1597. The number of sheets herein 13 with 18 leaves of every sheet, in all 244. The price of the parchment 10/- and for the bindynge 2/-."

William Cooper, Vicar of West Bradenham, Norfolk, declares in 1603 that he had—

"Trully and faithfully colected word for word out of both ye olde Register Books from the Beginning of our Lord God 1538 in anno regni Henrici Octavi."

The register of Nether Compton, Dorset, which begins in 1538, was copied throughout by the rector in 1600.

Robert Travell, the minister of Weston Favell, Northants, who died in 1641, did a good work in copying fragmentary registers. He enters in the earliest register book :—

"Ab anno 1548 the names herein contayned with their moneths and yeares very rudely and imperfectly written in loose papers I have faithfully set doune without any alteration according to my copies."

On the inner cover of the first register book of Plympton, Devon, which begins in 1616, are the following lines by the transcriber :—

"Walter Winsband His book
The Lord of Haven upon him look,
And so correcke him with a rod
that he may be a child of God
And when for him the bel doth dole
the Lord of haven recive his soul."

In at least one case the transcribing was the work of a woman, as is shown by the following entry in the registers of the parish church of Peterborough :—

"1564, August. Sarah Stowkes, the Daughter of Henry Stowkes, was christened the x day, who afterwards in the yeare our Lord God 1599 did coppye this Register Book with her own hands, then being the Wife of John Lansdune."

As to admittedly faulty registers, there are a variety of quaint entries, such as the one which occurs in the first book of Earls Barton, Northants :—

"1593. Understand gentle reader that from 1592 untill 1597 Renold Eastwood the Clercke was put in trust to write the weddings, christenings, and burialls, wch in part he somewhat negligentlie did, but ommitted w^t I have unorderly yet treulie sett down as I learned there names and tymes of there freindis."

Scores of registers bear witness to the natural irregularity or cessation of entries during the Civil War and Interregnum, a selection of which are subsequently cited in the historical section. But space may be found here for a long and gravely worded extract from the registers of Carshalton, Surrey.

"Good Reader tread gently :

"For though these vacant yeares may seeme to make me guilty of thy censure, neither will I symply excuse myselfe from all blemishe; yet if thou doe but cast thine eie uppon the former pages and se with what care I have kepte the annalls of mine owne tyme, and rectifyed sundry errors of former times thou wilt beginn to thinke ther is some reason why he that begann to build so well should not be able to make an ende.

"The truth is that besyde the generall miserys and distractions of those pretermitted years wh it may be god in his owne wysedome would not suffer to be kept uppon record, the special ground of that pretermisseon ought to be imputed to Richard Finch, the parishe clerke, whose office it was by long proscription to gather the ephemeris, or dyary of the dayly passages and to exhibite them once a yeare to be transcribed into this Registry ; and though I often called upon him agayne and agayne to remember his chardge, and he always tould me that he had the accompts lying by him, yet at last perceaving his excuses, and resolving uppon suspicion of his words to put him home to a full tryall I found to my great griefe that all his accompt was written in sand, and his words committed to the empty winds. God is witnes to the truth of this apologie, and that I made it knowne at some pish meetings before his own face, who could not deny it neither doe I write it to blemishe him, but to cleere mine owne integrity as far as I may and to give accompt of this miscarryage to after ages by the subscription of my hand.

"March 10, 1651. (Signed) WILLIAM QUELCH, B.D. Vic."

Nor did irregularities at once cease with the Restoration, as is shown, *inter alia*, by the two following entries in Northamptonshire registers :—

"The very true reason why this register, is found as imperfect in some years as from 1669 to 1695 is because the parishioners could never be persuaded to take to see it done, nor the churchwardens as yᵉ canon did require, and because they refuse to pay such dues to yᵉ curate as they ought by custome to have payed. (*Brington*)

"Memorandum that the Register booke being neglected two or three yeares notice was given two severall times in yᵉ church to desire all parents and others to give in yᵉ names of all yᵗ ought to have been registered and yᵉ time when baptized married or buried. But not more was brought in but what was set down in this and yᵉ two next pages.

"SAM. GEORGE, Minister, 1670 (*Long Buckby*)"

After the Restoration, it was generally the custom to procure substantially bound parchment volumes to serve as register books. The price of these often occurs in churchwardens' accounts, and occasionally in the actual books. Thus at Kidderminster a register book was bought in 1674 for £1, 15s. A new register was purchased for the Derbyshire village of Tickenhall, in 1693, for 8s.

"A register for yᵉ parish of *Ravenston* (Derbyshire) bought by Robert Ayre and Thomas Grant Churchwardens yᵉ 1st of Septembᵣ 1705, price 16 shillings."

The second volume of the registers of *Wellington, Somerset* has inscribed on the first page :—

"This Book was Bought by Cornelius Marsh, the 21st day of May, Anno Dom. 1726: and it cost the sume of 01*l.* 07*s.* 06*d.*

"Baptism, Matrimony, and the Winding Sheet,
As Times do come, Within this book do meet.
CORNELIUS MARSH"

The following entries respecting the Register Stamp Act of 1783 in the register of Whittlesey St. Mary, Cambs :—

"1783, Oct. In the beginning of this month the nasty three penny Tax took place, and as I expect, from the great number of poor, and the Rebellious Humour of the parishioners, to collect but few threepences I shall mark those that pay with V in the Baptisms and

Burial. *N.B.*—As people are most frequently openhearted on the day of Marriage, I expect most of my parishioners will pay yᵉ 3d on that occasion. I shall therefore mark those that do not pay with a V. I squeezed 3d from many a poor wretch ill able to give even so much to Government I am afraid. I think I ought not to urge quite as hard."

The fees for the one year in the parish amounted to £1, 0s. 9d., upon which the curate entered this further note :—

" 'Tis very much more than I expected or than I shall have next year, for as Poverty is admitted as a plea, it will be frequently urged."

The beginning of the Christian year in England has been subject to various changes. The year was reckoned from Christmas Day, 25th December, after the sixth century until 1066; from 1st January to 31st December, from 1067 to 1155 ; from the Annunciation, 25th March to 24th March, 1153 to 1750–51 ; from 25th March to 31st December, in 1751 ; and from 1st January to 31st December, from 1st January 1752 up to the present time. The last of these changes was brought about pursuant to Statute 24 Geo. II, c. 23; the alteration excited a great deal of comment, adverse and otherwise, particularly with regard to the omission of eleven days in September, to bring about a true balance of the calendar. It is not therefore surprising to find occasional reference to this subject in the church registers. The following entries occur in the books of All Saints, Northampton :—

"1752, Jan. Whereas the supputation of the year of Our Lord, (in the Church of England) did heretofore begin on the 25th day of March, it is now, by virtue of an Act of Parliament passed in the 24th year of His Majesty's reign and in the year of Our Lord 1751 to begin on the first day of January.

"1752, Sept. According to an Act of Parliament passed in the 24th year of His Majesty's reign, in the year of Our Lord 1751, the Old Style ceased on the second day of this month and the New takes place. So that all the eleven intermediate nominal days from the second to the fourteenth are omitted, or rather annihilated this year: and the month contains but nineteen days."

A highly unusual note accompanies the first entry of the year 1539 in the Chelmsford register book, which was kept by Mr. Richard Wolston, the curate. Under the date of 13th January 1539, Mr. Wolston writes:—

"Beginning at the first Daye of Januarye after the maner of the Astronymers and soe we truste to procede."

Mr. Wolston was evidently far in advance of his times.

In the register of Whilton, Northants, is another exceptional calendar note at the end of the year 1737:—

"*N.B.*—Before this I began the year as the common almanack does. But from this place shall follow the ecclesiastical year, beginning on the 25th of March."

A parish register ought to be no respecter of persons. The clerk (using that term in its widest significance) ought ever to bear in mind George Herbert's line—

"All equall are within the Churches gate."

The offices of the Church of England for Baptism, Marriage, or Burial are identical, whether used for prince or pauper, for peer or peasant. But those who made the entries were by no means always of the opinion of the writer in the register of Ruyton, Salop, who penned an appropriate stanza beginning:—

"No Flatt'ry here, where to be born and die
Of rich and poor is all the history."

Those who were best acquainted with original registers cannot fail to be aware that they not infrequently find, as they turn over the pages, certain entries written in a far

larger and bolder text than the remainder. On examination
it will always be found that the register writer has been
vulgar enough to reserve this prominent big lettering for the
great people or squires of the parish. This vulgarity is usually
more noticeable in seventeenth or eighteenth century register
books than in earlier examples; but it is occasionally to be
found in those of Elizabethan date. A single example will
suffice; the register book of Elland, Yorks, has the following
entries in great staring lettering:—

" 1566. Henricus Savile de Stainland gen. sepult. 12 Oct.
" 1567. Johes Thornell de Fixbie Gen. sepultus 27 Aprill.
" 1582–3. Jana   Filia   Johis   Savile   de   Bradley   Ar.   baptiz.
    16 February."

CHAPTER III

CHANGES IN RELIGIOUS FORMULARIES

Much Wenlock Register—Death of Henry VIII—Accession of
  Edward VI, Mary, and Elizabeth—Bidding Prayer of 1545—
  Use of English Service *temp.* Edward VI—Commonwealth
  changes

EXTRACTS from the register of Thomas Butler, vicar
of Much Wenlock, beginning 26th November 1538,
and ending 20th September 1562, transcribed by that
careful antiquary, the late Rev. C. Hartshorne, were printed in
the *Cambrian Journal* in 1861. This early register, written
on paper in a clear bold hand, was unhappily destroyed in the
fire that consumed the mansion of Sir Watkin W. Wynne,
at Wynnstay, in 1859, where of course this parochial register
had no business to be stored. This register, judging from
the fairly full extracts fortunately taken by Mr. Hartshorne,
was most exceptionally interesting in the full comments it
supplied as to the religious changes of the reigns of
Henry VIII, Edward VI, Queen Mary, and Queen Elizabeth,
and of incidents connected with the latter days of the
Cluniac Priory of Wenlock, which held the advowson of the
vicarage of the adjacent parish church up to the time of its
dissolution.

The Monastery of Wenlock, as stated in this register,
surrendered on the morrow of the Conversion of St. Paul,
1539.

The register stands out so distinctly and individually in

the character and freedom of its entries, that it seems better in this place to print the selected excerpts in a collective form and in chronological order, rather than break them up among the subsequent sections. It is somewhat singular to note that Vicar Butler, appointed to his living by the monks of the priory, and with his natural leanings to the unreformed faith, could reconcile it with his conscience to follow out the various changes in tongue and services that occurred during the twenty-two years that he kept this parish register. The vicarage was but of slight value, and it is not necessary to think that he retained the post of parish priest from merely mean motives. He may have enjoyed the responsibility and prominence of the position, but it is kinder to believe that Sir Thomas Butler, in common with others of the old priests, recognised that the main essentials of creed and worship remained the same under the varied changes, and that it was his duty to do the best he could for the flock he had been called upon to serve during this upheaval of formularies.

It must have caused him deep pain to record the burning, on 7th November 1547, of the bones of St. Milburge, to whom the priory was dedicated, and he made the bare entry in Latin. There is unrestrained joy about his long notice in English of the accession of Queen Mary, and of the dates on which the various Latin services, after the Sarum Use, were resumed, and genuine sorrow when the time came for recording the death of that Queen. But the simple way in which he at the same time urged his flock to rejoice over the accession of Elizabeth, and to join in the local festivities, is pleasant reading, whilst one of his latest entries states that the celebration of the Divine Service in the " Englysh Tonge" was once more begun on 25th June 1559.

" 12 March 1540–1. Thro lycens was christened at Wylley, Agnes the daughter of Ric. Charlton of this towne of Wenlok and of

THE PRIORY OF WENLOCK

Jane his wife, gossibes were Sir Thomas Butler of Wenlok, aforesaid Vicar, and mistress Agnes wif of Maistr Ric. Lacon, Lord of Wylley aforesaid, and wif of Wm. Davys of Apley Lode.

" Memorandum that the 10th day of this instant month of Febry. in the year of our Lord 1541, here was buried Wm Lowe a Cheshire man born, which William was a lad of 18 years of age or thereabouts, cast by the verdict of 12 men at the s^d Sessions holden here before the s^d Justices the day as it is written in the last of the leaf next preceding, which Sessions were prorogued till friday because of the absence of the ordinary, forasmuch as the s^d William desired the Priviledge of the Church, saying that he could read ; and on friday the 10th day of this february, when the Justices were sitting, the Ordinary Mr. George Dycher parson of Stretton, Dean of this Deanery, being ready in presence. It was found he was no Clerk, and so was put to execution of the law and buried the same day, confessing openly both in the Hall and at the place of Execution on the Edge Top that he had robbed divers persons of their goods.

" 1541–2, 5 Feby. Agnes Pyner a poore woman of thage of vi score er old and above as shee sayed unto h^r Gostly fad^r. Sr Richard Doghty who mynistred the blessed sācmẽts of thaltar unto her to dayes befor her departing.

" 1542, 17th June. John Mynsterley thrise bailiff of this borowe of Moch Wenlok whose corpus lyeth humate in this parish churche of the most holy Trinite befor the first stepp to the Pulpitt befor thimage of our Lady of Pitie and Elizabeth his wif lyeth ther buryed uppō the right hand of him southwards.

" 1542, 5 Nov. on Sonday aft^r the feste of Alhallows all Saincts in this parish Church sange his first Masse, Sr Rychard the Son of John Doughty of Burton w^{t}in this parish and of Julyane his wif, at whose said first Massinging was offered to his use a p'sent.

" 1543–4, Feb. 21. Here was buried out of the Almhouses John Treessingham, a Cheshire man born, an aged lame man, for on Saturday before his departing, he said unto me, Sir Thomas Butler, Vicar of the Church of the Holy Trinity of Moch Wenlock, that he was of the age of seven score years, and I said it could not be so, and he was, as he said, of the age of four score years at the Battle of Blower Heath, and since that, there were three score years (count altogeder said he, and ye shall find seven score years, rather more than less), and said also that some time he was servant to the old Sir Gilbert Talbot, Knt. at the manor of Blakemore besides Whitchurch.

"1542-3, 5 March. Agnes daughter of John Chistoke departed, somtyme deacon or Clerk of this Churche, who departed of the pestilens the first day of September in the er of our Lord God MDxxxij who was a full honest server of the Churche and taught scolers playne song and prick song full well so that the churche was well served in his tyme ; buryed he was in the churche yard on the knapp uppon the right hand as ye entre into the Porche abowte vij cloth yards frō the porch, whose sowle God Almighty take to m̄cy. Amen.

"1544, 15 Sep. John Gogh at that tyme Curate otherwise called Sʳ John Castle sōtyme moncke in monastre of St. Milbge preŝctor in Moch Wenlok and prior of the cell in Preen, the last Priest that ther was whose body is buryed.

"1546, 26 May. Here was buryed out of the Strete called Mardfold out of the two Tenements nexte unto Sanct Owens Well on the same side of the well, the body of Sʳ Willᵐ Corvehill Priest, of the Service of Oʳ blessed Lady St. Marie, within the Churche of the holy Trinite &c. which two hows belōging to the said Sv̄ice he had ī his occupacion, wᵗ their apperteñ and parte of his wages, which was viij markes, and the said hows in an overplus : whose body was buryed in the chancell of our blessed Ladie befor thaltʳ under the Ston in the myddle of the said altare, upon the left hande as ye treade and stand on the heighest steppe of the thre, befor the said altare; whose fete streche forth undʳ the said altare to the wall in the Eest of thaltare, the body ther lying wᵗin the Erth in a tomb of lyme and ston which he caused to be made for himselfe for that intent ; after the reryng and buldyng of the new Ruff of the said chansell, which rering framyng and new reparyng of thaltare and chancell was doñ throw the councill of the said Sir Wᵐ Corvehill, whoo was excellently and singularly experte in dyv̄se of the vij liberal sciences and especially in geometre, not greatly by speculacon, but by experience ; and few or non of handye crafte but that he had a very gud insight in them, as the making of Organs, of a clocke and chimes, an in kerving, in Masonrie, and weving of Silke, an in peynting; and noe instrumente of musike beyng but that he coulde mende it, and many gud ghifts the man had, and a very paciant man, and full honeste in his conversacon and lyvng ; borne here, in this borowe of Moche Wenlok and somtyme moncke in the monastrie of St. Mylbg̃e here. Two brethren he had. One called Dominus John, Monke in the said monastrie, and a Secular prieste called Sr Andrew Corvehill who dyed at Croydon beside London, on whose soule and all Christian soules Almighty God have mc̃y. Amẽ. All this contrey hath a great losse of the death of the s^d Sir Wm Corvehill for he was a gud Bell founder and a mak^r of the frame for bells.

"1546, 9 Julii. Ad ultimam missam ego dominus Thomas Boteler Vicarius huj. Ecclie in Pulpito legi proclamacionem dñi R. nr̃i Henrici octavi propter condempnationem librorum hereticorum istor. Vz. Fryth, Tyndale, Wycliff, Joy, Roie, Basilie, Bale, Barnes, Cov̄dale, Toñer, Tracy, anno regni predicti xxxviii.

"1546, 7 February. Memorandum that the same 5th day of month and year as it is above written, word and knowledge came hither to this s^d Borough of Moch Wenlock that our Sovereign Lord King Henry the 8th was departed out of this transitory life, whose soul God Almighty pardon.

"1547, 17 July. Eodem die fuit communis ludus apud Hopton Monochorum cuj^s ludi fuit director Richd Lawley.

"7 Nov. Quo die combusta fuerunt ossa dive Virginis Milburge in fori ĩtroitu cimiterii cũ quatuor imagor^s vz. S^{ti} Jo. Bapt. de Hopebowdlar, Imagines S^{ti} Blasii de Stanto long, imagines Ste Marie Vg̃is Matris Xti de Acton Roñde, et imagines ejusdem Ste Virginis Mariæ.

"25 Decr. Departed and dyed in the man^{or} place of Madeley about IX of the clock in the nyght Sir John Baily Clercke the last Prior of Moncks that was in the Monastre of Moch Wenlock prior ther at the tyme of the Surr̃edr thereof, whose bodie was buryed on the morrow, v^z fest of St Stephen in the parish churche of Madeley aforesaid.

"1551-2, 22 March. Out of Calowton John France Fermer of the Chief ferme ther, beyng at the tyme of his death of the yeres of one hundred vij ; five Score yeres, and seven yeres above the C as he himselfe in his lif tyme befor diverse of his neighbours did declare.

"(Richard Philips who hanged himself) at the ynde of the Lane going toward Calowton at the plotte of grownde wher somtyme was a Crosse of tymbre called Hamñs Weales crosse.

"1553, Mem. That as some say King Edward the VI by the Grace of God died the 6th day of this instant month of July, in the year of our Lord God as it is above written, and as some do say he died the 4th day of May last preceding, in the same year of our Lord, and upon Mary Magdalenes, which is the 22nd day of this instant month, at Bridgnorth in the fair, there was proclaimed Lady Mary Queen of England, &c., after which proclamation finished the people made great joy, casting up their caps and hats, lauding, thanking and praising God Almighty with ringing of bells and making of Bonfires in every street. And so was she proclaimed Queen the same day at Shrewsbury, and at the Battlefield in the same evening with the like joy of the people, and triumphal solemnity made in Shrewsbury, and also in this Borough of Much Wenlock.

"1553. Here was buried out of Brosely the body of Sir Thos. Parkes, priest, sometime a White Monk of the Cistercian order in the monastery of Buildwas.

"1553, 3 Sepʳ. Quo die Ego doˢ. Thoˢ. Botelar hujus Ecclie poc̃hlis Sancte ac individie Tñi vicarius, divina servicia ac etia missam Latinis verbis more antiquo et secūdum usu Sarum auctoritate excellentissime Vg̃is Mariæ Reginæ nostræ Angliæ celebravi, sicut et ceteri curati hujus decanatus, ac ecciar com. Salop fecerunt. Et in Vesperis, Rege Edwardo defuncto Vesperas, de Placebo et dirige ac Cetera p defuncto, cum missa de Regnina etiam in Crastino.

"1553, 7 Oct. A child first Christned in the Latyne tongue by the booke called the Manuale.

"1553, 31st Oct. A child first buryed after the Coronac̃on of the Queen's Majistie in the latyne tongue after the use of the Church of Sarum.

"1554, 16 June. The altar of our blessed Ladie within this Churche was consecrated and of newe reedified and made up·

"1554, July 6. Memorandum that in the 6th day of this instant month of July in the year of our Lord God as it is above written, and in the first year of the noble reign of Marie, by the Grace of God, of England, France and Ireland Queen, &c., here sat Mr. John Herbert of Buildwas, Wm. Charlton of Wombridge, Thomas Eyton, and Richard Lawley, Esqʳ., in

THE PARISH CHURCH, WENLOCK

commission directed to them from Lord Nicholas Bishop of Worcester, Lord President of the Marches of Wales, for the examination of the lands sometime belonging to the Chauntry or service of our blessed Lady within this parish Church of the Holy Trinity of Moch Wenlock.

" 1554, 16 July. That the same day last above written my Lord the Bishop of Worcester Dr. Nicholas Heath, Lord President of the Marches of Wales coming with Justice Townesynde in company with him from Salop, and riding towards Bridgenorth about two of the clock in the afternoon, was desired by the Burgesses of this Borough of Wenlock to drink, and so they did alight and drank, sitting in the house of Richard Lawley Gent. at the Ash, hanged and decked in the best manner the sᵈ Burgesses could, with clothes of Arrras, Covering of Beds, Baneards, Carpets, Cushions, Chair Forms, and a Cupboard covered with Carpet and a cloth, whereon stood the silver plate whereof they drank, borrowed for the time of Mrs. Agnes the wife of Mr. Thomas Rydley, sometime wife of Mr. Richᵈ. Lakyn of Willey; the table covered with Carpet Cloth of diaper and napkins of the same, three dishes of Pears, and a dish of old apples, Cakes, fine wafers, wyne white, and claret, and sack, and bread and ale for the waiters and servants without, at their pleasure, where my said Lord and Mr. Justice sat the space of half an hour, and then arose, giving the said Burgesses great and gentle thanks for their cost and chear, and so departed towards Bridgenorth. The names of the Burgesses that were the cause of this sᵈ Banquet hereafter do follow as they come into remembrance.

Edmund Sprott, deputy to Mr. Richᵈ Benthal, Bailiff of this Borough of Moch Wenlock and the Liberties of the same.

Ralph Leigh, Gent.	Richᵈ Leg	Christopher Morall
Wm. Moore	David Llĕn	Edward Dyke ⎫ Constables.
John Bradeley	Wm. Jeffries	Wm. Fennymer ⎭
John Sothorne	Thomas Hill	John Wildcocks de Burton.

Richard Wildcocks Serjeaunt of the sᵈ town and Liberties, and divers other of the Burgesses both of town and country. The sum of the costs of the said Banquet was 11s.

" 1555–6, 4th February. Here was christened Richᵈ the son of Thomas Lawley Gent. and of Beatrix his wife, dwelling within the site of the Monasterie of St. Mylburge the Virgin : the gossibs were Mr. Acton of Aldnam besides Sherlet, Richd Benthal of Benthal, and Ann Chidde widow, the wife sometime of Thomas Chidde Gentleman, sister natural of the said Beatrix, who hath been and brought into this world in Matrimony by her two husbands with this s^d child 17 children.

" 1558, 7 May. At Bridgenorth wtin the Churche of St Leonarde was buried the bodie of Dominus Richard Marciall othwise called dominus Richard Baker, sōtyme Abbot of the Monasterie of the Holy Apostles Petre and Paule in Shrowsburie, whoo succeeded in the Abbatie the dominus Richard Lye abbate of the same, whose bodie lieth buried in the churche of the Spittle of St. Bartholomew in London at Smithfield.   The s^d Richard Martiall resigned the s^d Abbatie to Dominus Thos Botelar who was Abbate at the suppressyng of the s^a Monastrie and after lyved and died in Bridgenorth, and his bodie buried ĩ the Churche of St Leonard ther.   And the resignation made, the s^d Ric. Martiall was Prior of the Cell in Northfield whose Sowles Almightie God take into his mercie.   Amen.

" In remembrance to be had it is, that the 17th day of this instant, month of November, in the year of our Saviour Jesus Christ, 1558, in the morning of the same day departed by death the noble Queen Marie, in the 6th year of her reigne the daughter of King the 8th, and of Queen Catherine his first wife ; and the same day of her departing at 11 of the Clock, with the whole assent of the nobility, was Elizabeth the daughter of the said King Henry proclaimed Queen of England &c. in London.   And upon St. Catherine's day, as Sir Thomas Botelar, Vicar of this Church of the Holy Trinity of Moch Wenlock was going toward the Altar to celebration of the Mass, Mr. Richard Newport of High Ercal Esqr then being Sheriff of Salop, coming late from London, came unto me and bad me that I after the Offertorie should come down into the Body of the Church, and unto the people here being, should say these words in open audience and loud voice.   Friends ye shall pray for the prosperous estate of our most noble Queen Elizabeth, by the Grace of God Queen of England France and Ireland, defender of the faith, and for this I desire you every man and woman to say that Pater Noster with ave Maria, and we in the Choir sang the Canticle Te deum Laudamus, pater noster, ave maria, cum collecta pro statu Regni prout stat in processionale in adventu Regis vel Reginæ mutatio aliquibus verbis ad Reginam. And then went I to the altar and said out the mass of St. Catherine, and after mass forthwith went the same Mr. Sheriff with all the people out of the Church and by Laurence Rindles the cryar he caused her noble grace to be proclaimed Queen in the Market Place at the Church Yard Style before the Court Hall; he the s^d Mr. Sheriff giving him instructions thereto as is above written; and then the honest men both of this Borough of Much Wenlock and of this parish brought and accompanied him to the house of Richard Dawley the younger, then Serjeant to Mr. Francis Lawley, then Bailiff of the Franchises and Liberties of the same, and this done he went homewards, they bringing him on the way; and he taking his Horse rode forth, and upon Sunday next after (the 28th of the same month being Dominica proxima adventum domini) Mr. Richard Lawley in the name of himself and of his Bailiff (who then was absent) came with Wm More, Richd Legg, and John Sothorne, with others, and willed me before (them?) that we should go in procession to repeat and to say in the body of the Church to the people assembled the same, saying in words that Mr. Sheriff willed me to pronounce with some addition of words as here it followeth after, and hereupon I having upon me the best cope called St. Milburges cope, said unto the congregation in this wise.   Friends, unknown it is not unto you that our Sovereign Queen Mary is out of this transitory life departed, for whose soul ye shall pray to Almighty God to take unto his mercy, and ye shall pray also for the prosperous Estate, &c. ut supra.   And for this I desire you every man and woman to say Pater noster and Ave Maria &c. Then I said, Friends, Mr. Bailiff of this Town and of the liberties of the same, and Mr. Richd Lawley his father, with other that have been Bailiffs, have willed me to shew you that are poor folks that ye may at afternoon about one of the clock resort to the Bonfire where ye shall have Bread and Cheese and drink to pray unto God Almighty for the prosperity of the Queen's noble Majesty, and this said we went forthwith in procession with Salve festa dies &c. sicut in dedicatiōe ecclesie, and at our return unto the quire we sang by note Te deum laudamus, and ended with Keerie, Christe (Keerie Eleeson?) pro nos ave Maria, cum precibus et collecta pro bono statu Regine prout est in processionale.   This done I went to mass

3

and after evening the bonfire was set on fire where the poor folks were served.

"1559, 25 June. It is to be had in Remēbrance that the celebration of the divine Svice in the Englysh Tonge was begun this day in crastino Nativitat S^{ti} Joh^{is} bapt."

The following are some of the more remarkable and definite references to the religious changes of the sixteenth and seventeenth centuries, noted in the parochial registers up and down the country, beginning with one in the latter days of Henry VIII.

Under the year 1545, the Bidding Prayer to be used before the service is written out in the register of Kirkburton, Yorks. The sentence, "our most holie father the pope wyt all his true college of cardenalls," is crossed out. This erasure was probably made by Archbishop Holgate during his diocesan visitation of 1546. The prayer runs—

"Yow shalt pray for the whole congregation of Xrystes churche wheresoever it be dyspersed throught out all the worlde and especyally for this churche of England and Hyreland wherein I commend unto your devout prayer our most holie father the pope wyt all his true college of cardenalls and for all archebyschopes byschopes parsons vicars and curates who hayth care and charge of soules and especyally for the vicar and curat of this churche who haythe care and charge of your soules."

All references to the Bishop of Rome were ordered to be "utterly abolished, eradicate and rased out" in 1537 by a definite royal injunction; but the order was in this case boldly disregarded for eight years.

"1547–8. (*St. George Tombland, Norwich*). Agnes Rogers nata fuit viij. Februar 1547, et baptizat xj. die Februar 9, minister non vult eam baptizare in lingua anglicana ideo differt' baptism set nihil p' valuer' quia baptizavit eam in lingua anglicana.

"1549 (*Soberton, Hants*), 12 May. This tyme began the Ingles service.

"1549 (*Staplehurst, Kent*). The ninthe daye of June. This day

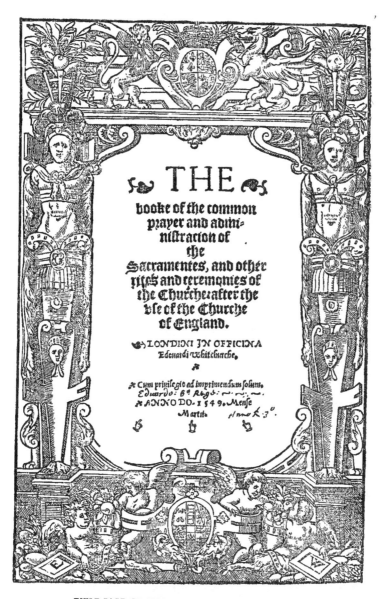

𝕾𝖔 THE 𝖊𝖘

booke of the common
prayer and admi-
nistracion of
the
Sacramentes, and other
rites and ceremonies of
the Churche: after the
vse of the Churche
of England.

LONDINI IN OFFICINA
Eduardi VVhitchurche.

Cum priuilegio ad imprimendum solum.
Eduardo 6º Regis
ANNO DO. 1549. Mense
Martii.

TITLE-PAGE OF FIRST PRAYER BOOK IN ENGLISH.

being Whitsunday (wherein the Booke of the Common Prayer and Administration of the Sacraments and other rite and Ceremonie of the Churche, after the use of the Churche of Englande began to be executed) there was first baptized Marie the daughter of Richard Besiley parsone of this py'she Churche borne the last Thursday hora fer' quintu ante meridiam of his lawful Wif Jane who were maryed the year before, and in the first day that the holly comunion in the English tonge (after thorder that now is was here mynystered), they bothe w^t others most humblye and devoutlie communicating the same. The parsone Christined his owne Childe."

Under an entry of births in the register of Oundle, Northants, on 6th July 1645, is written :—

"These set doune according to ye Directory set forth by ye synnod and alow'd by both houses of Parliment."

According to the Directory, which superseded the Prayer Book in 1644, the child was to be baptized in church, but

"not in the places where Fonts in the time of Popery were unfitly and superstitiously placed."

It is also therein stated that the minister

"is to baptize the child with water : which for the manner of doing it, is not only lawfull, but sufficient and most expedient to be, by powring or sprinckling of the water on the face of the child, without adding any other Ceremony."

"1645 (*Whitworth, Durham*), July 27. James, son of Ambrose Bell, was the last Baptism with the Book of Common Prayer in this Parish.
"1646 (*Fitz, Salop*), July 7. Alce, d. of Richard Ferington and Amias bap. This Alce d. of Richard Ferington was the first that ever was baptized in Fittz Church without the signe of the Crosse at the instance and earnest desyer of him, that is of Richard, was the signe of the Crose omitted.
"1647 (*Ibid.*) Nov. 16. John s. of Joseph Lloyd and Elnor bap.

A
DIRECTORY
FOR
The Publique VVorſhip of *G O D*,
Throughout the Three
K I N G D O M S
O F
England, Scotland, and *Ireland.*

Together with an Ordinance of Parliament for the taking away of the Book of

C O M M O N ‑ P R A Y E R :
A N D
For eſtabliſhing and obſerving of this preſent DIRECTORY
throughout the Kingdom of *England,* and Dominion of *Wales.*

Die Jovis, 13. *Martii,* 1644.

ORdered by the Lords and Commons aſſembled in
Parliament, That this *Ordinance* and *Directory* bee
forthwith Printed and Publiſhed:

Joh: Brown, Cleric.   *H. Elſynge, Cler.*
Parliamentorum.   *Parl.D.Com.*

---

march 18th L O N D O N :
Printed for *Evan Tyler, Alexander Fifield, Ralph Smith,* and
John Field ; And are to be ſold at the Sign of the Bible
in Cornhill, neer the ROYALL‑EXCHANGE. 1644.

TITLE-PAGE OF "DIRECTORY" OF 1644.

The infant was the first baptzd after the new forme of the Directorie and not by the Common Prayer Book.

" 1650 (*Moze, Essex*), July 6th. Francis yᵉ daughter of Mr. Thomas Sherman of Harwich Physitian and Francis his wife was baptized by me Mat: Duerdon rector of Mose by ye booke of Common Prayer at Mr. Shermans house in Harwich.

" 1660 (*Whitworth, Durham*). Charles 11 proclaimed at London, May 8th, and at Durham, May 12th, on which day I, Stephen Hogg, began to use again the Book of Common Prayer."

The registers of Nassington, Northants, contain the following :—

"Memorandum that on Sunday the viii day of Febuary in the yeare of our Lord 1662–3, being the second Sunday after the Revised Book of Common Prayer was brought him, John Laurence, vicar of Nassington, after Morning Prayer, publiquely and solemnly read (as it is by the said Booke appointed) and declare his unfeigned assent and consent to the use of all things in the said Booke conteined and prescribed according to the Act of Parliament on that behalfe in the presence of us whose names are underwritten and of the whole congregation then assembled." [No names, however, follow.]

CHAPTER IV

BAPTISMS

Births and baptisms — Casting nativities — Puritans and fonts — Exceptional baptismal entries—Adult baptism—Godparents— Godparents to bastards — Baptism by midwives — *Creatura Christi*

I T is very rare to find birth as well as baptism entered in registers until the Commonwealth period is reached; but from other sources it is quite clear that in mediæval days and throughout the sixteenth century baptism followed far more speedily after birth than has now for a long time been customary.[1] For instance, in a commonplace book of Arthur Mowen of Woodseats, Derbyshire, mention is made of Alice Mowen, born on Monday night, and christened at Dronfield church on the following Wednesday, 13th March 1593; of George Wilson, born on Tuesday, 13th September 1590, and christened on the Thursday; of Frances Wilson, born on Saturday about xj of the clock, 7th July 1599, and christened in Tickhill church, Yorks, on the morrow; and of George Mowen, born at Milnethorpe on Saturday 19th of April 1600, and christened at Dronfield on the following day by his uncle. There are many other entries of baptisms of his posterity the day after birth, and one of the latest is still more remarkable:—

[1] By the ecclesiastical laws of King Ine, A.D. 693, a child was ordered to be baptized within 30 nights; if otherwise, the father was to make satisfaction with 30 shillings. The laws of the Northumbrian priests shortened the period, in 950, to 9 nights, under a penalty of twelve ore. The canons under King Edgar, made in 960, extended the period to 37 nights.

"George Mowen my son and Hellen his wife had issue, and she was brought to bed of a goodly boy on Sunday at morn, between 1 and 2 of the clock, being the 12th of June 1628, at Woodseats, and christened at Barley the same day, between morning prayers, by me Arthur Mowen, his grandfather."

The earlier part of the first register book of Chislet, Kent, is a remarkable exception to the general rule. The birth is always recorded, and the entry is made in Latin, either as *natus et baptizatus*, or *natus et renatus*. It was obviously the rule in that parish to baptize on the birthday. Out of 15 baptisms in 1544, 13 were baptized on the day of birth; in 1545, 8 out of 11; and in 1546 the whole of the 16 entries were of that nature.

The expression *renatus* for baptism is not infrequent in Latin register entries; it is the form usually adopted in the registers of Hughley, Salop, from 1576 to 1616; it also occurs in the Shipton registers of the same county.

The following is the preface to the 1653 births and baptisms in the register of Barnstaple, Devon :—

"Here beginneth a Register of the dayes of the Birth of Children here in Barnestaple as it is comanded for Authoryty of Parlam^t more exact than formerly."

The list begins with William, son of Henry Drake, born 4th December 1653. Parallel columns opposite the names are prepared for "Born" and "Bap." Out of the 40 names entered as born up to the end of the year 1653 (24th March), only one is entered as baptized, and only five more up to the end of August 1654. As, however, from this latter date up to the close of the Commonwealth period baptisms are almost invariably entered after the births, the omission of the former for some months in 1653-54 is apparently accidental.

Occasionally births are entered of a much later date, as suggested in accordance with the Stamp Act of 1783. Thus the third register book of Askham, Notts, which begins in 1784, records both birth and baptism. The following is the first entry :—

"1784. Mary, daughter of William Pankerd, born 15 June, bap. 27th."

In the same year occurs Isaac Hilton, born 22nd May, baptized 20th June; and Mary Clark, born and baptized on 2nd April. The double entries continue down to 1812.

A belief in the follies of astrology caused certain registers to be disfigured by the occasional exact entry as to birth, in order to give facilities for "casting the nativity," or telling the fortune of the child. It is a wonder that the profanity of associating holy baptism with such an unscriptural attempt to fathom the future did not check such entries. Four examples are here given out of about a score that have been noted :—

"1574 (*Hawsted, Suffolk*). M^d. That Mr. Robert Drury, the first sonne of Mr. William Drury, Esquire, was born 30 Jan. betwixt 4 and 5 of the clock in the morning, the Sunne in Libra, anno 1574, at Durham House, within the Parish of Westminster.

"1586 (*Exton, Rutland*). Mr. Henry Hastings, Son and Heir of Mr. Francis Hastings, was born on St. Mark's Even, April 24, between the hours of 10 and 11 of the clock at night, Sign Sagit: secund: die pleni lunii Marte in Taurum intrato die precedente; and was christened May 17.

"1600 (*Brundish, Suffolk*). The xxvjth daie of October was Baptisid Thomas Colbye the sonne of Thomas Colbye gent and Annye ux' beeinge borne the xiij daie of October the signe beeinge in Taurus at the hower of vij of the clocke in the eveninge.

"1636 (*South Pickenham, Norfolk*). Elizabetha filia Jacobi Hunter ex Anna Uxore ejus in ipsius plateis sub Australi parte Magnæ Ulmi October 9 in Lucem Edita est, et eodem die sacro baptismate aspersa est."

The Puritans had an innate dislike to the use of a

baptismal font, and preferred to use an ordinary basin as necessitating more sprinkling, and belittling the importance of the initial Sacrament of the Church. The Elizabethan injunctions strictly forbade the use of basins, but when the Puritans gained the ascendancy in the Commonwealth days basins were ordered to be substituted for fonts, and not a few of the latter were broken up or ejected from the churches.[1]

The use of anything save a proper font for baptism was not only prohibited by Elizabeth in 1584, but is strictly forbidden by the reformed Canons of the Church of England. Nevertheless the use of basins by the Puritans had obtained such a hold that this irreverent custom was not wholly abolished at the restoration of episcopacy; in fact, it is still in practice in a few out-of-the-way parishes of slovenly habits. At Hillingdon, Middlesex, basin-baptizing continued for ten years after its renewed prohibition, as the incumbent admits in the register :—

"Elizabeth, the Daughter of William Pratt, Feb. 25, 1671–2. The first that in eleven years was baptized with water in the font, the custom being in this place to baptize out of a bason, after the Presbyterian manner, only set in the Font, which I could never get reformed, till I had gotten a new clerk, John Brown, who presently did what I appointed to be done."

We give two out of several register references to new or restored fonts immediately subsequent to the Restoration :—

"1660 (*Cathedral Church of Peterborough*). Hellin Austin, the daughter of Humphrey Austin, was born the 20th of February being Wednesday, and baptized the 7th of March in the Cathedral Church, being the first that was christened in the Font there after the setting it up. The said Font being pull'd down and the lead taken out of it by Cromwell's soulders. Anno Dom. 1643.

[1] See Cox & Harvey's *Church Furniture* (1907), pp. 160–235, and Bond's *Fonts and Font Covers* (1909).

" 1661 (*Whittington, Lancashire*). Mary daughter of Johne Johnson bapt. the second day of February in the New font the first child in the said font erected in the 14th year of the Reigne of our Soverign Lord Charles the second."

The following are a selection of somewhat unusual entries from baptismal registers arranged chronologically; they need no comment :—

" 1575 (*Christ Church, Newgate Street*), Sep. 26, was christened 4 dau's of Roger Abraham, pulter

Elyzabeathe
Margerett } these 4 dau's were borne at one byrthe
Dorathye } by his wyfe Joone.
Marye

" 1588 (*Mitcham, Surrey*). William Anselm, the sonne of William Anselm Vicar of this parish of Mytcham was borne upon Friday beinge the firste of Novembre and the festivall day off all Saintes betwene the hours of one and two of the Clocke in the afternone of the same day and was baptized the sonday sennight after being the x of the month aforesaid.

" 1604 (*Nunney, Somersetshire*). Roger Starr, baptized Dec. 17. He clymed up a ladder to the top of the house, 23 Oct., 1606, being seven weeks and odd days less than two years old.

" 1613 (*Holnest, Dorset*). Marye Dober, Hanna and Arthur Dober, the ii daughters and sonne of Thomas Dober, were all three borne at one tyme, and were baptized the xxixth daye of Marche.

" 1624 (*St. Peter's, Canterbury*). Elizabeth Fuller, d. of Thomas Fuller, a baker of St. James his p'ish in Dover (the mother in her jorney overtaken w'th her travaile being delivered here with us at the Cherrytree) the sayd Elizabeth Fuller baptized Septemb. 5.

" 1634 (*Stock, Essex*), 15 Mar. John s. of John Fisher (as was said) and of Margaret a stranger, brought to bed at ye 'Cocke' some 4 days before was baptized ye same time being ye 15th of March, on which day in ye night the sayd Margaret as they called her and her sayd sonne were together with one whom they called her sister, secretly conveyed away, the host and hostesse not knowing thereof. Meretricium certe hoc fuit facinus.

" 1635 (*Drypole, E. R. Yorks*). George the son of Robart Johnson was baptized on tuesday the 26th of Januarie about foure of the clocke in the morninge being weake and abortivelie borne. The said George Johnson was buried on Wednesday the 27th of Januarie.

" 1642 (*Nassington, Northants*). Rich. Forsters child christned at Fotheringhay by Mr. Welby and not signed wth the signe of the Crosse 2 June."

Allusion has already been made to the changes in connection with baptism under the Commonwealth. This change is commented upon in several registers; it will suffice to give two of such references, the one in Latin, the other in English:—

" 1645 (*Wing, Rutland*). Michael Winge filius Michael Winge et Annæ Haule uxoris ejus baptizatus fuit vicesimo sexto die Octobris. Iste infans fuit primus qui baptizatus fuit secundum Directorium parliamentarum.

" 1647 (*Blatherwick, N'hants*). Marke the sonne of Ferdinando Broun and Anne his wife was baptized Mar. the 25th, beeing the first baptized according to the Directory.

" 1646 (*Moze, Essex*). Mattheus Duerdenus filius natu maximus Matthei Duerdeni Rectoris de Mose et Elizabethæ uxoris natus erat 15 die Octobris Ano Dom 1646 inter horas primum et secundum nocturnas baptizatus Octob. 22 in ecclesia parochiali de Mose. Sponsoribus.

" 1651 (*Eastbourn, Sussex*). Rich Boulté, the Son of me John Boulté, was born January 19th, and was baptized January 20th, he being my 26th child.

" 1655 (*St. Botolph, Aldgate*). William Clark, a Soldier, and Thomasine his Wife, who herself went for a Souldier, and was billetted at the Three Hammers in East Smithfield, about seven months, and was afterwards delivered of this Child the 16th day of this July, and was baptized the 17th in her lodging, being one Mr. Hubler's House. She had been a Souldier, by her own confession, about five years, and was sometime Drummer to the Company.

" 1661 (*Hackness, Yorks*). James the sonn of Thomas Moore gentleman borne the second of September in the morneinge baptized the tenth day privately it is supposed by a popish prieste beinge a straunger then at the mannor. Mr. Thomas Moore was then at London.

" 1664-5 (*Grinton, Yorks*), Mar. 24. Anthony, son of Mark Raw of Blades, baptized in ye presense of ye Great Grandfather, and Grandfather and other witnesses then having received ye holy communion : he was aged 2 yeares at Martinmas before.

" 1667 (*Abington, N'hants*). John, sonne of Clement Spicer chirothecarius (glover) and of Elizabeth his wife, was made a X^an 24 Novemb.

" 1689 (*Thornton, Bucks*). Richard ye son of William How and of Elizabeth his wife was baptized 15th day of September. Called out of Church in midst of sermon to baptize it, bee likely to die.

" 1692. Debora ye dearly beloved wife of Robert Jenney Esq. dyed ye 24th of October and was buryed the 26 of ye same Month leaveing 2 pretty Babes Offley and Debora behind her whereof Debora dyed ye 28th of May and was buryed ye 30th 1693.

" 1703 (*Corby, N'hants*). Presbyterians, Nathaniel Chambers and Rebecca his wife had two children a male and a female, born May 22, 1703, as I am told, whom one Davis of Rothwell has made Christians, they will call (them) Richard and Rebecca.

" 1709 (*Hepworth, Suffolk*). Joseph son of Robert Beever of Hepworth junr. baptized with a conditional Baptism the 15th day of May, because it was said that the Dissenting Minister Mr. Jo. Biram had baptized him before, but the said Robert Beever being interrogated about it, could not tell mee that the said Mr. Biram had done more than sprinkled it and prayed with it, injoyning him to bring the child afterwards to Lidget meeting to be baptized there.

" 1712 (*St. Alkmund's, Derby*). Bap. Nov. 5 Elizabeth and Honeylove the daughters of John Key. Note Elizabeth was about 3 years old. The reason that she was baptized at the same time in the church when Honeylove the infant was, was this, I (Revd H. Cantrel M.A.) had some time before preached concerning baptism, and proved that the dissenting teachers have no authority to baptize, and consequently that children that had been sprinkled by 'em, ought to be baptiz'd by an Episcopal Minister. The Father was so fully convinced by what was said, that he came to me and desired me to baptize the said child.

" 1767 (*Church Broughton, Derbyshire*). May, daughter of Humphrey

Morley, was born and baptized June 2nd. N.B. This child had two Teeth cut when born. I saw the teeth when they brought the child to me to baptize it. Jno Dimott, Vicar.

" 1771 (*Slaley, Northumberland*), Feb. 25. Then was baptized John, son of William Durick and Mary his wife, a travelling dansing master and mistress.

" 1772 (*Stanwell, Middlesex*). Robert, John, and Mary Nash, trines (*i.e.* triplets), baptized Feb. 7, buried Feb. 14.

" 1796 (*St. Peter's, Canterbury*), Dec. 25. Esther Owen, d. of William Owen, Drum Major in the Royal Glamorganshire Militia and Ester his wife, privately baptized about the 16th day of October, 1794, on Maker Heights in the County of Devon or Cornwall, was received into the congregation, being 2 years of age, in this Church. This Battalion in October 1797, being then in camp on Maker Heights."

The following instances, selected from many entries as to the baptism of those of riper years, possess some interest. It will be noticed that three of them refer to persons of colour :—

1663 (*Westminster Abbey*). Drell Pead, one of the King's Scholars, ab^t 16 y^{rs} of age, was bapt^d by the Deane publickly in the font newly set up, April 18.

" 1674 (*Great Hampden, Bucks*). Colliberry Winkfield and Jane Winkfield, the daughters of John Winkfield and Elizabeth his wife were baptized the 23d of Sept., the first being about 9 yeares old and the other about 4 years old.

" 1693 (*Bishop Wearmouth, Durham*), March 27. A person aged about 20 years, a Tawny, borne at the Bay of Bengal, in the East Indies, and being taken captive by the English in his minoritie was (after due examination of himself and witnesses) baptized, and named John Weremouth, by me T. O., Curate.

" 1719 (*Bobbingworth, Essex*). John Reade (son of John Read an Anabaptist) born Dec. ye 19th 1698 was at his own request baptiz'd this 22d day of April.

" 1736 (*Dunster*), Feb. 15. A black man was baptized William, being about 22 years of age, and desired to be called William Dunster in remembrance of his new birth.

" 1757 (*Stokesby, Yorks*). Memorand. Jonathan Hill Physician and Chirurgion aged 66 bapt Apr: 24th.

" 1763 (*Thurcaston, Leicestershire*), Nov. 19. John Cragg of

Thurcaston, an adult, in his 75th year, being bed-rid, was privately baptized, at his own request. N.B.—His Father and Mother had been rigid Anabaptists.

R. HURD, Rector

"1788 (*Chislehurst, Kent*), Jan. 20th. Thomas West, a negro of about 6 years of age, who had been sent over as a present to Lord Sydney from Governor Orde of Dominica."

Entertainments at the time of baptism were customary among the well-to-do classes. Strype tells us that when the son of Sir Thomas Chamberlayne was baptized at St. Benet's Church, Paul's Wharf, in 1559,

" the church was hung with cloth of arras, and after the christening were brought wafers, comfits, and divers banquetting dishes, and Hypocras and Muscadine wine to entertain the guests."

There is an entry of a choral baptism in 1636 among the registers of 1636 at St. Margaret's, Westminster :—

" May 26. Baptized Mrs. Alice, daughter to Sir Robt. Eatan, Secretary to King Charles I. The Quire attended : the boys had £3, 16s. 8d."

When Cardinal Ximenes put forth his great influence in 1497 to secure the due registration of the baptism of children throughout Western Christendom, this step was mainly taken to correct the laxity of morals whereby divorces had become frequent on the score of alleged spiritual relationship or affinity, arising out of acts of sponsorship. Hence it was ordered throughout the diocese of Toledo, and the custom ere long became general throughout Spain and Italy and elsewhere, that the names of the sponsors should be registered at the time of baptism.

"Godfathers and godmothers," as Mr. Chester Waters puts it, "were regarded by the Church as spiritual parents, who, with their husbands and wives and children, were spiritually related to each other and to the infant of whom they were sponsors, within the prohibited degrees. When, therefore, two persons wished to dissolve the bond of marriage, they had only to allege that they had previously contracted some spiritual relationship which rendered their marriage canonically invalid; and from the absence of any record to test the truth of the allegation, they were, by an easy collusion, enabled to separate and marry some one else."

Divorces on the ground of spiritual incest were fairly common in England in pre-Reformation days. Thorpe's *Customale Roffense* supplies various instances in Rochester diocese during the fifteenth century of divorce or punishment for such offences. The marriage between John Trevemook and Joan Peckham was annulled in 1465 on the ground that John's former wife, Letitia, had been godmother to one of Joan's children. William Lovelesse, of Kingsdown, was cited in December 1472 on a charge of having married his spiritual sister—that is, a woman to whom his mother had been godmother. John Horsthan, of Tunbridge, was sentenced in 1463 by the diocesan official to be whipped three times round the market-place and church for marrying Dionysia Thomas, a goddaughter of his former wife.

The following entry in the register book of East Quantock's Head, Somerset, is the last instance known in England of the remarriage of the persons who had been divorced for spiritual incest:—

"1560, Aug. 7. Thomas Luttrell esquier and Mrs. Margaret Hadley married."

This Thomas Luttrell was a cadet of the ancient and distinguished family of the Luttrells of Dunster Castle. During the lax times of Edward VI he had been contracted in marriage with Margaret, the infant heiress of the Hadleys of Withycombe, notwithstanding the fact that she was the goddaughter of his mother, Dame Margaret Luttrell, and therefore in the eyes of the Church the spiritual sister of

Thomas. The bride came to full age in the time of Queen Mary, when the laws of the Church were strictly interpreted, with the result that the offenders were divorced, and ex-communicated. Appeal was made for a dispensation to Pope Paul IV, and by his decision the culprits were released from excommunication in November 1558, on condition of a new marriage being celebrated in the face of the Church. The remarriage, however, did not take place until the new conditions of things under Elizabeth were established, when all references to Rome and questions of illegality were ignored, and the couple were remarried according to the reformed rite, the bride in her maiden name.

It is highly probable that in a large number of parishes, and possibly in the majority, the names of the sponsors were added to the baptismal entries so soon as the general law of registration came into force in England. It is known that this was the case in several instances, but the vast majority of the registers which date back to 1538-9 are mere abstract transcripts dating from the close of that century, wherein every superfluous word beyond the barest record is obviously omitted.

It would appear, from some of the earliest entries in the now missing register of Much Wenlock, Salop, that god-parents were there known by the old English term of "gossips." The word is more correctly written "gossib," for it is derived from the Anglo-Saxon *sib*, alliance or relationship, hence one related in the service of God.

"Jan. 21, 1538-9. Gossibes Sr Thos Butler Vicar of this churche and dominus Jas. Ball monke of the Monastre of Sainte Milburge.
"18 Feb. Gossibes Ric¡ Lawley Gent. and Johan the wif of Jas. Fenymer Porter of the Monastre."

The following entry of the year 1542, in the register of Ickenham, Middlesex, is probably due to the distinguished

4

position of the sponsors, and not to any adherence to a then general Catholic custom :—

"Katherine, the Dowgter of the Lord Hastyngs, and the Lady his Wyff, was borne the Saturday before our Lady Day, th' assumption, being the 11 day of August, and was christened the 20 of August, the godmother, Queene Kateryn by her debite, being her syster, one Mr. Harbard's Wiff; the other Godmother, the Lady Margaret Duglas, the Kyng's nece, and the Godfather, the Lord Russell, beying the Lord Prive Seale, by hys debite, Master Francis Russell, hys Son and Heyre."

In the preliminary Articles of Visitation drawn up by Cardinal Pole, in Queen Mary's reign, the final question "Touching the Clergy" is—"Whether do they keep the book or register of christenings, buryinges or marriages, with the names of the godfathers and godmothers?"

The first register book of Chislet, Kent, shows compliance with the Marian orders, but the godparent entries ceased on Elizabeth's accession :—

"1556. Thomisina filia Thome Clipson erat baptizata 10 die Julii patribus et matribus rob'tus alen Thomisina blaksland Elizabet Hinckton.
"1558. Gilbertus Androwe filius Johani Androwe baptizat⁵ fuit 3 die Augustii compatres gilbert⁵ penj et Thomas Wylkys co'mat'r Juliana Lyon."

The earlier pages of the well-kept registers of the parish church of Chelmsford also show obedience in this respect to Cardinal Pole's injunctions. The following are among the few cases wherein we have noted the more or less regular entry of godparents in the baptismal registers of Elizabethan days: Mertsham, Surrey, 1559-1562; Selattyn, Salop, 1560-1574; Birchington, Kent, 1564-1606; Burton Fleming, Yorks, 1577-1599. At Ledbury, Hereford, the entry of the sponsors began, according to order, in 1556, and was continued down to 1576.

CARDINAL REGINALD POLE
(ARTIST UNKNOWN)
From a painting at the National Portrait Gallery

The registers of St. Martin's, Micklegate, York, give the names of the godparents of baptized children for the years 1571–75; they are in each case termed "sureties," to which term "witnesses" is added in two or three instances.

"1571. Barbara Vandighteryng, doughter of Sir James Vandighter-ynge, Flemyng and . . . hys wyf, was baptysed this eleventh day of november—surties, Mr. Cotton, archedecon of cleveland, Mrs. Trew, and Mrs. Cuttes."

Godparents are also named in the registers of All Hallows-in-the-Wall for several years, beginning in 1584:—

"1585 (*All Hallows-in-the-Wall*). Roose Raman, the daughter of John Raman being yeaman purvyar unto her Majestie was Baptized the xiiij day of novembre, and had to her witnesses John burton currier of this parish, and Roose Willis the wyfe of John Willis of the parish of St. peters the poore, and Martha Smyth, the wyfe of Richard Smyth one of her majesties trumpets, of this parish."

In the registers of Holy Trinity, Chester, the names of the godparents are set forth for each baptism from 1600 to 1624, thus :—

" 1601, 6 January. To Ashton Baker a sonne named Raf. G. F. Mr. Rose Berkenhead and Rafe Crosse, G. M. Mrs. Elizabeth Thropp.
" 1620, 14 March. Margret, Dau. to Robt Flecher Baker; Rafe Cratchley, Margret Harndy and Marg[t] Blanchard, Gossips."

The registers of Mansfield, Nottinghamshire, occasionally supply the names of godparents under the baptismal entries from 1600 (the beginning) to 1625. In each entry the sponsors are termed "witnesses." Thus under 1612 occurs :—

"Christopher Reane sonne of Nicolas Reane and Eme his wyfe was baptized the xvj day of June Robt Cockrell, thomas myles and Mrs. Mary Jackson wyttnes."

As to the various names, in addition to witnesses or sureties assigned in the registers to godparents, it may be mentioned that in the early Selattyn entries they are invariably called " Goshipps," and at Birchington " Susceptores," " Compatres," or " Fidejussores." The last of these terms is also used in the registers of Startforth, Yorkshire.

In the time of Elizabeth there was no necessity to continue the entry of sponsors in our registers on the ground of avoiding the danger of spiritual incest, as such an impediment to marriage was no longer maintained by the Church of England. The custom, therefore, generally fell into abeyance. But in many a register, more especially in country parishes, isolated entries of sponsors are found to accompany the baptismal record. In almost all such cases, we are sorry to say, the reason for this exceptional setting forth of sponsors is the innately vulgar one, particularly odious in a Church record, of doing supposed honour to the family of the squire or other magnate. This vulgarity is not infrequently still further emphasised by such entries being made in an exceptionally large text.

At Askham, Westmoreland, the Sandforths were lords of the manor ; throughout the latter part of Elizabeth's reign, and down to 1662, the children of that family bore the unique distinction of having their godparents' names set forth in full. A single instance is given as a sample :—

" 1592. Oct. 20 was Thomas the chyld of Mr. Thomas Sandforth esquier borne and chrystened the fyrst day of Nov. being All Saints day, his godfathers was Thomas Lord Scrope by his substitute Mr. John Mydleton esquier and Mr. Thomas Salkeld esquier, his godmother was Mrs. An Bellingham."

The only mention of godparents in the registers of Stokesley, York, which begin in 1571, is a single instance, the entry being obviously made for the poor reason of exalting the dignity of a family which could command the presence of such exalted sponsors at the initial sacrament of the Divine Carpenter :—

"1602–3. Margrett the doughter of the Right Worshippfull Sir William Eure Knight being borne the xth of December was Baptized the xviijth daie of Januarie The God Father my Lord Arch Bushopp hys Grace Bush. of Yorke and the God Moothers the Right Honorable Countesses of Kent and Cumberland."

It must suffice to give but two or three other examples, out of many that we have noted, of the preferential treatment in church registers of the children of the great people of the parish, when dedicated to Him who knew not where to lay His head. The Bowdens, of Bowden Hall, were the most ancient and wealthy family of the widespread Derbyshire parish of Chapel-en-le-Frith. Hence their children are singled out for elaborate entry :—

"Barnby Bowden was born ye 5th day of August, 1653, about 6 of ye clock in ye morning, and was baptized ye 16th day of y^t same, Thomas Barnby and Peter Foljamb Esquiers godfathers, and Katharine Wentworth, wife of Michael Wentworth, of Wody, Esquier, godmother.

"Thomas Bowden was born ye 4th of October, 1654, about 3 o'clock in ye morning, and was baptized ye 18th day of ye same. Henry Bagshawe, of Ridge, and Tristram Stafford godfathers, and Mrs. Wooderofe, godmother."

The same principle obviously regulates such exceptional entries as the following in the registers of St. Margaret's, Westminster :—

"1708, June 28. Charles Grahame, son to Very Rev. Wm D.D. Dean of Wells, by Alice, baptized by Jno Ld Arch Bishop of York. Her Majestie being godmother, and the Dukes of Somerset, Queensberry and Dover, godfathers—Born ye 6th.

"1720, June 22. Lord George Jonnstone, son to the Most Honorable William Lord Marquess of Annandale, by Lady Charlotte his Marchioness. His godfathers, His Majestie King George (by proxy the Earl of Orkney), the Lord Viscount Allington the

other: and Her Grace the Dutches of Hamilton his godmother."

After all this servility, it is a relief to recollect that there
are in our English parish registers just one or two very rare
cases where the minister does honour to the lowly. The
most touching entry of this kind that we have met with is
that penned by the parson of West Thorney, Sussex, who
was not ashamed to make known in the register that he was
sponsor to a base-born infant. Surely the boy's unusual
name was the clergyman's choice; spinola is a small briar
rose.

" 1615 ⎧Spinola, the Sonne of Dorothy Dumpar, base borne baptised
⎪   the tenth day of March, his Godfathers were Godfrey
filius ⎨ Blaxton P'sone of Thorney, and Thomas Roman, and
terræ ⎪ Widdowe Toogood Godmother; God's blessing be uppon
⎩   him, Amen."

In connection, however, with infants of illegitimate birth,
it must be recollected that now and again there are register
entries of sponsors whose names are obviously recorded in
order that they might serve as witnesses, if required, in
matters which might be charged on the parish, not unlikely
to arise in cases of bastardy. This is the explanation of the
following entry, of the year 1580, in the registers of St.
Michael le Belfry, York :—

"Dorothye Atkingson, Daughter to M'garett Atkinson, unmaryed,
and begotten as she did confesse, in the tyme of hir laboure,
before the wyves there present, by one Roger Nuton, cov'lett weaver.
The godfather name of it is Thomas Maryson, servant to Mr.
Henry Maye; godmothers are Dorothy, ye wyf of one Edward
Walker, and one Ephame, the wyfe of Laurence Graye, baptized
the xxvth day of April."

The same explanation holds good with regard to the
entry of sponsors in the two following register excerpts :—

" 1607 (*Holme Hale, Norfolk*). James, ye bastard of one Maria, who sayeth she hath or had a husband called Cockson; was bapt. 6 April. She sayeth y^t James Barbye was ye father of y^t; one Peter Whytyng of Walpole was godfather, Ann Cooke and Ann Bateman were Godmothers.

" 1614 (*St. Oswald, Durham*), May 8. Richard Elleson, supposed to be the son of Richard Elleson of the parish of Pittington, bassebegotten with Ezabell Raw, the wife of Cuthbt Raw decesed. Godfather John Sim; godmother Alice Dun, the wife of Georg Dun, with Sr Wright Curatt that did christen the saide child."

In the registers of the last of these two parishes, there are similar sponsor entries at the baptism of bastards for the years 1609–12.

A baptismal entry in the Elizabethan registers of St. Olave's, Hart Street, mentions such historical characters as "witnesses," that the exceptional registration honour done to the infant viscount can be pardoned, especially as the saintly Bishop Andrews, then vicar of St. Giles', Cripplegate, was the celebrant :—

" 1590–1, Jan. 22. Robert Lord Deaveraux Vicount Hereford, sonne and heyre of Robert Earl of Essex, in my lady wallsingham's howse, mother to the Countis, Sir francis Knolls and the lord rich with the countess of leicester wittnesses. Doctor Andrewes preached and babtized the child."

The condescension of two well-born men in standing as godparents to the child of a mere common sawyer, in the reign of Charles I, was thought well worthy by the rector of Albrighton, near Wolverhampton, of being honoured in the parish register :—

" 1638, May 12. John, sonne of Edwarde and Cisley Davies, of Albrighton, sawier, was baptized the 12th day of May, being Whitsunday even. Sir John Corbett Knight barronett, and his kinsman Mr. Thomas Riton coming from London accidentally being ye two godfathers who desired to doe good unto a poore man and so baptized his childe."

The rector of Methley, Leeds, had such an extraordinary tale to tell of the godparents at a baptism in his church, in 1683, that he may readily be excused for making a special entry :—

"John, the son of Savile Salsterston bapti^d the 16 of May, and it weare confirmed and had its sureties on the 24 day of May, and his sureties was these : his granfather and his great granfather and great granmother, all by the father."

The Canon Law has always held that the rite of baptism could be administered by any person in case of necessity. Midwives in the Church of England, both before and after the Reformation, were particularly enjoined to baptize if there was any risk of the child dying before a priest could arrive. The midwife was licensed by the bishop; to obtain a licence, the woman had to be recommended by matrons who knew of her skill, and also by the parish minister, who was to certify as to her life and conversation, and that she was a member of the Church of England. By her oath she was sworn to be "diligent, faithful, and ready to help every woman travailing of child, as well the poor as the rich, and not to forsake the poor woman and leave her to go to the rich," and she was also bound to "in no way exercise any manner of witchcraft, charms, sorcery, or invocation."

Curates were enjoined openly in the church "to teach and instruct the mydwiefes of the very wordes and fourme of Baptisme, to thententes that they may use them perfictly and none oder."

Several examples of entries referring to baptism by midwives are here set forth, both from the earlier and later parochial registers :—

"1539 (*Goodnestone, Kent*), July 19. Francis Sladde, Son of Henrie, who was also christened by ye midwife at St. Alban's Courte.

"1555 (*North Elmham, Norfolk*). The ij chyldren of Johne Brow and Agnes hys wyffe, wer chrystened by ye mydwyffe at home ye xvj day of Apryll, and was buryed yt same dye, it was esterne Tuysday.

" 1567 (*Herne, Kent*). William Lawson, an infant, christend by the woemen, bearyed 21 Martii.

"1568 (*Bobbingworth, Essex*). M^d that John Browne was Christened at home by the mydwyfe beinge in greate perill the ix day of November and after his recoveringe was brought to the Church to receave according to the Lawe.

" 1569 (*Ibid.*). M^d that George Bourne the sonn of William Bourne was Christened at home by mother Wryte the mydwyffe of the parish and in the presence of ix other honest women of the parish then beinge present accordinge to the lawe thorowe great pearill and dainger the xvj day of Februarie.

" 1578 (*St. Michael le Belfry, York*). John childe, sonne to Thomas childe, baptized at home in the house by the mydwif, mother todd, and afterwarde brought to the church, the iij^d day of may.

" 1582 (*St. Mary Woolnoth*), Sep. 12. Cislye, daughter of Roger Tasker, Goldsmythe, witnes by Roose Preest, Mydwief, that it was so weke that it coulde not tarry untelle Sundaye.

" 1589-90 (*Mitcham, Surrey*). George Tyrwitt the sonne of William Tyrwitt of Kettlebey Esquier was baptized by the hannde of the Midwife in Mrs. Rutlands house the Childe being in greate daunger. Jan. 1.

" 1591 (*St. Mary's, Lichfield*), Oct. 12. Magarett, D^r of Walter Hemingham, of Pypehall, baptized by the midwyfe, and as yett not broughte to ye Church to be there examyned and testified by them that were then presente.

" 1730 (*Bishop Wearmouth, Durham*). Robert, daughter of William Thompson, bap. 15 Feb. the midwife mistaking the sex, ebrietas dementat.

" 1731 (*Hanwell, Middlesex*), Daughter. Thomas, Son of Thomas Messenger and Elizabeth his Wife, was born and baptized Oct. 24, by the midwife at the Font called a boy, and named by the godfather Thomas, but proved a girl.

" 1787 (*Clunbury, Salop*), Augt. 5. Thomas* s. of William and Ann James was baptised.

> * "His name was not Thomas but William. He was the only son and was born on the 16th June, 1787, as appears by Mrs. Hold's (the midwife's) Book. B. Morgan, subcurate."

Creatura Christi. — It will be noticed that the three

last extracts by midwives all relate to mistakes made as to name or sex. It was, perhaps, from this liability to error in hasty baptisms during dangerous confinements that the midwives or others in mediæval days now and again styled the infant Creatura Christi, or simply Creature, a term equivalent to Child of God. This term is met with in several parochial registers of the sixteenth century. It probably had its origin from Tindall's version of the New Testament text, 2 Cor. v. 17. "Yf any man be in Christ, he is a newe creature."

"1547 (*Staplehurst, Kent*). Then was baptized by the Midwyffe and so buryed the childe of Thoms Goldham called Creature.

" 1 Edw. 6 the xxvij of Apryle, there was borne ij Childre ofAlexander Beerye the one christned at home and so deceased called Creature, the other christned at church called John.

"1561 (*St. Peter-in-the-East, Oxford*), June 30, the chylde of God, filius Ric. Stacy.

"1563 (*Ibid.*), July 17. Baptizata fuit in œdibus he^{ri} Humfrey (Bishop) filia ejus quæ nominata fuit Creatura Christi.

"1563 (*Ibid.*), July 17. Creatura Christi filia Laurentii Henfeldi sepulta fuit eodem die.

"1565 (*Staplehurst, Kent*), March 3. Ther was buryed the sonne of John . . ., which dyed imediatly as he was borne, being named Creature.

"1573 (*Kidderminster*), April 14. b. Gods creature, the sonne of John and Jane Glazzard.

"1588 (*Elmley Lovett, Worcester*). Bur. Creature the daughter of Robert Briges being christ^{d} by the midwife, was buried the xith day of December."

Sometimes, however, the little ones then baptized lived to mature age.

"1579 (*Staplehurst, Kent*), July 19. Marryed John Haffynden and Creature Cheseman yong folke."

CHAPTER V

CHRISOM CHILDREN, FOUNDLINGS, ETC.

Chrisom children—Foundlings—The foundlings of the Temple—
Nurse children—Confirmation—Churching—Bastards—Terms
for illegitimacy

REGISTER entries of the burial of " Chrisom Children "
are of fairly frequent occurrence throughout England during the sixteenth and seventeenth centuries,
and more rarely during the earlier part of the eighteenth
century.

The chrisom was the white linen cloth or vesture placed
on the child at the time of baptism. In the mediæval Church
of England, the priest anointed the child with the chrism
or holy oil, in the form of a cross, on the breast and between
the shoulders, and the idea of the chrisom cloth was to
protect the chrism marks and to preserve them from hasty
removal. The chrisom was worn as a vesture by the child
for seven days, or until the mother was able to be churched.
At the time of the churching, the chrisom was presented to
the church. The chrisoms were afterwards used by the
priests for ablutions and such-like purposes in the church.
If, however, the child died before the mother's churching, the
infant was termed a chrisom child, and was shrouded in the
white baptismal vesture, which was bound round the little
body with ornamental folds or strips of linen.

The anointing with chrism, unlike other incidentals of
mediæval baptism, was not given up by the Church of

England in her early reformed service, and the use of the chrisom was also for a short time maintained. The following is the pertinent passage as to the chrisom from the first Prayer Book of Edward VI (1549):—

" Then the Godfathers and Godmothers shall take and lay their hands upon the child, and the minister shall put upon him his white vesture, commonly called a chrisom, and say, 'Take this white vesture for a token of the innocency which by God's grace in this holy sacrament of Baptism is given unto thee; and for a sign whereby thou art admonished, so long as thou livest, to give thyself to innocency of living, that after this transitory life thou mayest be partaker of the life everlasting.'"

The use, however, of both chrism and chrisom was erased from the second Prayer Book of 1552. Nevertheless, though no longer enjoined, the use of the chrisom or special white vestment lingered in certain parishes for many a long year after the disappearance of the word from the Book of Common Prayer, together with its presentation at the time of churching. Thus in the register book of Wickenby, Lincolnshire, is an undated entry made early in the seventeenth century to the following effect:—

"The chrysom and a gracepeny is always to be given at ye woman's churching. The chrysom must be half a yard of fine linnen long and a full yard in width."

We have met with several late Elizabethan depositions, both in Derbyshire and Somersetshire, wherein the actual use of the chrisom at baptisms is named in manorial inquisitions, godmothers testifying that they had carried the chrisom to the font at the baptism of an heir, or had placed it on the child. A survival of the custom may even yet be noted in some quiet country churches, where the godmother is wont to place a clean cambric handkerchief, generally a new one, over the infant's face immediately after the actual baptism, and whilst the rest of the office is proceeding.

The custom was so engraven upon English minds that the application of the term chrisom child to those babes that died in their innocency, and who were shrouded in their chrisoms, was fairly general throughout the seventeenth century. Two entries from the registers of St. Peter's, Northampton, for the same year may serve as examples :—

"1632. A crisom woman childe of Ann Nelson widow buryed the xxx of March 1632. A chrisom child of John Taylor was buryed the vii of October."

It was not necessary to be of legitimate birth to obtain this title. Thus at Hinckley, Leicestershire, a few years earlier, occurs this entry among the burials :—

"1627. One Crysome, base, of Rebakca Dunning, March 16th."

The registers of St. Sepulchre's, Northampton, have an unusual number of chrisom children burials. They occur under the years 1622, 1631, 1632, 1633, 1634, 1637, 1643, 1644, 1646, 1659, 1663, 1664, 1665, 1667, 1668, 1680, 1684, 1687, and one at the exceptionally late date of 1716.

Like entries occur with unusual frequency in the registers of Aldenham, Herts, during the second quarter of the seventeenth century. There are two in 1637, four in 1642, six in 1643, three in 1644, two in 1645, two in 1646, and four in 1647 ; they are continued down to 1657.

Chrisom children occur in the parish register books of almost the whole of the churches of the city of London and of Westminster. One of the most interesting occurs at Westminster Abbey :—

"The Princess Anns Child a Chrissome bur. in yᵉ Vault, Oct. 22, 1687."

Occasionally the term chrisom or chrisom child was lengthened into chrisomer. This is the case in the registers of St. Botolph, Bishopsgate, where the terms "male

chrisomer " and " female chrisomer " occasionally occur.
Chrisomer is also used with some frequency in the registers
of St. Columb Major's Cornwall, between the years 1603
and 1618.   The register of Boughton-under-Bleau, Kent,
for the year 1617, has the following entry:—

"The 6th day of March buried a Female Chrisamer, the
daughter of Thomas Pudall."

Though the term is oftener found in seventeenth-century
registers than in those of the sixteenth century, yet there are
exceptions.   Thus there are three such entries in the register
of Kirkburton, Yorks, under the year 1568:—

"The xxvj of November was Margere Kay buryyd.   A Crysm
chyld.
"The ix day of December was Jhon March buryyd.   A Crysm
chyld.
"The xxviij day of december was Eyllyn Lytyllwood buryed.
A Crysm child."

There are four like entries in these registers for the year
1569, two in 1570, three in 1571, and seven in 1572; they
are continued at intervals down to the year 1710.

The following double entry as to twins, one of whom
was a chrisom child, which occurs in the register of
Broxley, Salop, for the year 1669, is sufficiently curious for
transcription :—

"April 2. Hugh twin son of Will'm Gough deceased and Eleanor
his relict :
"April 2. A chrisom son being the other twin of the s^{d} Will'm
Gough, deceased : "

A survival of the presentation of the chrisom to the parish
priest lingered for a long time in certain country parishes,
where it was customary for a woman at her churching to
make an offering of a white cambric handkerchief.   This is
stated to have been the use in the parish of Dutton, Essex,

in Morant's history of that county, which was published in 1768.

Representations of chrisom children are not infrequent on monumental brasses of the sixteenth and seventeenth centuries ; one occurs on an incised slab at Croxall, Derbyshire.

The baptism, only too often followed by the speedy burial of foundlings, is of frequent occurrence in town and suburban parishes, and occasionally in country districts. The naming of the deserted infant was left to the vestry in towns, and to the overseers of the poor and churchwardens in the country. It was usual to give the name of the parish as the surname, and of the Saint whose day was nearest to the discovery of the child as the Christian name. This is exemplified by the two following entries from the first register book of St. Denis (or Dennis) Backchurch in the City :—

INCISED SLAB OF EDWARD MYNER, CROXALL : A CHRISOM CHILD.

" 1567, Dec. 14. A chylde that was found at the strangers dore in Lymstrete whych chylde was founde on Saynt petter day, and founde of the p'ishe coste. Wherefore they named the chylde by the day that he was founde, and surname by the p'ishe, so the chyldes name ys Petter Dennis.

"1585, April 23. A man child was lead at Sir Edward Osbourne gate and was christned the xxiii of Aprill named Dennis Philpot, and so brought to Christes ospitall" [Philpot Lane was a street in this parish].

The registers of another City church, St. Nicholas Acon, supply two interesting instances :—

"1585, Nov. 5. A man child a foundling named Nicholas Acon after our Parishe Church name, was laid in this p'ishe.

"1618, Oct. 26. Elizabeth Acon. This child was found in the streete at one Mr. Wythers dore in St. Nicholas lane upon the nynteenth of this presnt moneth of October being as it was supposed some two monthes old but we not knowing whether it was baptized before or no, baptized it by the name of Elizabeth Acon after the name of this p'she."

The church of St. Dunstan West affords several curious examples. A child found in 1594 was baptized "Relictus Dunstan"; a foundling of 1618 was named "Mary Porch," doubtless from the porch where it was discovered; to another foundling, buried on 16th January 1629–30, the strange but not inappropriate name of "Subpœna" was applied; whilst an infant found in Chancery Lane in 1631 was styled "Elizabeth Middlesex."

The most marvellous surname bestowed on any City foundling was that chronicled in the following entry in the registers of St. Helen's, Bishopsgate, under the year 1612 :—

"Job Rakt-out-of the Asshes, being borne the last of August in the lane going to Sᴵʳ John Spencer's back gate, and there laide in a heape of old cole asshes, was baptized the First daye of September following, and dyed the next day after."

The first register book of All Hallows-on-the-Wall supplies the following :—

"1592. Benett Fincke being a man child of vj weekes old, being a foundling, in the p'she of St. Benett Finckes, the xvjth daye of

Septembre, and was brought to be nursed wth the good wyfe Hill dwelling within the vyne on the wall: was buryed from thence the xviijth of Septembre."

A quaint conceit gave the names of "Moyses and Aaron" to two male infants found in the street on 26th December 1629, as entered in the register of St. Gregory-by-St. Paul's.

Burn supplies the following from the Kensington registers as to treasure-trove in that parish, but neglects to give the year:—

"A woman child, of the age of one year and a half or there-abouts, being found in her swadlinge clothes, layed at the Ladye Coopers gate, baptized by the name of Mary Troovie, 10th October."

The registers of St. Mary Woolnoth's for the year 1699 give two instances descriptive of the clothing of foundlings:—

"March 28. Joseph, a male child, $\frac{3}{4}$ old, with a Blew Tamarett coat and English calico printed frock, was taken up at Mr. Man-wood's door. [In margin] Sent for away by the mother April 3.

"Sept. 28. Michael, a child taken up between Deputy Moor and Mr. Mark Gilbert's house, with a striped white coate and printed frock, put to Nurse Bramwood at Wirehall in Essex."

The following are a few of the entries of occasional foundlings culled from various provincial registers; they will suffice as examples, out of a large number of instances, of the style of names usually bestowed upon these deserted innocents:—

"1600 (*Lee, Kent*), Feb. 1. Vicessimo quinto die mensis Januarii infantula juxta viam communem relicta et inventa fuit, quæ (ignotis parentibus) primo die mensis Februarii in baptismo nominata fuit Fortune Founde.

"1669 (*Chipping, Lancashire*). Moses a child found within the forest of Bolland bap 28 March.

"1674 (*Great Hampden, Bucks*). Mary Lane, a child that was

5

found in the Lane by the street, whose father and mother we know not, was baptized (being about eleven months old) the 23d of Sept.

" 1689 (*Plympton, Devon*). Charity that was found in the strate of Plympton Morrish was baptized the 12th of Desember.

" 1713 (*Thornton, Bucks*). John reputed son of Catherine Cartwright of Ockhamstead (found hanging in a basket on the gates which open out of the great yard into the Highway) was baptized ye 4th of Oct.

" 1732 (*Walesby, Notts*). Ignotus a male child found in the Parish of Palethorpe, bap. March 31."

The Foundlings of the Temple during the eighteenth century were almost proverbially and scandalously numerous. The coarser cynics of the times sharpened their wits on the long-continued custom of abandoning these luckless infants amid the intricacies of the Temple precincts. The following is the first entry of a foundling baptism in the Temple register :—

" Ellenore Temple, being so named, found in the Middle Temple, was baptized on the 7th June, 1700."

The last is :—

"Mary Temple, a foundling of the Middle Temple, supposed to be now about ten months old, and on the 13th November, 1845, baptised."

The first entry of the burial of a foundling is :—

" Ann Temple, an infant, found in the Inner Temple, and buried in the Temple Churchyard the 21st May, 1695."

The last is :—

" Charles Temple, a Foundling, was buried in the Churchyard on the 2nd June, 1830, aged six."

In no other instance is the age of a Temple foundling given, but a comparison of the baptismal and burial registers shows that their life was usually very brief, often extending over only a few days. There is one entry, under 26th August 1763, of the burial of a murdered foundling :—

"A male child found dead in King's Bench Walk, Inner Temple, and according to the verdict of the Coroner's Inquest, murdered by a Person or Persons unknown."

During the eighteenth century there are actually 240 foundling baptisms, and 170 foundling burials recorded in the Temple registers. To almost the whole of these the name Temple or Templer was assigned.

The lack of any form of legislative protection of infant life caused the foundling scandals of London to be a grievous blot on the social condition of the metropolis. Even the establishment of the Foundling Hospital in 1739 did but little for a long time to mitigate the prodigal sacrifice of child life. It is stated that within four years of the establishment of that hospital 14,934 infants were admitted, and that out of that total not more than 4000 survived.

"Among the persons buried," writes Mr. Pegge in his valuable transcript of the first register book of Chesham, Bucks (1538–1636), "a considerable number of 'nurse children' from London are mentioned. This illustrates a curious difference in the family relations of the time from those which now prevail. Children received little attention at home, and were generally sent away as soon as possible to spend their early years elsewhere. Londoners who could afford it put them out at nurse with people in the country, ostensibly for the sake of the benefit supposed to be derivable from country air. But that so many of these children should die away from their parents and be buried unnamed affords ground for conjecture as to the real motives which prompted the sending of them to a place so far from London and so out of the way as Chesham was ; and it does not require a very imaginative mind to read an occasional tragedy between the lines of these simple entries."

The burial of a nurse child is first entered in 1575, and from that year up to 1635 there are forty-five cases of such burials. Of the large majority, it is specified that the child came from London. Sometimes no name of any kind is given to the child, only the name of the Chesham woman who had the infant in charge. Usually the name of the London father or mother is given, but only in one single instance (namely, Henry, son of George and Mary Linford, of Hornsey, buried in 1600) are the names of both parents supplied. Mr. Pegge's surmises as to these nurse children are far too charitable ; the probabilities are strong that in almost every instance these infants were born out of wedlock, and the supposed care of them would be now termed "baby-farming."

The mention of the burial of these nurse children is fairly common in the registers of the Home Counties or of other shires within reasonable distance of London, and occasionally near other large towns such as Bristol and Norwich. Without making any special search, we have incidentally noticed them in the registers of twenty-seven separate parishes. Several seventeenth century instances occur in the records of Aldenham, Herts, Stoke Pogis, Bucks, and Orpington, Kent. The following explicit instances of the latter part of Elizabeth's reign are taken from the registers of Mitcham, Surrey :—

"1589. Paul Toobast a fleminge sonne being a Norschilde from Loundoun bur. April 21.

"1590. Mary the dau. of John Water a Norsechilde of Loundoun being drewes norsery bur. Jun. 12.

"1590. Elizabeth Beresley a Nurschild of Londoun her father being a Joyner borne in St. Olife's parishe, bur. Nov. 13.

"1591. Mary Porter a Norschild of Loundoun being a habbardasher daughter, bur. March 19.

"1591. William son of John Platt of Barmondsy Streete being a

Norschilde of Loundoun with Mr. Frances tenannt beyound the River, bur. Apil 2."

Lewisham, Kent, with its township of Sydenham (usually spelt "Sipenham" or "Syppenham"), seems to have been a favourite resort of these baby-farmers on the fringe of London. They are first mentioned in these registers in 1576, and are of frequent occurrence between 1690 and 1703.

The name given at Holy Baptism has always been regarded by the Church as indelible, save for one exception. The Western Church from an early date reserved to itself the power of altering the baptismal name at the time of confirmation. Thus Charles IX of France only assumed that name at confirmation, having been baptized Maximilian. The like transformation was effected in the cases of two of this king's brothers, Edward - Alexander and Hercules being respectively changed at confirmation to Henry and Francis. After the Reformation, it was a disputed point whether the civil law of England would recognise a revised confirmation name. Serjeant Thomas Gawdy, who lived in Elizabeth's reign, had two sons, both of whom had been baptized Thomas. To avoid confusion, the younger brother's name was changed at confirmation to Francis. Both of them went to the bar, and both rose to be judges. The younger brother died in 1606 as Chief Justice of Common Pleas, but he did not venture to use the name of Francis in purchases and grants until the advice of all the judges had been taken that it could be safely done.

The registers of Holme Hale, Norfolk, furnish an instance of a change of name being duly entered when Queen Mary was on the throne :—

"1554. Deci'o nono die Novembris. Baptizat' filius Richi Lorington et Cecilie consor' sue et no'iat' Samuell et mutat' nomen ejus ad confirmacionem et noiat' Willm̄us."

A learned canon of the Church of England, who has taken a considerable share in a recent church history in several volumes, has made the strange blunder of stating that English mediæval bishops must have much neglected the rite of confirmation because there is hardly ever any reference to this sacrament in the extant episcopal registers ! If there is anything substantial in so flimsy an argument, it certainly follows that the post-Reformation bishops were equally guilty of this grave lapse, for not only are their registers equally silent, but it is most exceptional to find any reference to confirmation in the parochial registers. Five such instances are given.

At the end of the first register book of Pakenham, Suffolk, is the following entry :—

"The names of those Children within ye Parrish of Pakenham, which were confirmed in Church of Tostock by the Reverend father in God Matthewe Ld: Bishop of Norwich, September 21. Ao dni 1636."

The names appended are Samuel Cross and seven other boys.

The registers of Bamburgh, Northumberland, supply a list of those confirmed in that church by Lord Crewe on 22nd July 1676, namely, 11 males and 3 females. On that occasion the following extraordinary entry was made in the registers :—

"Mem: y^t ye most Rev'end father in God did honour Tho. Davison then presbyter of Bamb' with his attendance and acceptance of a glass of sack, sydar, and March beer in honorem parochiæ dictæ."

A most monstrous mixture of liquors !

" 1693 (*Tideswell, Derbyshire*). The fourth day of July, the Reverend Father in God William Floyd, Lord Bishop of Lichfield and Coventry, came to Tideswell church about 11 o'clock, and preached, and after Sermon did confirm four hundred and ninety and five persones."

A memorandum in the Basingstoke registers records that on 26th September 1732 the Bishop of Winchester confirmed 319 persons at the parish church. The Tarrant Hinton, Dorset, registers for 1809 contain a note of

"Bishop's Visitation Sep. 1. Elizabeth Frances and Leonora Diggle confirmed."

A ridiculous and vulgar instance of the abandonment of a long-held baptismal name, on the specious authority of the King's sign-manual, is recorded by Mr. Chester Waters : Sir Onesiphorus Paul, Bart., changed his name to George in 1780, when he was pricked as high sheriff of Gloucestershire.

If the absence of allusions to confirmation is to be taken as a proof of the neglect of that ordinance, still more so is this the case with regard to the Purification of women after childbirth. The register references to Churchings are most scarce. Here are two of Elizabethan date from the first register book of Kirkburton, Yorks:—

" 1567, 30 Sept. Rychard Wrygth howyth my Mr. for churchying of y⁵ wyf.
" 1567, 26 Oct. Rychard Crosland hath payd for churchying of hys wyffe.
" 1585. Hursselle Houssie daughter unto Hurselle Houssie was baptysed the vjth daye of Auguste. At the churchying they dyd put in this name Hursselle Houssie alias Houghesonne."

Burn mentions that at one period Churchings were entered in the register of Staplehurst, Kent; he gives the following extract, but omits to supply the date:—

" The xii day of May was churched Wyllyam Bassoke's Wyffe and Willyam Foller's Wyffe."

Entries of illegitimate birth are for the most part sadly frequent.

The register book of Bramfield, Suffolk, which begins in 1539, has a summary of the parish baptisms at
the end of each year up to 1558, in which cases of
bastardy are specially mentioned. At the end of 1539 is
entered :—

"The holle yeare Christened xiiij Children, whereoff Men
Children xj, whereof Bastards ii, Women Children iij."

The other instances of bastards were, 1540, three ; 1544,
one ; 1548, one ; 1549, one ; 1550, one ; 1555, one ; 1556,
one ; and 1557, one.

As a rule, registers bear witness to a growth in the
number of illegitimate births as time went on. This is
shown after a striking fashion by a table based on the
registers of Letheringham, Suffolk :—

1588 to 1600	.	.	none		
1601 to 1650	.	.	1 : proportion per births, 1 in 144		
1651 to 1700	.	.	1	,,	,,	1 in 74
1701 to 1750	.	.	3	,,	,,	1 in 33
1751 to 1800	.	.	7	,,	,,	1 in 21
1801 to 1812	.	.	3	,,	,,	1 in 10

Not a few registrars, in making entries of the baptisms of
illegitimate children, set at naught the order in such cases
of the Roman Church — *Omnis tamen infamiæ vitetur
occasio.*

It is certainly more seemly to have such entries made
in Latin. In the first register book of Mitcham, Surrey,
where the following Elizabethan baptismal entries are to be
found, the Latin and the vulgar tongue are promiscuously
used :—

"1568. Edwardus filius populi sed mater erat Anna Moris bapt 18
    die Janarii.
"1575. Johes filius nescio cujus sed mater erat Johanna Wagstaffe
    meretrix bapt. 30 die Januarii.

"1586-7. William White his father unknowen, bapt March 1
Anni d. of Martha Hedge the father unknowen, bapt
March 18.

"1588. Isabella filia nescio cujus sed mater erat meretrix, qua et
reliquet eam cum Jasper Dob, bapt 13 Januari.

"1592. Annis Parker, the daughter supposed of Thomas Parker, of
Mordoun, beinge lefte in the Churche portch by that harlot her
mother, bur. Dec. 18.

"1599. Johannes filius populi sed mater erat communis meretrix
serva Johannes Clay de Hollens bapt. 6 April."

The following chronologically arranged entries are taken
from registers in every part of England :—

"1550 (*St. George Tombland, Norwich*). Margareta filia cujusdam
Elizabeth ex fornicatione nata, decimo octavo die augusti,
1550, batizat' fuit.

"1553 (*North Elmham, Norfolk*). John Curbye, borne in bast:, ye
sone of Margaret Curbye, Synglewoman and begote by one
Thomas Wardy Syngleman, as it is seyd, whom he hath
p'mysed to marye, and was Chrystened ye xjth day of Maye,
w'ch was Thursdaye.

"1560 (*Chesham, Bucks*). Bridget and Elizabeth the daughters of
Adultery bapt. Jan\y 1560.

"1560 (*Chesterfield*). Rian, the mother's name Ashe, a bastar\d
gotten in London, bapt xiij March.

"1571 (*Idem*). Alicia Charles et Margreta Charles, filiæ Luca Charles
de Newbold, bastardes, bapt. fuere xxij July. Stephen Lu
father as she sayth.

"1583 (*Rochdale*), Dec. 15, bur. Jacobus filius Jacobi Earn-
shawe et Alice Hallowes boothe of Yorkeshyre and the sayde
Alice did lye in the house of ux' of James Collinge in
Butt'worth the woman hath done her penance.

"1591 (*Aston-by-Birmingham*). A bastard out of Yardington was
baptized 12 May, a travellinge woman brought a bedd in
the streete. Hard harted people.

"1594 (*Barnstaple, Devon*). Rycharde, base son of Jerymie
Payment, baptized 16 Aug. Fond uponne Island of Loundye,
being aged 1¼ years when baptized.

"1597 (*Mansfield, Notts*), March 26. Elizabeth, bast. born
child of Eliz. Stones, whose reputed father is Martin

Bridghouse, was, by the tollerance of the Vicare of Munsfield, baptized at Plesley.

"1602 (*Broseley, Salop*), July 18. Alicia fil, Izabelle Nocke et Johi's Berick putavi patris: bap.

"1613 (*Ibid.*), Nov. 14. Thomas Croyden fil. Alicie Croyden et Ludovici Poell, ut dicitur: bap.

"1606 (*Wigan*). William the sonne of one Gould borne by channce, bap. 20 Maye.

"1616 (*Harrow-on-the-Hill*), May the 4th, was baptized Lucretia Wilblud of Sudbery sojourner at Iles, one William Wilblud was with me acknowledging hymselfe to be the father, he sent xxˢ to be given to Alice Bateman the mother.

"1625 (*Adel, Yorks*), July 3. Grace, a base child, nominated by the mother to be the doughter of Expofer Kirke, of the Brecke.

"1633 (*Petersham, Surrey*). Nicolas, the sonne of Rebecca Cock, filius populi, bapt. 28 Jan.

"1658 (*Morden, Surrey*). Peter, the unlawfully begotten Son of Ann Major, bap. Jan. 6.

"1662 (*Forcett, Yorks*). Anne supposed daughter of Sir Jeremiah Smithson, fathered yᵉ said Jeremiah in the church, bap. 9 April.

"1717 (*Ramsden Bellhouse, Essex*). Diana daur of John Billy and Diana Waker, proles spuria, bap. Jan. 13.

"1732 (*Neentone, Salop*), April 11. Brazener Margaret Barret bur. Supposed to be the Bastard child of one Sarah Barret, a servant at Boreton in the p. of Much Wenlock, and to be born at one Brazeners of Cressidge in the p. of Cond but left by night in the Beast-house of John Wall of this p., about sixteen months before its death: the sᵈ Sarah Barret having liv'd in service some years before in this p. Tho. Nash, Curat.

"1743 (*St. Pancras, London*). William, Son of Lord Talbot, per Dutchess of Beaufort, ut asseritur, born November 1, 1743, bap. Mar. 24, 1743-4."

The commonest register term to denote illegitimate birth is "base-born"; but the variants of this unhappy nomenclature are exceedingly numerous. A selection is appended:—

1554	St. Martin's, Birmingham	Filia populi (a common form)
1560	Cheshunt, Bucks	The Son of the People
1564	Chelsea	Filius meretricis
1569	Croydon	Filius vulgi
1579	Wimbledon	The Daughter of an Harlott
1580	Stepney	Begotten in adultery
1582	Croydon	Filius terræ
1583	Herne, Kent	Filia fornicatoris
1590	Twickenham	A scape begotten child
1595	Eckington, Derby	Ye daughter of noe certain man
1603	Isleworth	Filia uniuscujusque
1608	Ulcombe, Kent	Filius scorti
1620	Minster, Kent	Filia adulterina
1652	Marden, Surrey	Begotten in fornication
1676	Wilby, Northants	One of ye children of ye people
1683	All Saints, Newcastle	Lanebegot
1685	Lambeth	A merry begot
1688	Do.	A byeblow

CHAPTER VI

MARRIAGES

Terms of entry—Marriageable age — Hours of marriage — Forbidden seasons—Marriage by banns—Forbidding of banns—Marriage by licence — Marriage of the defective — Marriage in smock—Marriage of bishops—Commonwealth marriages —Conviviality — Exceptional entries — Act of 1753 — Clandestine marriages and lawless churches — Fleet Street and London—Dale Abbey—Peak Forest

MARRIAGES are as a rule found to be entered in our parish registers with greater care and regularity than either baptisms or burials. This doubtless arose from the obvious importance to persons of all ranks of possessing a faithful record of their union, both for their own sake and as a legal proof of their children's legitimacy. The terms of the marriage entry were usually very simple, recording the fact that the contracting couple were "married" on such a date, the word being occasionally changed to "wedded," or "coupled together in matrimony." Most, however, of the registers of the sixteenth and early seventeenth registers are in Latin, and that tongue affords greater variety in the expression of the matrimonial union. *Nupti erant* is the commonest phrase; among other variants may be noted *copulati sunt in matrimonio* (Croydon), *contraxerunt matrimonium* (Heston), *conjuncti fuere* (Debtling), *mariti fuerunt* (Wilton), *alligati fuerunt* (Great Wigston), and *connubio juncti erant* (Bobbin).

The age of consent for espousals, in the mediæval Church,

was seven years, at which the infancy of both sexes was supposed to end. The canonical age for the completion of the contract or actual marriage has long been laid down as twelve in the woman and fourteen in the man. Consent given by males and females of these respective ages was held to be valid up to the passing of the Marriage Act of 21 Geo. II, c. 33. By this Act the legal age of consent was fixed at twenty-one for each sex, but with the consent of parents or guardians the much earlier ages remained valid.

It is exceedingly rare to find the ages of the contracting parties set forth in the old registers. An Elizabethan exception occurs in the first register book of Burnley, Lancashire, under the year 1582:—

"Edmunde Tattersall of ye age of xiij yeares and Lettice Hargreves of thage of xv° yeares mar^d 14 May."

For such a marriage, in the case of the boy, a dispensation or licence must have been obtained from the bishop or his official.

Exceptional cases of marriage at an early age can sometimes be detected by careful examination of the registers, as is the case in the following entry of the boy-and-girl union of two important local families, probably for estate reasons:—

"1611–12 (*Middleton, Lancashire*). Edmund Hopwoode gent and Dorothie Assheton were maried uppon Sundaye the seconde daye of Februarie in thaffore noone in the tyme of Divine service by me John Walkden Curate of Middleton with the Consente of bothe their parents accordinge to Lawe and theffect of a licence granted from Chester dated the first daye of thabove named monithe of Feb. ano 1611."

Previous entries in the Middleton register show that both groom and bride were but fourteen years of age. The bride lived until 1641, but the groom died within four days of the wedding, apparently from some virulent disorder, as is shown in the burial register:—

"1611–12. Edmunde Hopwoode, of Hopwoode Esquire, deceased the sixte daye of Februarie about Eleven of the Clocke before noone And was buried Att Middleton before tenne of the Clocke in the nighte of the same daye."

Various early canons provided, in order to secure due publicity, that marriage should only be celebrated at seasonable hours. As the nuptial Mass formed part of the ceremonial, it could not take place save in the forenoon.

The register of Soberton, Hants, has several entries about the year 1580 of marriages "at iiij yͤ cloke in ye morning," and one of "an oure before day breke by licence fro the chancelur."

Canon lxxii of 1603 ordered that no minister, under pain of suspension for three years, "shall join any person in marriage at any unseasonable times, but only between the hours of eight and twelve in the forenoon." [1]

The Commonwealth Directory of Public Worship merely named that the marriage was to be "at some convenient houre of the day." In the case of the following marriage, darkness was probably chosen because of its illicit character:—

"1659 (*Great Staughton, Hunts*). Lucy Cosen, widdow, was married to Jn Cosen (brother of her former husband) the 15th day of December at St. Neots, by the Mynister of the Towne, and at seaven of the clocke in the nighte."

As early as the fourth century, the Council of Laodicea (*c.* 365) forbade the celebration of marriages during Lent. Ere long the seasons of canonical limitation were extended. According to the rubrics of the Sarum manual and missal, the prohibited seasons in England were from Advent

---

[1] The new canons of 1888 extended the hours to three in the afternoon.

to the octave of Epiphany, from Septuagesima to the octave
of Easter, and from the Sunday before the Ascension to
the octave of Pentecost. The close time was restricted to
Advent and Lent by the Council of Trent, but for some
time after the Reformation the Church of England adhered
to the three periods prohibited by the use of Sarum. An
entry of the forbidden times was not infrequently made in
the parish registers.

In the first register book of Cottenham, Cambs, which
begins in 1572, is this Latin triplet :—

> " *Conjugium Adventus prohibet, Hilarius relaxat,*
> *Septuagena vetat, sed paschæ octava remittit,*
> *Rogamen vetitat, concedit Trina potestas.*"

The like occurs in Latin in slightly altered phraseology
in two or three other places, as at Dymchurch, where it is
dated 1630.

The four-lined form in the register of Lamport, Northants,
under the year 1628, runs thus :—

> "*Regula quæ matrimonium inhibet*
> *Conjugium adventus vetat Hillariusque relaxat*
> *Septuagena ligat solvitque octavia Paschæ*
> *Rogamen prohibet, Liberavit Trina Potestas.*"

On the last page of the first register book of Dunster,
Somerset, which begins in 1559, is a somewhat confused
Latin entry :—

" De temporib' in quid' non licet matrimonia solemnizare.

" Solemnitas nuptiarum facienda non est Septuagesimo in Octava
Pasche, et prius die rogatione in mane clauditur illa Sollemnitas
et Durat xhibitio ad octaviam diem post Pentecosten inclusionem, et
prima Die Domminicæ Adventus usque ad Epiphaniam non Debent
nuptua Celibrari.

"Tho. Smith "

A mingled Latin and English version of the forbidden

times is set forth in the register book of Horton, Dorset, under the year 1629. The Latin begins:—

"*Conjugium Adventus tollit, Hillarius relaxat.*"

The English version is particularly explicit:—

" 1. From ye Sounday moneth before Christmas
    till ye 7 day after twelf day.
2. From ye Sounday fortnight before Shravetyde
    till ye Sounday after Est^r weake.
3. From ye rogation Sounday till 7 dayes after
    whit Sounday, and ye 7 last days are in-
    cluded in ye prohibition."

In certain instances these forbidden seasons appear in English rhymes. At the beginning of the old register book of St. Mary's, Beverley, are the following rhymes:—

" *Rules for Marriage, the Time*

"When Advent comes do thou refraine
till Hillary sett ye free againe ;
next Septuagesima saith the nay ;
but when Lowe Sunday comes thou may ;
yet at Rogation thou must tarrie
till Trinitie shall bid the mary.
"Nov. 25, 1641 "

A somewhat later variant occurs in the register of Everton, Notts, where the lines run :—

" Advent marriage doth deny
But Hilary gives thee liberty.
Septuagesima says thee nay,
Eight days from Easter says you may.
Rogation bids thee to contain
But Trinity sets thee free again."

Archdeacon Cosin, in his Visitation Articles of 1627, inquired :—

"Whether hath your minister or curate . . . solemnized Matrimonie . . . in any time prohibited (that is to say) in Advent, Lent, and in the Rogations without a license first obteyned from the Archbishop or his Chancellour."

In the Durham Prayer Book, Cosin added in manuscript to the Table of the Vigils, etc. :—

"By the ecclesiastical laws of this Realm, there be some times in the year wherein Marriages are not usually solemnized, viz.—

$$\text{from } \begin{cases} \text{Advent} \\ \text{Septuagesima} \\ \text{Rogation} \end{cases} \text{Sunday until } \begin{cases} \text{8 days after Epiphany} \\ \text{8 days after Easter} \\ \text{Trinity Sunday.''} \end{cases}$$

This brief table is exactly copied in the register book of Wimbish, Essex, under the year 1666.

The register of the parish church of Lindisfarne contains the following prose version entered as late as 1660 :—

"Tymes prohibiting marriage. Marriage comes on y^e 13 day of January, and by Septuagesima Sunday it is out again until Low Sunday, at which tyme it comes in again and goes no mor out till Rogation Sunday, from whence it is forbidden again untill Trinitie Sunday ; from thence it is unforbidden till Advent Sunday, but then it goes out and comes not in again untill ye 13 day of January next after."

Almanacks and calendars of the seventeenth and occasion-ally of the eighteenth century gave tables of the forbidden times for the current year. Thus an almanack called *Galen*, for 1642, has the following :—

" *Times prohibiting Marriage this yeer*

From the 27 of November till January 13.
From Februarie 6 untill April 18.
From May 16 untill June 5."

A careful comparison of a large number of marriage registers up and down the country enables us to say that the ancient discipline of the Church of England with regard to the three periods was widely observed throughout the

6

whole of the sixteenth and seventeenth centuries. Thus the registers of Letheringham, Suffolk, which begin in 1580, contain only three marriage entries during March (the centre of Lent) for the term of 182 years.

On 8th February 1600 occurs the following remarkable marriage entry in the registers of Chislehurst, Kent:—

"George Ralins et Susan Switzer sine solemnitate omni propter diem hunc septuagessimæ."

The Twickenham registers for 1665 afford an instance of marriage by particular licence during the third period, which was as a season unforbidden throughout Western Christendom save in England:—

"Christoper Mitchell and Anne Colett married 4 June, by permission of Sir Richard Chaworth, it being within the octaves of Pentecost."

The term Banns is a Saxon word signifying a proclamation. It was laid down in the Church of England as early as 1200 that no marriage was to be contracted "without banns thrice published in the church" (Hubert Walter's *Canons at Westminster*, No. 11). The constitutions of Archbishop Reynolds, in 1322, provided that these three public banns were to be published "on three Lord's days or festivals distant from each other."

Marriage Banns were from time to time forbidden in past days as well as at the present time. The record of such an occurrence was occasionally entered in the register among the marriages. From several entries of this character, the three following, one from each century, have been selected:—

"1570 (*Bramfield, Suffolk*). M^d y^t the banes of Rychard Wappoll and Rose Simson was puplished the vj day of August and so was Asked ij Severall Sondays and ye last Sonday beyng ye xiij day of ye sam month did Thomas Neve forbid it no cause y^t he could lay against him but he sayd whan I am ordenary I shuld know.

"1681–2 (*Abington, N'hants*), Feb. 9. Henry Mason of Greens Norton and Mary Osborn were married by license. A shabby fellow came in and forbid the marriage, but wold neither tell his name nor shew any Reason thereof. I required Bond of him and securities on a sufficient caution that he would try the suite, but he ran away to Mr. Newmans the Aleman. I sent the clerk and Mr. Henry Osborne of Northton to the Alehouse to demand of him the reason of this act of his and to demand bond and securitie of him for trying the cause. He refused. Mr. Henry Osborne of Northton, Mason entered into bond of 40^l to keepe mee harmlesse. The bond hangs upon the file in my studie.

"1732 (*Mertsham, Surrey*). Married Joseph Benge and Betty Liew, Nov. 14. It is to be remembered that the Bans were publicly forbid in the Church by — Morphew spinster of this parish but upon her being then publicly told from the Desk how she must proceed according to the Rubrick, she was advised it seems by some to take another method to hinder this man's marriage and prove herself with child by him befor Justice Payton tho' in the end it appeared she was not."

A marriage could be legally solemnised without banns, by virtue of a licence granted either by the bishop or ordinary, or by the special licence of the Archbishop of Canterbury. The power of episcopal dispensing with banns was of ancient use, and is at least as old as the Constitutions of Archbishop Mepham in 1328. The subject of marriage licences was dealt with in detail in 1603 by Canons ci–civ.

Three examples of register entries making definite mention of the licence are here set forth; they are selected, almost at haphazard, from a considerable number :—

"1570 (*Bobbingworth, Essex*). M^d that Robert Younger principall of David's Inne in Holburne without London and Elizabeth

Brooke daughter of Robert Brooke were maryed together in
Bobingworth Church the 13th day of Aprill accordinge his
Lycense graunted therein.

" 1618 (*St. Margaret's, Canterbury*), Junii 9°.   Thomas Grenefeild
And Margery Stace Wyddow were publiklye maryed in the
p'she Church of St. Margaret in the Cittye of Cant: the
nynth daye of June by virtue of a lycence under the seale of
office of the Right Wor : James Hussey doctor of the law and
Commissarye gen'all for the dyocese of Cant.

" 1631 (*Bekesbourne, Kent*).   Richard Epps and Ann Pye were
married the 23th of June an° predict. by Mr. Arch-Deacon's
license."

Registers occasionally bear witness to unusual marriages
wherein one of the contracting parties is defective or
deformed.   A marriage at St. Martin's, Leicester, in 1576,
wherein the man was deaf and dumb gave rise to a long
entry :—

" Feb. 15.   Thomas Tilsye and Ursula Russel were maryed ;
and because the sayde Thomas was and is naturally deafe, and
also dumbe, so that the order of the form of marriage used
usually amongst others, which can heare and speake, could not
for his parte be observed.   After the approbation had from
Thomas, the Bishoppe of Lincolne, John Chippendale, doctor
in law, and commissarye, as also of Mr. Richd. Davye, then
Mayor of the town of Leicester, with others of his brethren,
with the rest of the parishe, the said Thomas, for the
expressing of his mind instead of words, of his own accord used
these signs : first, he embraced her with his arms, and took her
by the hand, putt a ring upon her finger, and layde his hande
upon his hearte, and then upon her hearte, and held up his
handes toward heaven.   And to show his continuance to
dwell with her to his lyves ende, he did it by closing of his
eyes with his handes, and digginge out of the earth with his
foote, and pullinge as though he would ring a bell, with diverse
other signes."

An equally long entry of the year 1618 occurs in the
registers of St. Botolph's, Aldgate, when Thomas Speller, a

deaf and dumb smith of Hatfield Broadoak, Essex, was married to Sarah Earle by licence granted by Dr. Edwarde, Chancellor of the diocese of London. The bridegroom appeared

"taking the Book of Common Prayer and his license in one hand and his bride in the other . . . and made the best signs he could to show that he was willing to be married."

The minister appears to have been nervous about the marriage, and required to be assured by the Lord Chief Justice of the King's Bench as to its lawfulness. He does not seem to have known of any precedent, and the entry concludes :—

"This marriage is set down at large because we never had the like before."

At a much later date, namely on 5th November 1832, there is a record at St. James's, Bury St. Edmunds, of the overcoming of a yet more serious impediment to the accustomed ceremonial of marriage :—

"Christopher Newsam married Charity Morrell. Charity Morrell being entirely without arms, the ring was placed upon the fourth toe of the left foot, and she wrote her name in this register with her right foot."

There must have been some special infirmity to cause the following entry in the registers of Sunbury, Middlesex, under 7th February 1663 :—

" Samuel Turner and Margaret Shase, widow, was married sitting in a cheare, in her house."

There was an old vulgar error, which lasted for several centuries, to the effect that a man was not liable for his bride's debts provided that he married her in no other apparel than her smock or shift. The strangest thing about this odious custom is that any priest or minister could be found to administer the sacred rite with the woman in such a guise.

> "1547 (*Much Wenlock*), Aug. 4. Here was wedded early in the morning Thomas Munslow, smith, and Alice Nycols, which wedded to him in her smock and bareheaded.
> "1714 (*Chitterne All Saints', Wilts*). John Bridmore and Anne Selwood were married, Oct. 17. The aforesaid Anne Selwood was married in her smock, without any clothes or headgier on.
> "1774 (*Saddleworth, Yorks*). Abraham Brookes, Clother, and Mary Bradley, of Ashton parish, Widow. By Banns 3 Feby, by Samuel Stones, Curate."

With reference to this last marriage, a passage occurs in Prescott's *Journal*, under date February 12th, 1774 :—

> "On Tuesday sen'night was married at the Parochial Chapel of Saddleworth, Abraham Brooks, a Widower, of about 30 years of age, to Mary Bradley, a Widow of near 70, but as the Bride was a little in Debt the Bridegroom obliged her to be married in her shift, and the weather being very severe threw her into such a violent fit of shaking as induced the compassionate minister to cover her with his coat whilst the marriage was solemnised."

The marriage of priests, after so many centuries of celibacy, as recorded in several registers of the time of Edward VI, must have caused considerable astonishment and resentment among the adherents of the unreformed faith. There must have been still greater surprise for them in the marriage of bishops. Here are two of the earliest of those episcopal entries, the one in Latin and the other in English :—

> "1551 (*Croydon*), Oct. 23. Reverendus Pater Johannes Episcopus Wynton duxit Mariam Haymond generosam in ista ecclesia coram multitudine parochianorum presente Reverendissemo patre Thoma Cantuar. Archiepo cum multis.
> "1560-1 (*St Dennis, Backchurch*), Jan 21. Edmond Scamlare, byshoppe of peterborowe and Julyan Franncys were married."

The former of these marriages cost the bishop his all, for Dr. Poynet was on that account deposed from the bishopric of Winchester on the accession of Queen Mary; he died in exile at Strasburg in 1556.

As examples of the form of record generally adopted for marriages under the 1653 Act, these two consecutive entries of 1654–5 from the register book of Marshfield, Gloucestershire, will suffice; in the one case the banns were published in the market-place, and in the other in the church.

"The twelth day of Februarie in the yeare abovesaid Stephen Browne and Jeane Simmons both of Westerliegh in the County of Glouc. being Three severall markett daies published in the Markett place between the hours of Eleavn of the clocke and Two of the clocke according to the Act and noe objection made to the contrary were married before John Gostlett Esq', Justice of the peace.

" The six and twentieth day of Februarie in the yeare abovesaide Robert Fry and Ellinor Barton both of the p'ish of Dynham being three severall Lords Daies published in the p'she Church of Dynham aforesaid and noe contradicion to the contrary were married at Marshfield in the County of Glouc. before John Gostlett Esq' Justice of the peace."

The entries of this period rarely omit the name of the Justice of the Peace before whom the civil contract was made; but this was now and again done for the sake of brevity :—

" 1657 (*Leek, Staffs*). Ralph Lees of Consal and a daughter of Hugh and Margaret Fynny were published three times at our Market Cross, and married April 22."

The full entry in the register of St. Martin's-in-the-Fields, of the civil marriage of Frances, the Protector's daughter, on November 11, 1657, is worth citing. It will be noted that both "Martin" and "Andrew" are childishly bereft of the saintly prefix which they had borne uninterruptedly for so many centuries.

Still greater brevity characterised a few of the Commonwealth marriage entries, as was the case at Staines, Middlesex.

FACSIMILE OF COMMONWEALTH MARRIAGE ENTRIES:
STAINES, MIDDLESEX.

"These are to certifie whom it may concerne, that according to a late Act of Parliament, entytuled an Act touching Marriages, and the registering thereof, etc., publication was made in the publique meeting place, in the Parish Church of the Parish of Martins in the Fields in the county of Middlesex, upon three several Lord's Days, at the close of the morning exercise, namely, upon the xxv. day of October MDCLVII., as also upon the i. and viii. of November following, of a marriage agreed upon between the Honorable Robert Rich Andrew's Holborn, and the Right Honorable the Lady Frances of Cromwell, of Martins in the Fields, in the county of Middlesex. All which was fully performed according to the Act without exception.

"In witness whereof I have hereunto set my hand the ix. day of November, MDCLVII.

"WILLIAM WILLIAMS"

Then follows, in the hand of Henry Scobell, the clerk of the Parliaments, and a Justice for Westminster:—

"Married, xi. Novemb., MDCLVII, in the presence of His Highness the Lord Protector, the Right Honble. the Earls of Warwick and Newport, Robert Lord Rich, the Lord Strickland, and many others."

An amusing account of the merriment that followed on this marriage has recently been printed in a contemporary letter from the historian Dugdale by the Historical Manuscript Commissioners:—

"1657, Nov. 14. On Wednesday last was my Lord Protector's daughter married to the Earl of Warwick's grandson; Mr. Scobell, as a Justice of the peace, tyed the knot after a godly prayer made by one of His Highnesses divines; and on the Thursday was the wedding feast kept at Whitehall, where they had 48 violins and 50 trumpets, and much mirth with frolics, besides mixt dancing (a thing heretofore accounted profane) till 5 of the clock yesterday morning. Amongst the dancers there was the Earl of Newport, who danced with her Highness."

Conviviality has been the usual accompaniment of weddings from scriptural days downwards, but it is very

rare to find any entry of such mundane matters in parish
registers. Here, however, is a dog Latin entry as to village
festivities on such an occasion, in a Norfolk parish, at a much
earlier date than the Commonwealth:—

"1606 (*Beeston, near Mileham*). Willmus Balye et Suzanna Byrch
nupti fuerunt ultimo die Julii. Celeberimus autem istorum
nuptialis dies habitus est apud domum cujusdem Hilarii Balye
(tam ipsius Willmi tam ipsius Margarete amicissimi avunculi)
die Jovis anno et tempore superdictis maxime tam cognatorum
tam amicoroum, cum concorsisque oppidinorum multitudine
multisque aliis ad idem conviviam. tunc temporis (ipsiusque
Hillarii solummodo expensis) congregatis ad numeram ut visum
est 300 aut circiter populorum, sive ut dictum est sexaginta
meases."

The following are a few of the somewhat noteworthy
marriage entries, selected from a large number of excerpts;
they do not call for any explanatory comment :—

" 1540 (*Sandbeach, Cambs*), 27 Nov. John Clarke and Mary Pearson
were coupled together in matrimony.
" 1560 (*St. Bridget's, Chester*). Willm Washington wedded 5 Feb. [no
bride mentioned [1]].
" 1588 (*St. Botolph's, Aldgate*). Michael Didyer, a stranger, born at
Marseilles in Province, a pilot under Mr Candish in his
voyage to the South Endyes, and Jaynete Desheaz, a maiden
born in Jersey, married 2 November.
" 1599 (*Brewood, Staffs*), June 4. William Hoyte and Joane Alporte
of Tettehall Parishe, married at Breewood at the request of Sir
Thomas Corbit, being a sicke and dying the same day.
" 1624–5 (*Bermondsey, Surrey*). James Herriott Esqr and Elizabeth
Josey, Gent. were married Jan 4. *N.B.* This James Herriott
was one of the 40 children of his father a Scotchman.
"1657 (*Chapel-en-le-Frith, Derbyshire*). There came from Tideswell
and Litton seventeen marriages all married by Randle
Ashenhurst Esquier justice of the peace.

[1] Burn states that in the parish register of " Hokington'" (? Hockerton, Notts)
there is no mention of the wife's name in marriage entries for a period of over
forty years.

"1659 (*Aldenham, Herts*). A Contracte of matrymony betwene John Towers and Elizabeth Edwardes both of this Parish, Published on March the 27 and Aprill the 3 and 10; But broke of and never maryed.

"1659 (*Hackness, Yorks*). Robert Coulson of Hagg house within the parish of Wykham and Marie Cockerell daughter of Henrie Cockerell of Sharpegate were married by Mr Francis Proude min^r of Hackness in the Church and in the middest of the marriage Mary dreeped down by reason of a swame and after she was had to the Queer Doore into the Ayre shee recovered verie well againe and there they were married in the presence of the Congregacon the xxv^th day of October.

"John Richardson
"Parish Register

"1688 (*Hexham, Northumberland*), 27 Feb. Thomas Locke, a pretended doctor, married to Jane Inglesby; y^t he after marryed one Mrs Elizabeth Clarke of Markett Welton in ye East Rideing, York, for which he was prosecuted, but pleaded his majestie's pardon.

"1712 (*Ashborne, Derbyshire*), May 11. James Dawson and Susannah Osbaston both of Derby. This was a fraudulent and wicked marriage. Dawson came to Ashbourn fair May 10th and applied himselfe to old Mr Hardister the Surrogate for License, who having examined him upon oath (as the Canon requires) the perjured wretch swore y^t there was no pre contract or other legall impediment against his marriage, so he obtained a licence and was married next morning being Sunday May 11th. But before noon I discovered that his first wife was living at Southampton.

"1750 (*Lee, Kent*), May 24. Samuel Woodward and Chasable Torkinton (the woman's Christian name was so spelt in the license by mistake for Chastity; which she said was the true name), both of St. Nicholas, Deptford.

"1752 (*Mayfair Chapel, London*), Feb. 14. James, Duke of Hamilton, and Eliza Gunning married."

Horace Walpole gives a lively account of the circumstances of this marriage :—

"The Duke carried off Miss Gunning from a ball, and notwithstanding the lateness of the hour sent for the rector of St.

George's, Hanover Square, to marry them. Dr. Trebeck, however, refused to perform the ceremony without licence and ring. The Duke swore he would send for the Archbishop; at last they were married with a ring of a bed-curtain at half an hour past 12 at night at Mayfair Chapel."

"1766 (*Melverley, Salop*), Dec. 17. Matthew Dodd and Elinor Foster married.

> "This morning I have put a Tye
> No man could put it faster
> 'Tween Matthew Dodd, the man of God,
> And modest Nelly Foster.

"JOHN LEWIS Clk."

The registers of Great Houghton, Northants, contain the following indignant protest against the penalty imposed on defaulters under the Marriage Act of 1753:—

"The marriages are entered in a Book provided for that purpose according to Act of Parliament which prohibits the clergy solemnizing marriage contrary to rules therein prescribed, under ye penalty of transportation for 14 years; a punishment little inferior to ye gallows and inflicted generally on ye most profligate and abandoned part of mankind."

"*Clandestine Marriages and Lawless Churches.*"—In the second edition of Burn's *History of Parish Registers*, published in 1862, there is a long chapter (pp. 130–169) under the above title. The same author brought out a *History of the Fleet Marriages*, which passed into a second edition in 1834. Those who desire to study the subject of the clandestine marriages of the latter part of the seventeenth century and the first half of the eighteenth century, which attained to scandalous proportions up to the time of their suppression by Lord Hardwicke's Act of 1754, must consult the records and information gathered together with much care by Mr. Burn. Up to that date a marriage by a priest of the Church of England, without either banns or licence, was valid and indissoluble, although the contracting parties were liable to ecclesiastical censure, and the minister to heavy legal penalties. But such penalties were practically inoperative where the celebrant of the marriage had neither liberty to lose nor benefice to forfeit. Hence it came about that, under the then careless management of prisons, binding marriages were therein performed by disreputable priests, more especially at the Fleet. Strange to say the Fleet registers abound with aristocratic names, but they have never been accepted as legal evidence. The earliest Fleet register begins in 1674. At one time these marriages were actually performed in the Fleet chapel; but as these Fleet parsons were generally prisoners enjoying the "Rules of the Fleet," it became usual for these disreputable men to enter into an evil alliance with the lowest class of tavern-keepers of the district, who fitted up a room as a quasi chapel; they shared not only in the fees but in the sale of the liquors which the wedding parties drank. These disreputable priests kept rough memoranda of these marriages with occasional notes as to disgraceful scenes, and these entries from their pocket-books seem to have been generally copied into the larger Fleet registers. On the day previous to Lord Hardwicke's Act coming into operation, 25th March, 1754, there were no fewer than 217 of these Fleet marriages performed!

In addition to these Fleet marriages, there were other equally clandestine and scandalous weddings (save in their surroundings) celebrated in what were termed the lawless churches or chapels. These churches or chapels had real or pretended exemptions from the visitation of the Ordinary, and claimed or exercised the right of marrying at once without either licence or banns. One of the most notorious of these was the church of St. James, Duke's Place. The rector, Adam Elliott, was suspended for three years in 1606 for marrying without licence or banns; but the scandal was soon resumed. The Mint, Southwark, Lincoln's Inn Chapel, and the prison chapel of Newgate were among other notorious places for illicit marriages which continued to defy the laws ecclesiastical until 1754.

The Fleet Marriage Act, by its comprehensive wording, also brought about the cessation of clandestine marriages in several places in the provinces. Two of these, which were much resorted to in the Midlands, were both in Derbyshire, namely Dale Abbey Chapel and the Chapel of Peak Forest.

The marriage registers of Dale Abbey begin in 1684. The yearly average of marriages in this small extra parochial district is three ; but in 1605 these weddings numbered thirty-eight, in 1606 there were forty-six, and in 1690 thirty-six. A literal transcript of the first register book, which extends to 1731, but is much mutilated, was printed in vol. xxii. (1900) of the *Journal of the Derbyshire Archæological Society.* These marriages appear to have been wholly illegal, for Burn states :—

"The marriages in the parish of Dale Abbey were, until a few years previous to the Marriage Act of 1754, solemnized by the clerk of the parish, at one shilling each, there being no minister."

The chapel of the extra parochial district of Peak Forest was begun to be erected in 1657, but not completed until 1668. It claimed to be extra-episcopal, and was a peculiar to itself. The minister's title was " Principal Official and Judge in Spiritualities in the Peculiar Court of Peak Forest." He had the right of granting marriage licenses, and held a seal of office, dated 1665, which is still extant. In consequence of this undoubted and exceptional privilege, the chapel in this wild moorland district gradually became the resort of runaway couples and of those seeking clandestine marriage from various parts of the kingdom. There are numerous

DALE ABBEY CHAPEL.

proofs of this in the earlier registers, which begin in 1665 but are in a fragmentary condition. So much did this practice increase that in 1728 a new register book was purchased, and endorsed "Foreign Marriages." It simply contains the names of the contracting parties, without any other particulars. It concludes with the year 1754, when Lord Hardwicke's Act put an end to this use of the chapel. The minister stated at that time that he lost thereby £100 per annum. These foreign marriages averaged about sixty a year.

CHAPTER VII

BURIALS

Burial entries not perfect—Singular burial entries—Characters
of the deceased—Centenarians—Burials of excommunicants
—The Recusants—Excommunicate Non-conformists—Post-
Reformation excommunication — Burials of suicides—Other
burials by night — Burials of criminals — Burial without
coffins—Burials in woollen—Mortuaries—Arrest of corpse for
debt—Burial offered to passing corpse

BURN'S statement that the parish register of burials,
as to correctness and fulness, came next to those
of marriage is undoubtedly correct.   Nevertheless, to
take the burial entries, as some parochial historians do, as an
absolute guide to local population or as complete evidence
of mortality at any given period is by no means a sound
conclusion.   The Abstract of the Population Returns, based
on the census of 1801, mentions that they are deficient from
the following causes :—

1. Many congregations of dissenters in towns had their
own burial grounds, as had also the Roman Catholics and
Jews in London.

2. Some persons, from motives of convenience or
economy, interred their dead without any ceremony.

3. Children who died before baptism were not registered
or had no ceremony.

4. Negligence in small benefices, where the minister is
not resident.

5. Many in army and navy (or merchant service) die abroad.

To these causes it ought to have been added that from very early times, and certainly through the whole of the

[facsimile of handwritten burial register, 1538–1540]

FACSIMILE OF FIRST PAGE OF BURIAL REGISTER, LYMINGE, KENT.

7

registration period, the Church forbade the ceremonial interment of all excommunicated or unbaptized persons, as well
as suicides unless bereft of reason, and that the insertion of
such burials in the registers was only fitful and irregular.

There are a great number of more or less noteworthy
burial entries that do not admit of any particular classification; a small selection of these is here set forth in chronological order.

"1551 (*Rotherham*), Dec. 24th vij litle wenches at Cutloffs
buried.

"1578 (*St. Michael le Belfry, York*). M^d y^t one Richarde Kendall, a
p'soner in the Bushoppes pryson, wch came frome Doncaster,
buryed the thirde day of Aprill, without any solemnytye,
saving that the curate and clarke and others p'sones weare
by and p'nte at his buryall.

"1580 (*Orpington, Kent*). A Poor Childe wiche died in an oxe stall
at my Lady Hart's house, buried 9 March.

"1588 (*Durnford, Wilts*), 20 Augt. Ludovicus Ria, vicarius de Durnford Magna, obiit mortem transeuntem per viam Ambrosiam
inter villam et domum suam Durnfordiæ. [He was not buried
until 17th Sept.]

"1589 (*Mitcham, Surrey*). William a little boy in a blew jerkine and a
blew paier of gaskins, being the livery of Bridewell, buried out
of William Swillinghurst his barne, he was supposed to be a
Cheshire boy as he reported, bur. Oct. 19.

"1591 (*Thorington, Suffolk*). It. one Derrowe a ladde of the age of
viijth yeares whoe as he saide came from Bunggaye and was
there borne, he dyed at our bricke kell and was buried the
viijth of December.

"1593 (*St. Martin in the Fields*). Tho. Finglas buried Augst 4, and ij
yeares after his bodie was taken upp and caried in a Truncke
into Irelande.

"1599 (*Great Burstead, Essex*). Elizabeth Wattes, widdow, sometyme
the wyffe of Thomas Wattes, the blessed marter of God, who,
for his treuth suffered his marterdom in the fyer at Chelmes-
ford, the xxlj day of May, in the an° dni 1555, in the reigne c^f
Queene Mary, was buryed the 10 day, 1599, so she lived a
widdow after his death xliiij yeres, and fro' the 22 of May to

the 10th of July, and made a good end, like a good Christian woman, in God's name pased.

" 1599 (*Methley, Yorks*). Robert Nelsonne was buried the xxviijth November, the said Roberte did breake his faste the same day and was in good healthe, and came to ye churche to ye buryinge of the foresaid Marioye Hagger, and did helpe to ringe a peale at ye bells, and withn one halfe howre after died in the p'sence of all the people in ye churche, and was buried within fowre howres afterwarde.

" 1615 (*St. Martin's, Ludgate*). Feb. 20 was buried an anatomy from the College of Physicians.

" 1617 (*Stanton Lacy, Salop*). Mem^d that there was a blacke cloath upon the hearse of Richard Joanes buried this yeare, which of right appertaines to the vicar, but I bestowed it upon the poore clerke.

" 1626 (*Wickham, Durham*). This present year one Annas Gaskell, wife to Anthony Gaskell, bore at one birth fower p'fect children, whereof one had life and stirred after it was borne, the rest all three still borne, and were all buried in one grave 25th of March.

" 1627 (*Great St. Mary's, Cambridge*), March 13. A boy that was anatomized in the Schools.

" 1643 (*Carlton, Suffolk*). Jane, the wife of Mr John Saunders, Parson of Carleton, dyed the thirteenth day of June, about six of the clock in the afternoon, being tuesday, and was buried in the upper end of the Chancell within a foot length of the wall upon the north syde of the sayd Chancell, the fifteenth day of the said month of June. Mr Gabriel Elend, vicar of Pratfield, preached at her buriall, his text was taken out of the Epistle to the Hebrewes, ix, 27.   This woman was (by her owne account) above the age of fourscore yeares, beinge borne in the North, in a Towne called Keswicke in the Countie of Cumberland. Before shee was married, her Name was Jane Williamson.

" 1644 (*Tamworth*), 24th March. Cast into the ground the body of Ellen wife of Richd Ensor, a popeling.

" 1646 (*Tamworth*), June 29. buried the body of Richard Harding, he was once one of the company but was put out bec: he was an ale seller.

" 1699 (*Esh, Durham*), 27 Jan. David Gordon a poor soldier beging his bread fell sick of a feaver and died in a Bakehouse att Usshaw.

" 1710 (*Ashbourne, Derbyshire*), 7 April. Buried old George Wood aged about eighty years, a person of good health and activity for his years and one that frequented the Prayers and Sacraments at Church continually. On Wednesday the 5th of this month having eaten his dinner well he came down to Evening prayers, and entered the Church with a lively fresh colour in his face, and went into the seat y^t is just opposite to ye Reading Desk, laid down his staffe and gloves on ye bench, and stood up leaning his arms on the side of the seat, when the sentences of Scripture and the Exhortation were read, but just as that was ended, and before ye Confession began, he fell down on the floor of the seat, and in two minutes time was taken up dead and carried home on a pillow upon the Bier. Matt. 24th 42–46.

" 1720 (*St. Michael le Belfry, York*). Bur. John Brookes, the first Hackney coachman, February 26th.

" 1773 (*Breadsall, Derbyshire*). Mr Joseph Jackson (a Miser under a Heap of Riches) buried May 18th.

" 1814 (*Long Buckby, Northants*). Edith Freeman, who from an obstinate temper kept to her bed 44 years, relict of the Revd George Freeman LL.D., buried 21 January, aged 74."

Now and again those in charge of the registers did not hesitate to express their opinion in writing as to the character of the deceased, whether good, bad or unusual. Here are some instances :—

" 1580 (*St. Oswald's, Durham*). Mayster John Watson of thage lxxx years, for wysdome, gravyte, honeste, sobryete, and other godly vertews, worthe to be pr'sed, was buryed the xxix day of June, beinge the feast day of pet^r thapostle.

" 1597 (*Aston-by-Birmingham*). Edward Vincent buried 3 June a great sinner and blasphemer he died desperately *qualis vita talis ita.*

" 1601 (*St. Peter's, Cornhill*), Sept. 22. Buryed David Powell Clothworker but free of ye Merchant Tailors : 54 years old, lies just in the mid ile.

> "This Powell was a plaine man and led an honest life,
> Hee loved peace and amitie, and shun'd debate and strife.''

" 1607 (*Aston-by-Birmingham*). Jeiss wife of Nicholas Eagles of

Erdington buried 25 Dec, a good churchwoman and good to the poor."

Following the entry of the burial of John Collen on 6th of July, 1613, the rector of Beeston next Mileham, Norfolk, writes :—

"Ipse autem per multos annos habuit in oppido *an alehouse* ad magnum hujus oppidi nocumentum.

" 1614 (*St. Oswald's, Durham*), Nov. 8. John Richardson, public notari, a verie honest nighbore and a good willer both for the good of this Churche and for the good of this parish, whose soule the lord Jesus receive in to his Kingdome. Amen.

" 1619 (*Kensington*), April 23. Mr Robert Fen the elder, Esquier, an ancient howshold servant unto Queene Elizabeth and unto our most gracious Kinge James, a faythful p'fessor of true relegion and a most charitable freind to the poore, of age 77, upon fryday night at 10 of the clock.

" 1624 (*Burstall, Suffolk*), Aprill 5. Jane Salter widdow buried when she had lived in the favor of God and all good people lxxi yeares.

" 1670 (*St. Nicholas, Ipswich*). Mrs Abigall Maninge widi whoe had tooe housbonds both Ministers her first housbond was that Reverend and holy man of God Mr Nathonile Smart whoe was Minister of this p'ish of St Nicolas fiveten yeares and dyed here in his Ministery whose precious ashes lyes Interred close to the Entrance into the vestery in the Chancel in whose grave rests the boddy of this holy Matrion waiting til her Redeemer comes whoe was buryed october 17th.

" 1671 (*Condover, Salop*), Mar. 20. Mr William Owen, the third son of Sr William Owen, Knight, Prebendary of Worcester and Minister of Pontesbury bur. He was a Reverend and learned Divine, a Loyeall subject, an excellent friend, a tender husband, and most endearing and indulgent Parent, in a word hee was a Person of y^t great modestie, humilitie, charitee, and hospitalitie which made him the best neighbor in the world. Hee was a publick loss and publickly lamented, for I never saw truer mourning and soe generall in all my life. Help Lord for good men decay !

" 1707 (*Ashbourne, Derbyshire*), 16 August. Mr Charles Chancey, Physician and Apothecary, and one of the Church Wardens of this parish. A man of good knowledge learning and experience in Physick, Pharmacy, and Chyrurgery; of a lepid and satyricall kind of conversation, but of great Integrity and good nature, and so helpfull and usefill to all sorts, that his loss was universally deplored, and his Corps was mett some miles from the Town, for he died at Darby in his return from visiting a Patient in Leicester, the Gout (with which he was much troubled) striking up to his stomach, and that occasioned (as was supposed) by eating cowcumbers and ffruit. He was sorrowfully (yet voluntarily and without invitation) attended to his grave by multitudes of the whole neighbourhood.

"1708 (*Ibid.*), 8 April. Nathaniel, son of Nathaniel Boothouse and Hannah his wife, vicar of this parish, who was born at Careington (where his father was then rector) June 22, 1704, and died here at Ashburne on Easter Tuesday the 6th of this instant month. A child he was of exceeding sweetness and prettiness both in person and temper, and of wonderfull quickness of apprehension and parts, far beyond his years. His death drew tears from many more eyes than those of his own Parents. He lies buried in the east end of the churchyard, his father esteeming Churches and Chancels to be too good to lay dead bodies in.

"The Lord gave and the Lord hath taken away, blessed be the name of the Lord.

"He was a flow'r of Sweetness, might have grown
In age and kindred to perfection,
But God's resistless Hand, by Death's surprise,
Transferred him to th' Heavenly Paradise.

"Verba haec (Lectores) maesto indulgete Parenti.

"1773 (*Clovelly, Devon*), Aug. 6. Catherine Rowe, a pattern of Industry and a good Neighbour.

" Aug. 7. Christian Meek, truly deserving of that name.

" Oct. 26. Emlyn, Wife of Richard Crews, eminent for a meek and peaceable disposition."

This is not the place in which to discuss the once much disputed point concerning Centenarians, as to which the late Mr. Thoms was so persistently sceptical. Suffice it to say that during the last fifty years there have been several score of deaths registered in England of those who have without any doubt exceeded the age of 100 years. In fact there is no lack of documentary evidence as to recent cases of decided super-centenarians. For instance, until a few years ago there still lived at Auberive-en-Royen (Isère) a certain Mme. Durand, known under the name of "Mère Girard," aged 135 years. Her birth certificate, registered in the parish of Saint-Just-de-Clast, bears the date of September 22, 1740. In 1864 she solemnly celebrated the hundredth anniversary of her marriage.

Two cases of extraordinary longevity have already been cited from the remarkable register of Much Wenlock, under the years 1541–2 and 1545. In the same register, under 1546, mention is made of Thomas Smith, subprior of the monastery, 115 years of age at his death.

The following are a variety of centenarian register entries, selected from about double the number, which we have culled from old parochial registers :—

"1586 (*Swainswick, Somerset*). Elianor Cox, wydow, being an hundred yeres old, was buried the 8th daie of Julie.

"1588 (*Minehead, Somerset*). John Williams was 100 years old.

"1591 (*Aston by Birmingham*). Ould Weddowe Seye was buried 30 March a woman of a hundreth years olde and more.

"1596–7 (*St. Peter's, Cornhill*), 14 March. Margery Mane widow, old, yet devout in often hearing ye word : in ye cros ile, (years) 100.

"1603 (*Stoke Newington*). Margaret Forster, widow, of the age of 103 years or thereabouts, was buried the 21st of Sept.

"1607 (*Great Marlow, Bucks*). The Eight day of Marche was Buried Emline Clarke widowe 100 yere olde.

"1611 (*Cathedral Church of Peterborough*), January. Bartholomew Barnaby, an oulde Faulkener, buryed the 5 day, above an hundred yeares old.

"1627 (*Dorking, Surrey*), Nov. 14. John Colcott aged 108 years was buried.

"1630 (*Swainswick, Somerset*). John Poule the eldest, beinge about an hundred years of age, was buried the 21st of Julie.

" 1641 (*Albrighton, Salop*), Nov. 1. Margarett Brooke, 115 yeares old and odder wife of Roger of the Harrits Haies of this p. : bur.

" 1650 (*Heyford, N'hants*). Thomas Ward senex centum annos errabundus, melancholitus, et inventus mortuus (on the uppermost Furlong beyond Depcambe) resepult : first Decemb 12.

" 1657 (*Stranton, Durham*). Richard Brantingham, of Seaton, bur May 29th, aged 106.

" 1661 (*Barton-under-Needwood, Staffs*), Feb. 13. Widow Reading, aged above an hundred, bur.

" 1663 (*Eyam, Derbyshire*), Dec. 30. Bur. Anna, the traveller, who, according to her own account, was 136 years of age.

" 1665 (*Alstonfield, Staffs*), Nov. 27. Eliz. wid. of Ric Baatt, reported to be about 100 years old, bur.

" 1683 (*Salehurst, Sussex*), Oct. 5. Bur[d] Peter Sparke aged 120 odd years.

" 1693 (*Edlingham, Northumb.*), 20 April. Barham Norris, widow, aged 100 years and more, buried in Edlingham church.

" 1703–4 (*Bywell St. Peter, Northumberland*), March 23. Ralph Seymor, of Rochelport, buried, aged 106 as is reported.

" 1706 (*All Saints, Northampton*). Old John Bales Button Maker buried the 14th April who lived part of y[e] Fifteenth century, the whole sixteenth, and part of the seventeenth century. The most probable conjecture of his age is that if he had lived to the August following he would have been 114, for we find in this Register a John Bales Bapt August ye 20th 1592.

" 1706 (*Cleobury Mortimer, Salop*), May 5. Frances Worston, widow, aged by computation 114.

" 1708 (*Bitterley, Salop*), May 20. Maria Smith, quæ ad centissimum vixit annum sep.

" 1709 (*Ibid.*), Jan. 21. Margaretta Williams, quæ annum præteriit centissimum, sep."

In the same register are entries of eight subsequent centenarians under the years 1714 (two), 1717, 1719 (two), 1756, 1794, and 1809, the exact age in these cases varies from 100 to 104.

" 1716 (*Haughton, Staffs*), May 9. Frances Cook, of Booden, aged 101, bur.

" 1717 (*Edlingham, Northum.*), 10 Oct. Edward Crisp, aged 102, Abberwick, in Bolton Chappell.

" 1723 (*Warkworth, Northumberland*), April 9. Johannes Lamb, annos natus 106, et Isabella uxor, annos natus 86, eodem die sepult. de Warkworth.

" 1731 (*Alstonfield, Staffs*), Jan 5. Margery Baddely of Hope, said to have been 107 years old, bur.

" 1739 (*Warkworth, Northum.*), 13 Jan. Henricus Richardson annos natus 101 de High Buxton.

" 1745 (*West Hallam, Derbyshire*). Old Sarah Baldack of Dale Parish, aged 103, buried Apr. 22.

" 1746 (*Norton, Durham*). Frances Wrench bur. October 9 in 110th year of her age.

" 1749 (*Warkworth, Northum.*), 15 Feb. Elisabetha Brown annos nata 105, de West Chivinton.

" 1749 (*Hartlepool*). Ruth Nicholson was bur. 10th of December, aged above 103 year.

" 1761 (*Selattyn, Salop*), April 2. William Sandland, aged 103, bur.

" 1763 (*Bothal, Northum.*), 5 Dec. Robert Turnbull, aged 104 years.

" 1774 (*Ibid.*), 1 Nov. Catherine Brown, Longhirst, aged 109 years.

" 1807 (*Linton-in-Craven, Yorks*). Margret Strorey of Bridgend, Aged 101 years, was Buried June 13."

Those under sentence of excommunication were not allowed any burial ceremony, and, strictly speaking, could not be interred in consecrated ground. Two post-Reformation register entries have been noted of interdiction by the bishop of all burials, for a period, owing to the infringement of this ecclesiastical rule.

" 1598 (*Chesterfield*). Robertus Eyre generosus sepult p'videntiam ab Hercule Foljambe xv die Decemb.

   " Upon the buriall of the said Robert Eyre being an excommunicate recusant (R. Catholic), our buriall was interdicted; in the tyme of the inhibitian, before it was released these persones followinge dyed, and were buried at other churches as followeth. [Here are entered four burials at Whittington, two at Brampton, one at Wingerworth, and one at Barlow.] The xiiij day of Januarie the interdiction was released."

The second instance occurs at a later date in the registers of Weedon-Beck, Northants, in the year 1615 :—

"William Radhouse the elder dying excommunicate was buryed by stealth in the night time in the churchyard 29 Jan. Wherefore the church was interdicted for a fortnight."

The persecution of the Recusants, that is of those who clung to the old unreformed faith, was carried on relentlessly even to the grave throughout the reign of Elizabeth; though their burial at night without any rite was winked at in various parishes, particularly where they were numerous. In the instances cited below, it can be proved that all were Romanists, though in some cases it is not so stated in the registers.

"1504 (*Leeds*). Richard Lumbye, of the Chappiltowne, being a papist, not comyng to the church the space of 12 years, being indycted at the generall and private sessions upon the statute, presented at the visitacions of papystry, excommunycate, dyed at Chappiltowne the third day of December, and was by hys kynsfolk and neighbours brought towards the churche to be buryed, but at the churchyard gate stopped by the Curate and Churchwardens where hys corps remained till the seventh day of the same moneth at night, and hys frends could not gett lycens to burye him ; going to York for yᵗ purpose, hys said corps was in the night conveyed and buryed."

It may be here mentioned that there are certain remarkable additions to some of the burial entries in the register of the parish church of Leeds under the years 1573–7. The pious old Catholic invocation *Cujus anime propitietur Deus* is added to the interment record in twenty-two instances. Possibly these were all at heart Roman Catholics, and the additions made by a broad-minded or sympathetic clerk. To two of the burial entries during this period is appended the absurdly irrelevant ending "God save the Queen," a kind of Erastian protest, we suppose, against the use of the ancient formula.

" 1594 (*Parham, Sussex*). Widow Duke on the Common, being excommunicated, was laid in the Churchyard Nov. 4.

" 1595 (*Longford, Derbyshire*). Margaret Bakewell, a maid of Auk-manton, buried excommunicated 14th of October being Sun-day after sun setting.

" 1602 (*Drypole, E. R. Yorks*). Thomas Cletheray a recusant of the North blockhouse was put into his grave in drypoll churchyard vii day of March, by the means of Henry Garrub, without the minister and without the order of buriall, according to lawe.

" 1604 (*Christchurch, Hants*), April 14. Christian Steevens, the wife of Thomas Steevens, was buried in childbirth, and buried by women, for she was a papishe."

There are various night burials mentioned in the registers of Stokesley, Yorks, all of which apparently apply to the interment of Recusants :—

" 1608. Anne Brasse buryed at midnyght 26 June.

" 1615. Agnes rountree of tantan was burd 29 August at nyght in inner churche yarde a recusantt.

" 1618. Wm pillye wif was bur the 7 Nov at nyght butt wher I can not tell.

" 1621–2. Xtofer hutcheson of Sto bud vjth day Fabruary upon the nyght by whom I knowe not.

" 1639. Frances George buried the 11th September at night but by whome it is unknone."

The Recusants were always numerous in the Derbyshire parish of Hathersage ; four of them were buried there and entered in the register in 1629, four in 1630, and five in 1631 —all by night.

" 1623 (*Albrighton, Salop*), May 19. Thomas Harrington, of Byshton, esquire, was buried in the night by commandment from the Byshop.

" 1626 (*Tarporley, Cheshire*). Richard Welch Papist and excommunicate bur 20 August at night.

" 1631 (*Methley, Yorks*). Prothasia Shaun buried the 25th of
December, in the night, but not by a minister.

" 1642 (*North Elmham, Norfolk*). Rose, ye wife of Robert Lunford
was buried y[e] 23 of December, she was a recusant papist, she
was buried in the night without the church ceremonies."

At Norbury, Derbyshire, an old seat of the celebrated
recusant family of the Fitzherberts, there are three entries
in the parish register, for the year 1723, of interments without
service; in two of these instances it is specified that the
deceased were " papists," and it was doubtless also the case
with the third.

There are various register entries which show that other
Nonconformists were treated after death as excommunicants
and denied (if they had desired it) formal burial.

" 1610 (*Beeston next Mileham, Norfolk*). Henery Surskey, widower,
by the order of his schismaticall sonne, who not only denyes
but contemnes and rayles agaynst the discipline of the Church
of England, and hates the ministers thereof, was put into the
grave in the churchyard of Beeston the 16th day of September
without minister or any but factious persons like himselfe,
which is heere set downe to his shame to posterity.

" 1614–15 (*Nassington, N'hants*). Jeane Burton was buried the 7th
of Februarie by moone light about two a clock in the morning
dying in childebed but not trimmed.[1]

" 1619 (*Albrighton, Salop*), Aug 20. Izable Keames of the Park Syde,
wyddowe, diceased the 18th day of August, and was buryed in
the hall orchyard neere unto the church wall upon the west
side thereof, the 20th day of August, Anno Dom 1619, being
an excommunicated person.

" 1642 (*Stock, Essex*), 7 May. Elizabeth the d. of Thomas Wood (an
Annabaptisticall and factious Separatist) and Eleanor his wife
(the grave being ready made) was (by the companie that
came with the childe) interred and layd into the ground before
the minister came: and without praiers, or the righte of

---

[1] The expression "not trimmed" is a puzzle, and it seems scarcely worth
while to guess at an explanation.

christian buriall according to the order of the Churche of England on Satterday."

The supposed liberty of conscience and freedom of worship under the Commonwealth is a baseless fable. Presbyterians and Congregationalists united in denying every kind of freedom to Romanists, Episcopalians, Unitarians, and especially to Quakers. To this the burial registers occasionally bear witness :—

" 1653 (*Hackness, Yorks*). Richard Cockerell dyed on Wednesday the xiiij[th] day of September and was buryed the next day being Thursday and there was many of them they call Quaker at his buryall. And Mr. Prowde did exhorte and argue with them at the Grave and they held out that that work wch they had in them was not wrought by the word wch I was sorry to heare but they sayd they made use of the word only to try whether it were right or not.

" 1656 (*Ibid.*). George Watson dyed the xij[th] day (July) and was buryed the next, beinge of the Quakers Sect and many of them were at his buryall but M[r] Prowde was not called to bury him, and after they see him buryed they wente away.

" 1658-9 (*Wing, Rutland*). William Sharp the younger (comonly called William Sharp) at the Townes End who was a whither witted sectary and a separatist from own congregacion, having languished a great while neglected of his owne wife and children at last died miserably soe far in dett that all his goods would not near make satisfaction. He died the 26 and was buried the 28 of February 1658.

" 1677 (*Bishop Middleham, Durham*), Jan. 31. Isabell, wife of Francis Williamson, was buried at 2 of the clock in the morn[g].

" 1679. (*Waterbeach, Cambs*), 10 Dec. Francis Wilson, excomunicated, buried in his orchard.

" 1695-6 (*Thornton, Bucks*). Francis Colman dyed March 3[d] but was not buryed in this paresh bec. he dyed excomunicate, and was fetch by some Anabapt. brethren to a Burying place of theirs at Stony Stretford.

" 1703 (*Corby, N'hants*). Thomas Seamark informed me y[t] one William Faukiner was buried in an orchard belonging to Emanuel Boone on y[e] 17th of Octob[r] 1703.

"1704 (*Bourton-on-the-Water, Gloucestershire*). Wm Wickser's wife, of Layborough, was buried in Widow Green's orchard at Lower Slaughter (a chapelry to Bourton) March 5.

"1726 (*Breadsall, Derbyshire*). Mary Daughter of Edward Wheatcroft died in January being under sentence of Excommunication and as I heard was interred ye 23^d of ye same month.

"1741 (*Spratton, N'hants*), Dec. 10. Mary ye wife of William Lansbury the younger being dipd and dying a profess'd Anabaptist was interr'd without ye office of ye Burial Service a little before six o'clock in ye evening.

"1741-2 (*Ibid.*), Feb. 10. John Lee ye Anabaptist teacher was interr'd without the Burial Service."

It must not, however, be supposed that all post-Reformation excommunications were on account of lack of conformity with the established formularies of religion, or, as was occasionally the case, for moral offences. Sentences of excommunication, as enjoined by archidiaconal courts, were of fairly common occurrence in connection with non-payment of tithes or Easter dues, or for other technical offences of an ecclesiastical nature. It was the attempt to enforce the full legal penalties involved in excommunication for offences of this character that gradually brought the whole system into contempt and secured its final disuse.

Amongst the parish muniments of Luccombe, a retired village of West Somerset, hidden away amidst the combes of Exmoor, are two or three original forms of excommunication, *temp.* Charles I.[1] According to English canon law, a sentence of excommunication was bound to be delivered in writing and under a proper seal. The most perfect of these documents is written on a half-sheet of foolscap lengthways, and has borne a large wafer seal, only the stain of which remains :—

"Samuel Ward doctor of divinity Archdeacon of the Archdea·

[1] These were discovered by the present writer as long ago as 1864 among a litter of discarded rubbish. See "Gleanings from a Parish Chest" in Andrews' *Curious Church Gleanings* (1896).

conry of Taunton to our well-beloved the Parson Vicar or Curate of the parish church of Luccombe within our Archdeaconry of Taunton sendeth greetinge in our Lord God everlastinge. Whereas Walter Pugslie, Moses Pugslie, and John Anton of yᵉ parish aforesaid for their manifest contempte and disobedience have been longe time justlie excommunicated and for excommunicate persons openly denounced in the face of the Church at the time of divine service in which dangerous estate without feare of God or shame of yᵉ world they still remaine in contempte of lawe and lawful magistrates. We therefore will and require yow that the next Sabath day or holiday ensuinge the Receipt hereof in your said parish Church at the time of divine service before the whole congregation assembled yow shall publiquely denounce those Walter Pugslie, Moses Pugslie and John Anton for aggravated persons and also then and there yow shall admonish all Christian people by virtue hereof that they and any of them henceforth eschewe and avoid the society, fellowshippe and company of the said-persons and that they neither eate, nor drink, buy, sell, or otherwise by any manner of means communicate with them, being members cut off from all Christian Society under the payne of excommunication by lawe in this behalfe provided until they shall submit themselves to be reconciled. And of yʳ doinges herein Certifie us or our Deputy the next court day ensuinge after fortye dayes after the denouncinge hereof and fayle yow not under the payne contempte. Dated under our Seale the three and twentye day of May Anno dom, 1628.

"Rɪc: Pᴇᴇᴋᴇ Reg."

It is a mere matter of surmise what had been the original offence of these three Luccombe parishioners, but it was probably non-payment of tithes. The offence would have been stated in the original sentence. This excommunication is a further declaration; for the excommunication was obliged to be repeated at the end of six months, provided the person or persons had not meanwhile purged themselves by submission and penance, and obtained the benefit of absolution. The reason of the mention of the forty days was because, according to the law and custom of England—which differed in this respect from all other parts of Christendom—the civil authority in the person of the sheriff was bound to step in and imprison excommunicated folk, until they made submission, provided that the desire *de excommunicata capiendo* was expressed by the bishop or diocesan official. On the same Sunday whereon these three Luccombe offenders were denounced in their parish church, and all Christian folk commanded to boycott them, the like excommunication was read during service in the Cathedral Church of Wells, and on the following day the names and offences of those excommunicated were forwarded to the Archbishop of the province.

In the neighbouring parish of Wootton Courtney, a paper dated 1st November, 1629, is pinned into the register book, wherein the rector expresses in naive terms his regrets that he had proceeded with the excommunication of two parishioners for considerable arrears of tithes, as the fees of the archidiaconal officials considerably exceeded the amount recovered!

At the beginning of the first register book of Great Preston, Northants, is a list of twenty instances of the excommunications or consequent absolutions of parishioners between the years 1607 and 1633. Bosworth (whose Christian name is missing), was "decreed excommunicate the 26 of March and denounced in Preston church Ap. 27, 1618." Another Bosworth was decreed excommunicate on 24th July of the same year and denounced in Preston church on 9th August. Henry Adkins excommunicated on 27th June and denounced 8th July 1621, "was absolved fro the sentence of excom: the ix of January 1622." From other entries in this list, it is clear that absolutions were decreed by the chancellor or his surrogate; there is no express statement that such absolutions were afterwards pronounced in church, but there can be little or no doubt that this was the case at Great Preston.

At the end of the second register of Bingley, Yorks,

are lists of persons of that parish excommunicated at the
time of the Archdeacon's visitations in the years 1639, 1664,
and 1682; the respective numbers were 24, 25, and 20.   There
are two other undated lists.

> " 1667–8 (*Scotter, Linc.*), June 19. Mem. That on Septuagesime
> Sunday one Francis Drury, an excommunicate person, came into
> church in the time of divine service in y⁰ morning, and being
> admonisht by me to be gon, he obstinately refused, whereupon yᵉ
> whole congregation departed ; and after the same manner in the
> afternoon the same day he came againe, and refusing againe to
> goe out, the whole congregation againe went home, soe yᵗ
> little or noe service perform'd yᵗ day.   I prevented his further
> coming in yᵗ manner, as he threatened, by order from yᵉ justice
> upon the statute of Q. Elizabeth concerning the molestation and
> disturbance of public preachers. Wᵐ Carrington, Rector. *O
> tempora !   O mores !*"

In the register book of Alstonfield, Staffordshire, there is
a list of "persons excommunicate in the Chancellor's Court."
In 1678, three names are given under 23rd June, and eight
under 1st September.   In the following year there are five
persons thus named; in 1680 seven; and in 1681 three.
The excommunicate of Alstonfield in the Archdeacon's
Court for 1678 numbered nine, in 1679 eight, in 1680 five,
and in 1683 twenty-nine.   The respective grounds for
excommunication are not named in these lists.

On the inside cover of the fourth book of the registers of
Stokesley, Yorks, which begins in 1723, are the names of four
women "under excommunication for fornication"; a weaver
under like sentence in 1745 "for refusing to pay his Easter
Offerings to ye minister"; and a widow excommunicated for
contumacy in a slander case at the York Consistory Court.
The widow in this last case was

"publickly Declared to be Absolved from yᵉ Sentence of
Excommunication in yᵉ Parish Church of Stokesley on yᵉ 19ᵗʰ of
April, 1755, by Tho Thwaites Curate of yᵉ sᵈ Parish."

8

Christian burial was denied in very early times not only to the unbaptized and the excommunicate, but also to those who had laid violent hands on themselves. In the case, however, of suicides, it is expressly laid down by the canons under Egbert of A.D. 740, and repeated at later dates, that this penalty is to be incurred by those who thus act *by any fault*, thus excluding those who commit the deed in madness or frenzy. It was customary in England to bury suicides at cross roads, but not unfrequently, for charity's sake, the body was interred in the graveyard without ceremonial. By an Act of 1821, the burial of one against whom a verdict of *felo de se* had been pronounced is ordered to be within the church-yard between the hours of nine and twelve at night.

The following are some selected instances of register entries of the burials of suicides :—

" 1556 (*St. Alkmund's, Derby*). Sepultus est Johannes Marriath pastor hujus ecclesiæ postquam sese laqueo videlicet funiculo minimæ campanæ suspenderat vitamque miserime finierat. Junii 14. Deus det aliis meliorem gratiæ mensuram. Nota, fregit campanam corporis gravitate et casu.

" 1573 (*Pleasley, Derbyshire*). [Loose leaf of an early register.] Tho. Maule f^d hunge on a tree by ye wayeside after a druncken fitte April 3. Crowners queste in churche porche April 5. Same nighte at midd nighte burried at ye nighest crosse roades w^t a stake yn him, manie peopple frome Manesfeilde.

" 1574 (*Chesham, Bucks*), June 30. Francis Cocker did strangle him selfe to death.

" 1579 (*St. Anne's, Blackfriars*), Aug. 4. John Hacone infamously buried, for killing himselfe desperately.

" 1594 (*Ibid.*). Robert Halle, servant to Jysse Cutler, who did hang himself, and was buried at the Thames, hard by Blackfriars Bridge.

" 1597 (*St. Alkmund's, Derby*). Concescit fato Johannes Wooddewise, parvæ Cestria, non sepultus, quia laqueo seipsum suspendit, Deus det aliis meliorem gratiam, Apr 3.

" 1597 (*All-Hallows-in-the-Wall*). Thomas Atkinson gentleman sometyme servant to the old Ladye of Pembrooke, and at this present dyd belong to Mr Thomas Compton, brother to the Lord William Compton : he was buried the iiijth day of June, who being sycke of a whole fever : wth a sworde in the anguyshe of his fytt, thrust y^t into his bellye : And so ended this mortall lyfe in the house of wydowe Olyver, the seconde daye of June at night, being but newlye come thyther, theyre to lye and to have his being.

" 1597 (*Drypole, E. R. Yorks*). Anne Ruter a singlewoman drowned herselfe and was buried the iiij daie of Julie on the North side of the church.

" 1600 (*Chesterfield*). Isabell Taylor widowe drowned her selffe in a well and was buried vij April.

" 1600 (*Chesham, Bucks*), July 11. Isbell the wyfe of Thomas Border being greate with childe most fearfully by drowning herselfe in a ponde ended this present lyfe.

" 1617 (*Elland, Yorks*). Thomas Gleidell generosus bur^d 31 Oct, corpse dug up 27 Nov. Carefully viewed by 16 sworn men because it was noised and said by some of his covet and envious near relations that he had k. himselfe with his own h^d—untouched and unwounded.

" 1620 (*St. Alkmund's, Derby*). A certayne prisoner brought unto ye gaole and guarded coming over the Mary bridge leapte over into the water and drownde himselfe, and was buried by the highway side close at the foote of the bridge, June 28.

" 1678 (*Bishop Middleham, Durham*), Oct. 20. Joseph Bowes, gent (being found to have laid violent hands on himselfe) was buried in a void place.

" 1698 (*West Hallam, Derbyshire*), April 13. Katharine the wife of Tho. Smith alias Cutler was found *felo de se* by ye Coroners inquest and interred in ye crosse ways near ye wind mill on ye same day.

" 1699 (*Twyford, Derbyshire*). Jacobus Hurd de Stenson bachalauraus qui in aqua Trenti immersus die Veneris vicesimo tertio sepultus fuit Sancti Johannis Baptis die, M^t. Charles Adderley Coroner sat upon him in Twyford Church,[1] June 24.

" 1706 (*Ibid.*), April 6. Quidam Gulielmus Smith Peregrinus veniens

[1] Among the Derbyshire county records are a variety of papers relative to inquests held by Coroner John Alderly from 1677 to 1699. A jury of twenty-four was always summoned ; the day of the inquest was usually Sunday, and the place of summons the parish church. The corpse was usually viewed in the porch. Unsuitable as this ancient place for holding inquests seems to modern ideas—it can

a Parochia de Utoxetu suspendit seipsum apud Twyford : sepultus autem erat in loco vulco appellato Hailslouts.

"1719 (*Overstone, Northants*), Dec. 6. Bur. Rebecca Adams, widow of John Adams (who cut his own throat July 5th last past and was buried at the corner of ye hedge by ye Northfield closes but twice clandestinely taken away by one Stephenson a Surgeon at Northampton in order to be made a skeleton).

"1719 (*Bothal, Northumberland*), 19 Feb. John Hurst, Gallow-house, who hanged himself with the cowband over the Ravel Tree.

"1734 (*Thorpe Achurch, N'hants*), Sept. 19. William Greenwood, a Dissenting Teacher of March in the Isle of Eley, cut his throat at a Publick House in our Parish, and after the Correnors Inquest was Bury'd behind the Church in Woollen according to law."

Other burials by night are also to be found in parochial registers in addition to the dishonourable ones in cases of excommunication and suicide. Some of these were inter-ments by torchlight, *causa honoris*, as something exceptional, reserved for persons of distinction, or handed down by family tradition. Aldermen of London, who had filled the office of Lord Mayor, were by ancient use buried by torchlight with great ceremonial; but these nocturnal funerals led to so much disorder that they were prohibited in the time of Charles I. At Westminster Abbey, Abraham Cowley in 1617, Joseph Addison in 1717, and George II in 1760, all had torchlight burials. Archbishop Hutton was buried at night, at Lambeth, in 1758, and John Wesley's funeral in 1791 was at so early an hour in the morning that lanterns and torches were required. The Berkeleys, of Bruton, Somerset, were for a long period buried at midnight in a crypt beneath the chancel, after a sermon had been preached in the church. The old custom of burying members of the Dyott family by

be traced back in Derbyshire to the thirteenth century—the palpable modern scandal of holding inquests in public-houses was unknown. See Dr. Cox's *Three Centuries of Derbyshire Annals*, vol. i. pp. 79–82, 391.

torchlight in the vaults of St. Mary's Church, Lichfield, is still maintained.

The three following register entries of the seventeenth century are clearly concerned with honourable burial:—

" 1609 (*Harrow-on-the-Hill*), August 23[d] being Wensday about sixe of the clocke at night dyed the right Worshipful M[r] William Gerarde and the body of the same M[r] Gerrard was buryed in the sepulchre of his father within the Churche of Harrow on Thursday the 24th day of the same moneth about nyne of the clocke at night By one Humphrey Wiltlud.

" 1635 (*Albrighton, Salop*), Nov. 15. The Right Honor[ble] Ladie the Countesse of Shrewsburie was buried at this Church upon Twelf day at nightt, being the sixth day of January 1635.

" 1668 (*Bruton, Somerset*), June 26. The Rt Honor[ble] Charles Lord Viscount Fitzharding was between 12 and one of the clock in the night, after a sermon preached by M[r] John Randall, then minist: of Brewton, buried in the vault in the Chancell in a coffin of lead."

In two or three parishes burial in the late evening or night became habitual. A striking instance of this is Wellingborough, as shown by the following parochial entry:—

" 1737, 11 April. Whereas there hath been and still is a custom and usage within the said Parish of Burying the Dead at the Houre of eight or nine at night in the winter, and somtimes later, which is found to be a very inconvenient and prejudicial custom both to the Minister and inhabitants—For the putting an end therefore to the said custom and usage, and for the future good and convenience of the said Minister and Parishioners, we the Minister and majority of the Principal Inhabitants of the said Parish being upon due and publick notice assembled in vestry for that purpose, do hereby upon mature consideration order and require all persons within the said Parish who shall hereafter bury their dead in the church or churchyard of the said Parish that they bring their said dead hither to be buried from and after the day of the date of these presents until the feast of St. Michael the Archangel next ensuing at or before the hour of seven in the afternoon, and from and after the 1st Feast of St. Michael unto the Feast of the Blessed Virgin Mary at or before the hour of four in the afternoone."

A fine of 1s. an hour was to be imposed for every hour after the appointed, one half to the minister and the other half to the poor.

In the old days executed criminals were usually buried in the consecrated ground of the parish where the gaol stood. For the most part the burial service was used; and this could scarcely have been otherwise, for the condemned criminal not infrequently received the Holy Communion, and sometimes was baptized on the eve of execution.

"1576 (*Cartmel, Lancashire*). Richard Taylor was buried who suffered the same daye at Blacragge Bridge end for murthering wilfullye Richard Kilner of Witherslacke."

In the seventeenth century the Surrey assizes were held at Dorking on several occasions. In 1635 two persons were condemned and executed; in 1636 five, and in 1668 five. The registers show that all these criminals were buried in the parish churchyard.

The register of Little Brickhill, Bucks, contains entries of the burials of forty-two criminals who were executed here between 1561 and 1620; it was formerly an Assize town. In this register occurs the entry:—

"Cecely Reves was buried the same day, burned."

This last horrible entry requires some explanation. The burning for heresy, as carried out under Henry VIII and Mary, was not a newly invented death torture. It was a form of capital punishment long reserved in England for women who were guilty of high or petty treason. Petty treason included not only the murder of a master by a servant, or of a husband by a wife, but even a minor crime such as coining, for which a woman was burnt in 1721; so that rarely a year passed by in England, down to about a century ago, without at least one such sickening spectacle. It is supposed that the last of these cases occurred in 1784 at Portsmouth, when one Mary Bayley, for the murder of her husband, was condemned "to be drawn on an hurdle to the place of execution on Monday the eighth of March, and burned with fire until she be dead." The punishment of hanging in such cases was substituted for that of burning in 1790.

The registers of St. Chad's, Shrewsbury, bear witness to another instance of this enforced cremation:—

"December 1647—23 of this month that a woman was burnt in the quorell for poysong her husband."

The burial of the partly burnt remains of other women subjected to this horrible penalty are, to our knowledge, recorded both at Derby and York, and probably elsewhere; but in those cases the register entry decently veiled the cause of death.

At Newcastle-on-Tyne, seventeen prisoners were buried in the graveyard of St. Nicholas on 13th August, 1632.

The following are a few other register entries of burials of executed criminals, selected almost at haphazard from a large number:—

"1631 (*St. Mary's, Reading*), Aug. 11. Bur. Symon Wilkes, gentleman, executed uppon presumpson of murder, but he denied it to death.

"1643 (*St. Andrew's, Holborn*), July 6. Nathaniel Tomkins Esq. who was executed at Fetter Lane end the 5th, being found to be one of ye conspirators against this City of London, was buried here.

"1679 (*St. Mary's, Reading*), Mar. 26. Robert Mathewe, Richard Fleetwood, Thomas Grinaway, John Vasey, hanged and buried.

"1722 (*St. Mary-le-Bow, Durham*), 30 August. Bur. James Graham, a felon, he was hanged ye same morning just after Bap."

The following somewhat ghastly entry reminds us that the custom of burying in coffins is a comparatively modern one save among the wealthy classes :—

"1608 (*Poyning, Sussex*). The xviij day of April was buried John Skerry a poore man that died in the place stable, and being brought half naked with his face bare, the parson would not burye him soe, but first he gave a sheete and caused him to be sacked therein, and they buried him more Christian like, being much grieved to see him brought soe unto the grave ; and at this time did one Thatchar dwell at the place."

Registers and churchwardens' accounts bear frequent witness to uncoffined burials throughout the sixteenth and seventeenth and early eighteenth centuries.

The register of Great Doddington, Northants, of 1560–1648, has a list of clerk's fees :— *

"For bell and grave in churchyard, for a coffin 1. o.
      ,,   ,,   for a man without a coffin 8d.
      ,,   ,,   for an infant without a coffin 6d."

At Birchington, Kent, in 1638, the burial fee for "a coffin'd person" was 8d., and for "a noe coffin'd person," 6d. A Table of Duties in Shoreditch church, dated 1664, names 8d. as the burial fee in the new churchyard without a coffin, and 6d. for burial in the old churchyard without a coffin.

The wording of the Burial Service in the Book of Common Prayer clearly anticipates uncoffined burial. The word coffin is not used; it is always "the corpse" or "the body," as in the rubric, "the earth shall be cast upon the body." In Wheatley's book on the Common Prayer, first issued in 1710, occurs the comment—"When the body is stripped of all but its grave clothes, and is just going to be put into the grave," etc.

In the registers of Melbourne, Derbyshire, for the year 1663, five out of the seventeen interments are specified as buried in coffins. But the custom made slow progress. In

1698 only one burial in a coffin is named out of seventeen funerals, and none in 1699 out of ten. In the eighteenth century coffins began to predominate; in 1718 there were only two uncoffined burials out of eight.

The Commonplace book of Mr. White Watson, of Bakewell (*Derb. Arch. Soc. Journal*, vol. xi. 159), has the following entry:—

"The custom of Interment in Wooden coffins (wooden Josephs) was on the Rev^d Mr. Monks coming to reside here [He was vicar from 1678 to 1724]. A corps from Sheldon was brought in swaddling clothes, which was abolished in 1797, and was detained in Church until a coffin was made, and the wife then took off the flannel for her own use."

The present writer has talked in the "sixties" of last century with more than one aged resident of Bakewell who remembered uncoffined burials in that churchyard, and with others who remembered the same in the churchyard of Duffield, in the same county.

It was the custom for each parish to provide a shell or coffin to rest on the bier for the carrying of the corpse to the edge of the grave, when it was lifted out and lowered into the grave in its shroud, which was wrapped round with strips of canvas, termed swaddling clothes in the Bakewell entry. References to these parish coffins are not infrequent in early churchwarden accounts, such as Louth, 1521 and 1593, and St. Michael's, Cornhill, 1554. Two Yorkshire churches, namely those of Easingwold and Howden, still retain the old parish coffins.

Various registers contain express reference to the time when the Act compelling registration of burials in woollen came in force. Thus:—

"*Finedon, N'hants.* On the first of August, 1678, the Act of Parliament for burying in Woollen came in force so that there is a New Book on purpose to enter Buryalls from that day.

" *St. John's, Peterborough.* The act for burying in woollen taking place August ye first, 1678, Xtianings and Marriages are only registered in this book, and burialls in ye New Booke provided for ye purpose."

The burials in woollen at Helmdon, Northants, from 1678 to 1783, are registered in a separate book. The earliest of these entries are couched in phraseology, by a would-be-facetious minister, to throw contempt upon this extravagant sumptuary law. Three examples will suffice :—

" 1680, June 16. Thomas Shortland, the son of Thomas Shortland of the Parish of Helmdon, being Dead was put into a Pit-hole and Bury'd in the churchyard of the Town above written. Memorandum That within the revolution of eight days after the Funerall obsequays of Thos Shortland Affidavit was brought from a justice of Peace that the said Thomas Shortland was well wrapt in a shirt of wollen and was let down into his dormitory with that vestment about his corps to the great satisfaction of a Law enjoineing that Habiliment as convenient for the Dead.

" 1682, December 7. Frances Pickeings widdow of the parish of Helmdon was then let downe into her grave made in the churchyard of the village aforesaid. Let the Beadle take notice that within 8 days after yᵉ Funerall obseqyes of Frances Pickeings Affidavit was brought from a neighboring minister that the abovesaid Frances Pickeings was shrowded only in a winding sheet made of the Fleece of good Fat Mutton.

" 1683, April 30. Betty Garland, the little Pretty daughter of Nump Garland was then Bury'd within that little territory of the Dead the churchyard of Helmdon. Noverint universi, that within 8 days after solemn obsequays of the said Eliz. Garland Affidavit was brought from a neighbouring Lerite that this very numericall Betty Garland was well wrapt in a shrowd of woollen."

The late Mr. J. E. Bailey, of Stretford, Manchester, made an interesting contribution to *Notes and Queries* (5th S. vi. 144) in 1876, wherein he stated that during the operation of the Burial in Woollen Act, the law was some-

times evaded by covering corpses with hay or flowers, called
" strewings."   He cited from "the registers of an adjoining
parish" entries of bodies, about the year 1706, "Buryed in

A Register of ý Burials in ý Parish of Littlebourne
in Kent since ý Act of Parliamt for burying in
Wooll only; made in ý year of oúr Lord 1678.

The Widow Dade was buried according to ý said Act
on ý fifteenth day of October 1678 Affidavit brought in
the 20th day of ý same Month:

Robert Johnson was buried according to ý said Act on ý
16th Day of Octob: 1678. Affidavit brought in on ý
20th day of ý same month.

Magdalene Impet Widdow was buried according to ý
said Act Octob: 18. 1678. Affidavit brought in on ý
20th day of ý same Month

Jone Howkins Widow was buried according to ý said
Act, on ý seventh day of November, Affidavit brought
in on ý 10th day of ý same Month.

Ellen ý Wife of Edward Goorly was buried according to
the said Act on ý 17th of December 1678. Affidavit
was brought in on ý 22th of ý same Month.

Martha Reader of Icham was buried according to ý said
act, on ý 29th day of December 1678. Affidavit
brought in January ý 4th following.

John Gostling Vicar:

FACSIMILE OF FIRST PAGE OF REGISTER OF BURIALS IN WOOLLEN:
LITTLEBOURNE, KENT.

sweet flowers only." In other cases it is said that the bodies were "not wounde up or Buryed savinge only in sweet flowers and Hay." The affidavits were made to that effect. Unfortunately the exact parishes where these curious and exceptional entries occur are not mentioned.

The following is an example of the affidavit which had to be brought to the minister within eight days of the burial, certifying that the requirements of the law had been fulfilled. Bundles of these affidavits are still preserved in a few parish chests :

" Elizabeth Bryant, of the parish of *Radmill*, in the county of *Sussex*, maketh oath, that Elizabeth Ford, of the parish of Radmill, in the county of Sussex, lately deceased, was not put in, wrapt up, or wound up, or buried in any shirt, shift, sheet, or shroud, made or mingled with flax, hemp, silk, hair, gold, or silver, or other than what is made of sheep's wool only; nor in any coffin lined or faced with any cloth, stuff, or any other thing whatsoever made or mingled with flax, hemp, silk, hair, gold, or silver, or any other material contrary to the late Act of Parliament for burying in woollen, but sheep's wool only. Dated the 16 day of Jan. 1724."

This may be appropriately followed by two examples of the disregard of the Act by the higher classes, who regarded it rather as a tax to be paid than a law to be observed : —

" 1603 (*Rushbrooke, Suffolk*), Jan. 10. The Right Hon[ble] Henry Jermyn Earl of St. Alban was buried in y[e] south side of y[e] Church. Because he was buried in Linnen contrary to an Act for burying in woolen only, therefore by order of a warrant from a Justice of the Peace fifty shillings was paid to the Informer and fifty shillings to the Poor of y[e] Parish upon the Sunday next following.

" 1708 (*Gayton, Northants*). Mrs. Dorothy Bellingham was buryed April 5 in Linnen, and the forfeiture of the Act payd fifty shillings to y[e] informer, and fifty shillings to y[e] poor of the parishe."

A mortuary, or corpse-present, had its origin in the idea that it was left by a man at his death to the parish church or priest as a recompense for forgotten or over-looked tithes or offerings; it was quite distinct from any burial fee to rector or vicar. It became customary to pay as mortuary to the rector the second best animal owned by the deceased, the best being reserved as heriot for the lord of the manor. In default of a beast, the mortuary claimed was the second best garment. In a receipt roll of 1539 for the Peak jurisdiction of the Dean and Chapter of Lichfield (*Derb. Arch. Soc. Journal*, vol. xi. 142–156), there is a list of 115 mortuaries, which vary from cows and oxen to tunics, super-tunics, and cloaks or coverlets. By an Act of 21 Henry VIII, the taking of mortuaries by rectors, a custom much abused, was considerably restricted, and only to be taken in money at a fixed rate. Ten shillings was the highest sum that could be levied, and that only when the deceased had goods to the value of £40. It was also forbidden to be taken on any one who was not a householder, or a traveller, or not a resident in the place where he died.

The rector of Rype, Sussex, coolly set this Act at defiance in almost every particular, as is shown by the following entries which he made in the parish register :—

" William Wade who died as a stranger, for whose mortuary, I, John Goffe, parson of Ripe, had his upper garment which was an olde coate, and I receaved for the same 6ˢ.

" 1634. I buried Alice Whitesides Feb. 22ᵈ who being but one weeke in the parish of Ripe, died as a stranger, for whose mortuary, I, John Goffe, had a gowne of Elizabeth her Daughter, price 10ˢ."

On a fly-leaf of the first register book of Stanton Lacy, Salop, there are entries of mortuaries of ten shillings each paid to the vicar in 1639, 1640 (two), 1641, and 1643 ; also of similar mortuary fees paid in 1664, 1666, 1667, 1671, and 1672.

The following note appears in the register of Eaton-under-Heywood, Salop, beneath an entry of the burial of one Thos. Linley, on March 3rd, 1717, viz.:—"A mortuary 2s. was paid for Thos. Linley by widow." In subsequent years there are many such entries, the amount being, in some instances, as much as ten shillings.

It is asserted in Phillimore's *Ecclesiastical Law* and elsewhere that it is a mere vulgar error to suppose that the arresting of a corpse for debt was ever legal. Nevertheless there was at one time a general belief that this was the case, as is testified by several registers. The last attempt to carry out this odious action was as late as 16th October 1811, as recorded in the *Gentleman's Magazine*, when a sheriff's officer presented a writ and seized a body from a funeral procession proceeding from Hoxton to Shoreditch. Here are two eighteenth-century register references to this outrageous and illegal practice :—

" 1659 (*Alstonfield, Staffs*), Aug. 30. Humphrey Dakin, buried about 2 of the clock in the night, feareing an arrest.
" 1689 (*Sparsholt, Bucks*). The corpse of John Matthews, of Fawler, was stopt on the churchway for debt August 27. And having laine there fower days, was by justices warrant buryed in the place to prevent annoyances—but about six weeks after it was by an Order of Sessions taken up and buried in the Churchyard by the wife of the deceased."

Demanding burial fees for a passing corpse was another absolutely illegal exaction, apparently claimed sometimes in an honest belief that it was a lawful custom. In the event of a corpse being carried through a parish for burial in a further one, the minister, clerk, and sexton not infrequently offered burial, and, if refused, claimed their full fees. We have found instances of this claim being successfully made at

Chelmsford, Wellingborough, Boston, Duffield, and about a score of other places. The following entry from the Godalming registers must suffice:—

" 1608, May 8. Ye lady Ford came through ye town and paid all duty to ye Minister Clerk and Sexton for proferring to bury her."

CHAPTER VIII

ACCIDENTS

Deaths from various accidents—The fate of Dorothy Matley—Deaths
through cold and snow—Mining disasters—Deaths through
drowning—Escapes from death—Freaks or prodigies

THE large majority of registers simply mention the
name and date of each interment from the beginning
to the end of the entries. In a minority, however,
of cases, a brief entry is made when the death was in any
sense unusual or caused by accident. A varied list of such
entries, which could of course be greatly extended, is here
set forth :—

" 1562 (*Dorking, Surrey*), Feb. 28. Owyn Tonny was christened ;
who (a later hand adds) scoffing at thunder, standing under a
beech was stroke to death, his clothes stinking with a
sulphurious stench, being about the age of twenty years or
thereabouts.

" 1569 (*St. Peter-in-the-East, Oxford*), 17 June. There was buried
Wyllyoun Willes a householder who was by misfortune kylled
withe the Whyle of his owne Weyne.

" 1575 (*Alstonfield, Staffordshire*), June 15. Thurstan Gybbe, s. of
Eliz. Gybbe, a bastarde, slayne in falling out of a wayne by a
blowe of a piece of woode called a sorner, bur.

" 1578 (*Kidderminster*), June 18. bd Wm sonne of Nicholas
Bettison which perrished by a fall out of the bell sellor in the
steeple and fell through all the flowers to the ground.

" 1579 (*Loughborough, Leicestershire*). Roger Shepherd, Son in
Law to Nicholas Wollands, was slain by a lioness which was
brought into the town to be seen of such as would give money

to see her. He was sore wounded in sundry places, and was buried the 26th day of August.

" 1583 (*St. Oswald's, Durham*), Dec. 2. John Mydfurthe, slayne by fallynge into a colepytt at Rayneton.

" 1589 (*Chesham, Bucks*). Moris Lewys of Kynges Langeley in the Count. of harts pedlar being slayne in a fraye by an other pedlar comying togeather to this towne on the fayer even was buried 16 July.

" 1591 (*Chesham, Bucks*). Hugh Doyot slayne by a faule out of a cherrytree was buried 16 July.

" 1600 (*Beeston-next-Mileham, Norfolk*). Thomas Threlkeld, filius Robti Threlkeld et Emme ux., cum in flore juventatis esset tempore reparationis pinnaculi ejusdem Templi audaciter minis ascendit in summitate ejusdem et supra Le Boule et crucem pinnaculæ, cruce autem frangente infeliciter cecidit in terram et confractis ossibus vivente tamen atque loquente per spacium duarum horarum mortuus est vicesimo nono Septembris et sepultus tricesimo ejusdem sequente.

" 1601 (*Blakesley, Northants*). Richard Tomason fallinge out of a tree as he was gatheringe ivie upon the Lordes daye tooke his death wound and was buried the xxij day of the moneth of December.

" 1601 (*Elland, Yorks*), Decembris 12. Hewyus Smith de Eland in putio carbonario occisus in Hollinghey lapsu casuque terræ qua fuit oppressus et suffocatus.

" 1602 (*St. Mary's, Reading*), July 22. Richard s. of Rich: Edwards, this child was killed by a blocke that fell upon him, which blocke was founde by the Couroners Jury to be guyltie of his death.

" 1603 (*Chesham, Bucks*). Elyzabeth widoe of John Atkins of Berkhamsted in the Count. of harts by falling out of a cherry tree was here buried the xiith of July.

" 1606 (*Elland, Yorks*). Henricus King de Cromblebotham ebrius amissus aqua suffocatus die dominico Decembris 7, 1606, inventum autem cadaver ejus in Flumine Calders Junii 11, et sepult. 13, 1607.

" 1608 (*Elland, Yorks*), Julius die 6. Johannes Marsh de Knowles excom. impræviso fustis ictu occisus subito, cujus fœtidum cadaver tentatum fuit in templo sepelire.

" 1608-9 (*Ibid.*), January 26. Johannes Horner de Elande senex tempore divinarum vespertinarum precum die dominico uxta

o

unam partem Strangstree aqua suffocatus, cadaver autem ejus inventum fuit infra fontem de Brighouse die mecurii et insemiterio sepultum die jovis.

"1609 (*Ibid.*), Julius. Richardus Gleedall juvenis filius spurius Henrici Gledall de Stainland occisus in Domo corfonaria (public-house) in ebritate sua, improviso ictu in caput, instrumento quo solent sordes a linteolis vestibus extundere. R. G. slain with a battel or batledore.

"1609 (*Ibid.*), September 2. Willimus Carter de Soiland cultro occisus Nathana Carter ipsius fratre manco ante et tunc ambo excommunicati olim in Hibernia milite.

"1612 (*Aston by Birmingham*). Henrie the sonne of Richard Blaxsiche of Erdington buried 10 Sept. who was most beastly and savidgelie slayne at Perrie wake by a company of lewde fellowes the vj day of Sept. which Henrie had one weapone but a walkinge staffe.

"1614 (*Elland, Yorks*). Henricus f. Henrici Ransley de Narland ætate 12 annorum die Dominico May 29, pomeridiano tempore juxta Woodhouse aqua suffocatus dum Rotam puerilis curriculi vel carri in aquam delapsum cum fratre suo natu minore comprehendere conatus fuit, frater tamen junior per aquam ad ulteriorem ripam onirifice salvus evasit Dei beneficio.

"1614 (*Holy Trinity, Chester*). John Brookes Mason who poynted the Steple 1610 and made many showes and pastymes on the steple of Trinity and also on the toppe of St. Peter's Steple as many thousands did witnesse, dyed 10 July and bur 11 July in the Church Yard broke his neck going downe a payre of Stayres by the Church.[1]

"1623 (*St. Nicholas, Ipswich*), Nov. 29, æt 4 months. John Steggoll buried w. fallinge into ye fire was burnt to death in his mother's absence, his forehead w^n he was taken out beinge as red as a cole.

"1627 (*Ibid.*), Dec. 7. Emme Wilbey daughter of Nicholas Wilbore was buried slaine by a brick fallinge down the chymney.

"1638 (*Marshfield, Gloucestershire*). vj die Augustij sepulta fuit

---

[1] Acrobatic feats on steeples, especially sliding down ropes extended from their summits, were not infrequent in bygone days. Both Edward VI and Philip were welcomed on entering London by rope-dancers' descents from the battlements of St. Paul's. Among other steeples similarly used may be mentioned those of Salisbury Cathedral, All Saint's, Derby, and St. Mary's, Shrewsbury.

Katherina Stockman who as she was a stealing Apples out of Mr. Michaell Merediths Orchard at Okeford gent, fell downe from the tree beinge the sabbath day at night and brake her necke.

"1654 (*Lyminge, Kent*), June the 30th. Henry Rolphe haveinge an hott Iron ramed into his body of wch he dyed was buried.

"1655 (*St. Mary's, Reading*), Dec. 15. Cathere Eldridge a servant and Mary Welbanck, a chield, drowned together att the second bridge from the Beare for want of a raile to the bridge in frosty weather.

"1656 (*Lyminge, Kent*). Mary the wife of Thomas Beene who dyed as shee was knelinge by her Bedside praying was buried the 7th day of Dec.

"1659 (*Hackness, Yorks*). Tewsday the Third of January was an exceeding stormie day and dyd drive snowe verie fearsely and that day towardes the Eveninge Richard Dickinson's wiffe of Trovdale (his house standinge under the north syde of the hill) shee beinge in the Chamber there fell a greate drifte of shelfe of snowe from the hill and drave downe the House all but the Chimney and the next day shee was found under the Thatch and snowe dead and their daughter and Child that war in yᵉ Chimney were saved alive and foure horses that were in the Stable were Laimed and Spoyled and dyed, there was also a waine broken: after she was buryed the Crowner came and she was unburyed the xxvth day of Jann. to be viewed, which was now as snowy and stormey as the Tewsday.

" 1667 (*Litcham, Norfolk*). Dorothee, the wife of Richard Collison, being rushed downe by a Trooper's horse as she was going in the street, June the 16th, dyed about an houre and a half after, and was buryed (when the coroner had sate upon it) June the eighteenth.

"1673 (*St. Benedict Fink, London*). April 23, was buried Mr. Thomas Sharrow, Clothworker, late Churchwarden of this parish, killed by an accidental fall in a vault, in London Wall, Amen Corner, by Paternoster Row, and was supposed had lain there eleven days and nights before any one could tell where he was. Let all that read this take heed of drink.

"1692–3 (*Rushbrooke, Suffolk*), Jan. 1. Mr. Thomas Jermyn, son of yᵉ Right Honoble Thomas lord Jermyn by Mary his wife, was buried in yᵉ South side of the Isle of Rushbrooke Church.

He was borne ye first day of December 1677, and was unfortunately slaine at London Dec. 27, 1692, about eleven in
ye forenoon, by ye fall of a Mast which ye Seamen were
raising in a stormie day, he being accidentally gotten into their
vessel. The young Gentleman was ye only survivinge heire
male of ye Honoble family of ye Jermyns, so that in all
appearance ye name and race ended with his life.

" 1699 (*Middleton, Lancashire*). Robert Lever, Batchellor of Arts
and Barrister at Law, son of Robt Lever of Altrington was
stript and murdered nere High Gate, in the County of
Middlesex the 11th day and there died and Anno ætatis suæ
27 and was buried 29 July.

" 1699 (*Renfield, Sussex*), Jan. 3. Bur^d Joseph Tysehurst a Boy
who on Whitsunday morning fell from climbing a mag pye
nest and was smothered in a pond of mud his heels sticking
upright.

" 1701 (*Barrow and Twyford, Derbyshire*). Robert Stevenson of
Draicott, in the Parish of Wilne, died suddenly in Barrow
Field, near to Swarkston Field ; he had a son-in-law with him,
whom he had sent before to Swarkston with his waggon and
six poor horses or mares (going towards the Ferry), loaden
with cheese. He was buried in Barrow churchyard, Sunday
20th, but died Thursday 10th ; I having a paper under Mr.
Charles Adderly's hand of Derby, coroner, to bury him Quod
vide. He sickened in Potluckland, as he came from Utoxeter
to Twyford and so towards Swarkston.

" 1701 (*Chapel-en-le-Frith, Derbyshire*). Edward Green, of Dor-
chester, was catching a young horse, which was laid to Mr.
Adam Bagshawe, a holding them up together, an old mare of
Mr. Richard Bagshawe, of Castleton, stroak him of the brost
that he dyed and was buried in the churchyard the 15 October.

" 1705 (*Mappleton, Derbyshire*). William Mawkin, a poor old man,
being long troubled with fitts of spitting and vomiting up blood
and being oftentimes brought very near to deaths door by these
fitts, was att last on ye 26 of October found dead in a field not
far from Okeover the same day that Elizabeth, wife of Rowland
Okeover, Esq., was interred at Okeover. The said William
Mawkin was buried at Mapleton, on Sunday, the 28th. of
October.

" 1707 (*Ibid.*), Dec. 8. Buried George Holmes butcher Butter-
ton in Staffordshire, who was found dead on Mapleton Calow

on Sunday morning last, viz. Dec. 7, having been at Ashbourn market on Saturday ye 6th, and being lost in a most
violent storm of wind and rain on Saturday night.

" 1796 (*Middleton Scriven, Salop*). Samuel Son of Richd. and Anne
Cork was buried Decr. 2d. He was killed by the kick of
a Horse, which was forfeited to the Lord of the Manor as a
Deodand.

" 1785 (*Eyam, Derbyshire*). Bur. 24 May, Mary Hall killed by
lightning while sitting in her corner chair.

" 1804 (*Chelsmford*), 26 Oct. Thirteen Hanoverians, who were
burned to death in the fire in the Spotted Dog in the backe
Street, Chelmsford, names unknown."

This is followed by the burial, on November 2, of another
Hanoverian, of whom it is also said, " name unknown." A
few particulars of this fatal disaster are given in the
Gentleman's Magazine of that date. Chelmsford, being
itself a garrison town and on the direct road from the port
of Harwich to London, frequently formed a resting-place for
moving troops. On this occasion 120 Hanoverians arrived
unexpectedly ; they were quartered on the premises of the
Spotted Dog, and most of them went to sleep amid straw in
the stables. The fire broke out in the night—it is supposed
through some of the soldiers smoking. When the alarm was
given, owing to these foreigners misunderstanding the working
of the latch of the door, many of them failed to escape. In
the morning the burnt remains of thirteen of the number
were discovered, and another soldier died shortly afterwards
from the injuries he had received. They were buried with
full military honours.

A highly remarkable entry in the registers of Ashover,
Derbyshire, warrants special mention and comment :—

" 1660. Dorothy Matly, supposed wife of John Flint, of this parish,
foreswore herself ; whereupon the ground open, and she sanke
over hed March 1st ; and being found dead she was buried
March 2d."

Full particulars of this strange event are to be found in that curious little known treatise of John Bunyan, *The Life and Death of Mr. Badman*, which was first published in 1680. Instances are therein quoted of sudden judgment for false swearing.

"But above all, take that dreadful story of Dorothy Matley, an inhabitant of Ashover, in the county of Derby. This Dorothy Matley was noted by the people of the town to be a great swearer and curser, and liar, and thief; and the labour that she did usually follow was to wash the rubbish that came forth from the lead mines, and there to get sparks of lead ore; and her usual way of asserting things was with these kind of imprecations—'I would I might sink into the earth if it be so,' or 'I would God would make the earth open and swallow me up.' Now upon the 23d of March (?) 1660, this Dorothy was washing of ore upon the top of a steep hill, and was there taxed by a lad for taking of two single pence out of his pocket (for he had laid his breeches by, and was at work in his drawers), but she violently denied it, wishing the ground might swallow her up if she had them. She also used the same wicked words on several other occasions that day. Now one George Hodgkinson, of Ashover, a man of good report there, came accidentally by where this Dorothy was, and stood still a while to talk with her as she was washing her ore; there stood still also a little child by her tub side and another a distance from her calling aloud to her to come away; wherefore the said George took the girl by the hand to lead her away to her that called her. But behold, they had not got above ten yards from Dorothy, but they heard her crying for help, so looking back he saw the woman, and her tub and sieve, twisting round and sinking into the ground. Then said the man, pray to God to pardon thy sin, for thou art never like to be seen alive any longer. So she and her tub twisted round and round till they sank about three yards into the earth and there for a while staid. Then she called for help again, thinking, as she said, she would stay there. Now the man, though greatly amazed, did begin to think which way to help her: but immediately a great stone, which appeared in the earth, fell upon her head and broke her skull, and then the earth fell in upon her and covered her. She was afterwards digged up and found about four yards within the ground, and the boy's two single two pence in her pocket, but her tub and sieve could not be found."

Deaths through cold and snow are chiefly met with in registers of mountainous or hilly districts. In addition to those here cited, other instances can be gleaned from registers of parishes round Exmoor, Dartmoor, and the Lake district.

" 1614–15 (*Stamford Baron, N'hants*). John Madisonne being perished on Spittlehill in the greate snow, buried March 10.

" 1616 (*Darley Dale, Derbyshire*). John the sonne of John Ward was buried 15 Dec. Perished with cold on ye moor.

" 1638 (*Ibid.*). Frances the wife of Robert Haslowe was buryed 28 Oct. Perished with colde on ye moor.

" 1664 (*Alstonfield, Staffs*), Mar. 10. Anne, w. of Tho. Hill, who was smothered in a snowy day on Calton Moor, bur.

" 1684 (*Willesley, Derbyshire*). Timothy Anderson of Ashley who was found starved to death with cold within this parish was here buryed upon the twenty sixth day of December.

" 1692 (*Eyam, Derbyshire*), Feb. 4. Bur. Elizabeth Trout, starved to death in a snow on Sir William (a hill 1200 ft. high).

" 1743 (*Ibid.*), Feb. 5. Bur. Stephen Broomhead, starved to death in a snow, Eyam Moor.

" 1772 (*Monyash, Derbyshire*), 5 Feb. Buried John Alcocke blacksmith and Richd Boham. [These two men were starved to death in coming from Winster market on Middleton Moor and brought down to Mid. Boham was a baker and was f^d he died as they were bringing him through Fr. Blackwall's y^d on a ladder on Monday morning. They were lost on Sat^d night 31 Jan., and found on Monday 2 Feb. Alcocke was dead on the entrance to Oneash farm, and Boham was f^d somewhere on Kenslow. The f^{ds} of the deceased were g^{ty} blamed for not having been in search on the Sunday (Woolley MSS 6700)]."

Considering the numbers respectively employed in various forms of mining, the accidental deaths in connection with such occupations were probably as frequent in the past as in the present. The following are a few of the register-recorded accidents of this class:—

" 1580 (*Chesham, Bucks*). Richard Moreton laborer was killed in a chalke pitt and buried 17 June.

"1582 (*Ibid.*). John Overstreete Jr. slayne in a pitt and buried
1 Sept.

"1601 (*Burnley, Lancashire*), 25 September. Georg Spenser of
Clyriger, slayne in a cole pitt.

"1604 (*Walsall*), August 29. Lawrence Wilcox and John Cartter
that were killed in the Colepitt with the earth damp.

"1669 (*Derby Pall, Derbyshire*). William Hogkinson and Robert
Sidwell were ·both buried 30 July, both dampt in a grove.
[Lead mining.]

"1673 (*Ibid.*). Denis Hodgkinson was dampt in a groove, buried 8 July.

"1677 (*Allendale, Northumberland*), June 11. Edmund Stout, a grocer
in Easterheads, who was killed in a groove, buried in the Church.

"1686 (*Duffield, Derbyshire*), Dec. 11th. Buried Matthew Harrison
of Belper Lane, who was killed in a pit on the Gibbett Hill.

"1712 (*Middleton, Lancashire*), 5 June. Jonathan Kaye of
Oldham p'sh killed with Damp in a pomp pitt (*i.e.* a well).

"1747 (*West Hallam, Derbyshire*). Joseph Mothershaw, John
Brown, and Charles Bennet all three killed by falling in of a Pitt
and all buried in one grave, June 7th."

The following are examples of interments after death
from drowning :—

"1574 (*Grantchester, Cambs*). Tres Norfolciences e Collegio
Corporis Christi, viz., Johes Butler, Thomas Orolls, Robertus
Smith, in Amne submersi ac sepulti, 17 Maii.

"1591 (*Desborough, Northants*). George Homes Schoolmayster to
mayster Vavyser his children at Rushton rydde to desbr in
the evening and was drowned in desbor ryver by the willowes
closse there uppon Munday at night betwene the houres of
vij and viij of the clocke being the viij of Nov. and
his horse sadle and bridle was founde in the willowes closse
uppon the friday following the xij day and so he was buryed the
satterday following, the xiijth day.

"1596 (*Whitburn, Durham*), Sep. 4. Thomas Sharppe, Thos.
Richeson, Thomas Willkinsone of Hartlepoule, was cast away by
a tempest of ye Sea and was buried.

"Sep. 16. Thomas Hart of Hartlepoule was cast away by the sea
and buried.

"1600 (*Chipping, Lancashire*), 15 Auguste. Isabell Gregson alias
Parker baste daughter of Thomas Parker of Grastonlee fil Meg

in Botland, being by misfortunat chaunce upon a heble (plank bridge) goinge over was drowned over a neede an ashe, beyond Grastonlee my fatheres late house for want of a good bridge and so carried them to Humphrey linne, were founde the same day being Wensday the iij day of Septembe the oulde bridge being driven dowen by a floode before.

" 1626 (*Whitburn, Durham*), July 17. bur. John Burne, of Shecles, beinge Casten forth of a Cobble and spent in the sea.

" 1654–5 (*Howden, Yorks*). The thirteenth of ye month of January being Saturday at Whitgift the ferry boat unfortunately sunke when John Pycocke and Marmaduke Marshall of Addingfleet with sixe other persons were drowned three escaped.

" 1573 (*Duffield, Derbyshire*). April 10th. Robert Randall of Denbigh who going from a Cockfight at Duffield and being drunk fell into water above Duffield bridge and was drowned.

" 1678 (*Wallingford*). Will Alcorne was buried May 17. The said William was drowned att Shillingford Ferry by rowing over himself; his horse leaping out of the boat threw him into ye river, as was testefied by two boys yᵗ stood on yᵉ shore."

The registers of sea-board parishes frequently record the burials of drowned mariners and voyagers. Entries from three such registers must suffice. The two first relate to the wreck of a troopship in the Bristol Channel; each parish was held responsible for the burial of those cast up within its limits.

" 1735 (*Minehead, Somerset*), February 22d. Thirty-five men women and children in one grave, drowned.

" February 23rd (*Ibid.*). One child and 7 men and women.

" 1735 (*Dunster*), Feb. 22. 19 soldiers, a boy and two women and two children were buried which were drown'd ye day before. [Their interment cost the parish £9, 4s. 9d]."

The registers of the sea-board parish of Whitburn, Durham, have frequent records of death by drowning; four in 1596, one in 1607, one in 1615, one in 1625, three in 1626, one in 1630, six Dutchmen in 1633, one in 1641, one each in 1701, 1705, and 1708, two in 1713, one in 1715, one in 1754, five in 1756, one each in 1759, 1766, and 1777, three in 1782, two in 1784, two each in 1794 and 1795, and three in 1799.

There are various eighteenth century entries of the burials of drowned sailors in the registers of the sea-board parish of Warkworth, Northumberland: six in 1728, three in 1754, one in 1757, one in 1762, one in 1769, seven in 1784, and two in 1799.

"1784 (*Long Houghton, Northumberland*), Dec. 10. 10 sailers, who were lost at sea in the great storm in Dec. 1784, bur.

"1785 (*Ibid.*), March 13. A mariner supposed lost in the late dreadful storm in Dec. last; the body much mangled, without head, legs, or thighs, bur.

"1794 (*Ibid.*), Jan. 25. 3 mariners, belonging to the May-flower of Alemouth, lost near Dunstenborough castle in the great storm of 25 inst."

Nor must a sad tragedy that occurred on fresh water in 1635 be omitted from these register records of drowning. In the register book of Grasmere, Westmoreland, for that year, occurs this entry:—

"The 6 of Oct. these were all drowned in Windermere Water in one boate coming over from Hawkshead."

The list is headed by Mr. George Wilson of Kendal, and this name is followed by 45 others, in addition to—

"2 more or 3 and 7 horses, and one that escaped."

One tradition has it that the victims were a large wedding party, but a more probable supposition is that it was the return ferry-boat from market which upset.

In connection with this grievous disaster, it may be mentioned that the parish register of Hawkshead, Lancashire, is exceptionally full of accidental deaths, although there is no reference to the wholesale catastrophe of 1635. Between 1599 and 1699 there are records among the burials of 14 cases of drowning, 5 of suicide by hanging, 5 instances of found dead, 1 murdered person, 1 murderer, and 10 of various fatal accidents.

Not only do registers contain fairly numerous references to accidental deaths, but now and again brief records of escape from disaster, of which two examples are appended :—

> "1661 (*St. Peter's, Sandwich*). The 13th of October, St. Peter's Church fell down. That day the same year was a Sabbath day, there were two sermons preached there that day, and it fell down within six or seven hours after the people were gone home, presently after one quarter of an hour past eleven o'clock at night. Had it fell at the time when the people were there, the chiefest of the Town and Parish had been killed, and buried under the rubbish and stone and timber; but the Lord was so gracious as to shew a miraculous mercy in that judgement, for there were no man, woman or child killed or hurt, and very few heard it. The Rubbish was three fathom deep in the middle of the church, the bells underneath it.

> "1701 (*Chapel-en-le-Frith, Derbyshire*). The great bell in our steple was taken down to be cast upon Friday, 27 June, and as it was coming down the pulleys broke and the bell fell to the ground and brought all before it. The man who was above to guide it was one Ezekiel Shuttleworth, a joiner in this town, he seeing the pulleys break could no ways keep himself but came after it, a ladder with himself and a little crosse of iron in his hand, and yet by God's great preservation had little or no harm. The great bell was recast at Wigan, 6 Aug. 1701."

The somewhat unsavoury subject of exceptional or monstrous births ought not to be omitted, as such entries occur from time to time in parish registers. A few examples are appended in chronological order :—

> "1545 (*Kelsall, Suffolk*). Ano regis Henrié 8, 37, in June was born a wonder, a monster, whose father was Richarde Baldway, of Kelsall, begotten in lawefull matrimonie, whiche childe from the sholders upwarde had growinge ij severall neks w^t ij feyr-heds standinge upon them in licke quantite eche heade having mothe, nose, eies, eares, and winde pipe goyng downe in y^e

throte unto ye breste, whose bodye was licke the forme and shape of all other children, wiche was sene to many credable people of Kelsall.

" 1565 (*Herne, Kent*). John Jarvys had two woemen children baptized at home joyned togethee in the belly, and havynge each the one of their armes lyinge at one of their own shoulders, and in all other parts well proportioned children, buryed Augt. 29.

" 1601 (*Chipping, Lancashire*). There was xtined at our p'ishe chuch at Chippin the 10th of December one litle small infant called John Parkinson sonne of Ric Parkinson borne by Jaine daughter of John Salbury of the Lund y^t was so small in all proporcens saving the length as a greate mans great long finger the head lyke an egg in quantit.

" 1655 (*Hackness, Yorks*). Grace the wyff of William Baxster beinge aboute three weekes before her tyme was brought in bedd the first day of December aboute three of the Clocke in the afternoone of two children. Their bellies were growne and joyned together from their breastes to their navells but their navells might be seen and their faces were together but the supposed man child was not soe longe as the daughter, in that his face reached but to the chine of the other. [The remainder of the long description is too unpleasant to print. These twins were buried on December 2.]

" 1672-3 (*Hillingdon, Middlesex*), March 12th. William, the Son of John Poker and Jane his Wife, natus, renatus, denatus die eodem, summa scilicet Dei miseratione tam in puerum quam in parentes, cum monstrosus fuit Infans non ex defectu sed excessu partium, una cum conformatione aliarum haud bona.

" 1688 (*Carsington, Derbyshire*), September 29. Sarah Tissington, a poor young woman, born into the world without any hands or arms, yet was very nimble and active in the use of her feet, with which she could not only take up things from the ground, and play at most childish games with her play fellows when she was a child; but also, when grown up, she could knit, dig in the garden, and do divers other services with her feet; she was aged 24 or 25 years, and departed this life the day and year aforesaid; born and buried at Carsington.

" 1690 (*Mitcham, Surrey*). Anne, the Daughter of George Washford, who had 24 fingers and toes, baptized Oct. 19.

" 1738 (*Dorking, Surrey*), May 16. Richard Madderson, aged

29 years, and was not above three feet and three inches high ; but in thickness grown as much as any other person. He was all his life troubled with a griping distemper, of which he at last died very suddenly.

"1758 (*Minehead, Somerset*). Christopher Jones who was born of April last without arms or legs but otherwise perfect."

CHAPTER IX

THE PLAGUE AND OTHER SICKNESS

The Sweating Sickness—The Plague in London—In Northampton-
shire—In Derbyshire—The Eyam episode—Plague burial in
Cheshire—The Plague in the Midland Counties—In the
North of England—In the Eastern Counties—In the South and
West—The tragedy of the Dawson household—The tragedy
at Great Hampden—Small-pox—Inoculation—Influenza—
Scarlet fever—Obstruction—Lithotomy—The Royal Touch for
scrofula

REGISTER entries making definite reference to the
"Sweating Sickness" of 1551 are very rare. They
were probably numerous in the originals, but were
omitted, with many other notes, for the sake of brevity,
when the parchment transcripts were made at the end of
Elizabeth's reign. The sweating sickness or "English
Sweat," a remarkable form of disease, apparently quite distinct from the plague or any kind of pestilential fever, first
broke out in England in 1485 with dire results, killing in
London in one week two successive Lord Mayors and six
aldermen. It broke out again in 1507, in 1517, and in 1528.
There was only one occurrence of it within the registration
period, namely, the fifth and last attack which happened in
1551. It first appeared at Shrewsbury on 13th April, and
after spreading to other towns in Wales and the Midlands,
reached London, where it caused the deaths of 751 persons
in a single week. By the end of July it ceased in London,
went through the east of England northwards, and died out

by the end of September. It has never, happily, again made its appearance. The disease began with suddenness, and was characterised by its extremely rapid and fatal course; it affected the rich more than the poor, especially those of dissipated life.

The registers of Loughborough, Leicestershire, have the following entry under 1551 :—

"The sweat called New Acquaintance, alias Stoupe Knave and know thy Master, began 24 June."

The registers of Uffcolme, Devon, make mention, in August 1551, of "The stupgallant or the hote sicknesse." These various names arose from the grievous way in which young men of fashion in full health and strength were seized almost in an instant. Hancock, in his *Autobiography*, says :—

"God plagued thys realme most justly for our sinns with three notable plages: The first was the posting swet, that posted from towne to towne throughe England, and was named *stop gallant*, for hytt spared none, for ther were dauncyng in the courte at 9 a'clocke thatt were deadd on eleven a clocke."

This awful sickness fluctuated to the beautiful valley of the Wye, Derbyshire. By the side of the marriage entries of the parish of Darley Dale for the year 1551 is written, "The sweate was this yeare." On referring to the burials, this note is found :—

"Nine persons were buried from the 5th of Julye till the 10th, which dyed of yᵉ sweatinge sickenes."

There are a few references to this visitation in the London registers. Three deaths are entered in the register book of St. Dionis, Backchurch, under 1551, as dying from this awfully sudden disorder, and eleven in the register of St. Antholin, headed, "In the time of yᵉ sweating July." At

St. Martin-in-the-Fields, two of the 1551 burials are followed by the words *ex sudore*.

In Canon Bardsley's elaborate edition of the register of Ulverston (1886), it is stated in the introduction that the town was visited by the plague in 1551. It came with great suddenness, and though it stayed but a fortnight, its ravages were calculated to fill the hearts of the people with horror. This is all true save for the word "plague"; for this should be substituted that totally different epidemic, the fearful Sweating Sickness. The registers do not name the epidemic, but the year makes it quite clear. In 1549 and in 1550 there was but a single interment entered for the month of August, but in that month in 1551 the burials numbered forty-two.

The name Plague, or *Pestis*, used to be given to almost any epidemic disease which resulted in considerable mortality; but by the time that registration began in England the term had begun to be chiefly applied to a specific and awfully fatal disease, otherwise known as Oriental, or Bubonic Plague.

The plague was bad in London in 1537–9, and again in 1547–8. In the year 1550 parts of London were afflicted; there are a considerable number of entries of deaths from plague in the register of St. Martin-in-the-Fields, beginning on 27th March. It raged with greater intensity in 1563–4, a thousand dying weekly, it is said, for several months. The first register book of St. Andrew's, Holborn, under date 23rd July 1563, has the entry—"Here began the great plague." This is followed by:—

"4 Feb. 1563–4. Here by God's mercy the plague did cease, whereof died in the parish this year to the number of four hundred four score and ten."

This year's epidemic was also severe in the parish of

St. Martin-in-the-Fields; there are 177 burials entered in the register, 145 of which are followed by the word *peste*. In the register book of St. Michael, Cornhill, under 1563, there is an entry before 11th June—" The beginning of the plague in this p'she"; there were 202 burials for that year, whilst the burials for 1562 and 1564 were 25 and 15 respectively. In many registers during this and later plague epidemics there is no specific mention of the plague, but the immense growth in the number of burials at once points to something abnormal. This is clearly shown in the following brief table, where the number of burials for 1562-3-4 are set forth as taken from the registers of six city parishes:—

	Burials.		
	1562	1563	1564
All Hallowes, London Wall .	15	85	8
St. Antholin	15	83	21
St. Mary, Aldermary . .	13	128	9
St. Mary, Woolnoth . .	15	88	8
St. Nicholas, Acon . .	5	58	8
St. Peter's, Cornhill . .	19	169	18

The registers of St. Margaret's, Westminster, show how grievous was the visitation in that parish. Its first record is on 23rd June. On 27th September 14 cases of plague sickness were interred. At St. James', Clerkenwell, the registered deaths during 1563 numbered 172, whereas the average about that period was only 30.

In 1575 a plague wave passed over Europe, and made some impression in England. At St. Martin-in-the-Fields there were fifty-three deaths from plague in that year, three in 1576, and thirteen in 1577. The registers of St. Margaret's, Westminster, contain plague entries from 1574 to 1583. The

City rector of All Hallows, London Wall, of this period, usually entered the cause of death in his register; for the year 1575 three deaths are recorded from plague, and among other causes may be mentioned "surfett," fever, pining sickness, "dyed of worms," "plurysey," "strangulation and the stone," ague, cough, "squinancie," and "pyning sickness and thought taking." Comparatively mild or local outbreaks continued to occur right through the reign of Elizabeth. Thus, in this same All Hallows register, eight cases of death from the plague are entered in 1581, nineteen in 1582, seven in 1583, and three in 1585. Thirty-three deaths from plague are entered in the register of St. Michael's, Cornhill, for 1582-3.

One of London's greatest plagues culminated in 1593. At St Martin's-in-the-Fields, 22 burials are followed by the word *peste* in 1592, whilst the like fateful words accompany no fewer than 169 entries in 1593.

The deaths in the three years preceding 1593 in the parish of St. Peter's, Cornhill, were 24, 28, and 17 respectively; but in 1595 they rose to 83. At the end of the entries for that year are the following comments :—

"Thear dyed in London in all, .	.	. 25,886
Of them of the plague in all, .	.	. 15,003
Within the walles and liberties,	.	. 8598
Without, in and out of liberties,	.	. 17,288

"In a thousand five hundred ninety and three,
The Lord preserved my house and me.
When of the pestilence theare died,
Full maine a thousand els beside."

There are 64 deaths registered at St. Mary's, Aldermary, as occurring through the plague in 1593. Out of the 122 burials during the same period at All Hallows, London Wall, 65 are entered as caused by the plague. In the small parish of St. Christopher Stocks, there were 29 burials during that year, and against 15 of them "plague" is written in the margin. The register of St. Dionis, Backchurch, records 83 deaths for 1593; the word plague only occurs in a single case, but it is quite clear that this heavy roll was caused by some unwonted epidemic, for the average burials of the period were only nine a year. The death-roll of St. James Clerkenwell, sprang up to 330.

There are a few definite plague deaths recorded in London registers for 1599, but with the accession of James I in 1603 came another terrible outbreak, which cost the metropolis about 30,000 lives. The register book of St. Peter's, Cornhill, has the following notes at the close of the year :—

> " From the 23 of December 1602 to 22 of December
>   1603, buried in this parish in all: num : .   .   158
>   Of them of the plague   87
>   Buried in all this yeare both without and within
>   the liberties, and in the 8 out parishes from 14 Julie 38,244
>   Of them of the plague   .   .   .   . 30,578 "

The burials in the parish of St. Mary, Aldermary, in 1603, numbered 104; in the following year they only numbered 12; but in 1605 the plague returned, and there were 97 burials. All Hallows, London Wall, records the frightfully heavy death-roll of 245; in 1602 the burials only numbered 23, and in 1604 but 20. In the parish of St. Michael's, Cornhill, the register enters 149 burials for 1603, most of whom are definitely said to have died of the plague; in 1604 the burials merely numbered 14. There was a like terrible ratio of increase in the death penalty in the parish of St. Mary, Woolnoth, for the burials numbered 117 in 1603, and only 7 in the following year. Although there is no mention of the plague in the register of St. Dionis, Backchurch, the burial roll, which averaged about 12, leapt up in this fateful year to 129. At St. James, Clerkenwell, the visitation was appalling, for the burials numbered 784 in 1603, and more

than twice the number who fell during the pestilence of 1593.
Out of these burials 336 of them occurred in the month of
August.

The plague raged vehemently in St Margaret's, Westminster, between June 1603 and September 1604. On 11th
September 1603, 20 who had died of the plague were buried,
and 21 on 20th October.

In the then thinly populated parish of Kensington the
visitation made itself felt. The register states, under 1603,
that "In this yeare was the great plague"; the burials in
1603 were 31, whilst in 1602 they were 9, and in 1605 only
5. Within a few days one Richard Spervigg, his wife, three
sons, and a daughter, were all buried. The entry as to the
wife says :—

"Nov. 2. Alce wife of Richard Spervigg, the most thicke and
stink'g misty day y^t ever was."

The plague continued to simmer on for several years.
In the register of St. Michael's, Cornhill, 13 plague deaths
were recorded in 1606, and 2 in 1607. The second serious
plague year for London during the seventeenth century was
1609, when the total mortality was 11,785.

From 1609 London seems to have enjoyed an almost
complete immunity from this epidemic. But the plague was
reserving its forces for the year of the accession of Charles I;
in 1625 the mortality bounded up to over 35,000.

"*St. Mary, Aldermanbury.* In the year 1625, Mr. Downing, the
Curate of this Parish, his wife, three of his children, and the Parish
Clerk, were victims to the plague, and the consequence was that a
hundred names were entered in the Register from recollection."

The burials in the parish of St. Mary, Woolnoth, for that
year amounted to 81. In the registers of the little parish
of St. Christopher Stocks, 33 of the deaths of 1625 are
marked "plague." The burials for that year in the parish

The Fearefull Summer:

OR,

Londons Calamitie, The Countries Discourtesie, And both their Miserie.

Printed by Authoritie in *Oxford*, in the last great Infection of the Plague, 1625. And now reprinted with some Editions, concerning this present yeere, 1636.

With some mention of the grievous and afflicted estate of the famous Towne of New-Castle vpon Tine, with some other visited Townes of this Kingdome.

By IOHN TAYLOR.

TITLE-PAGE OF "FEAREFULL SUMMER."

FIRST PRINTED IN 1625.

of St. Dionis, Backchurch, were 103, immensely in excess of
the average. It is noted that in eight cases they were buried
without a coffin, denoting hasty interment, for uncoffined
burials were only exceptional at that date in towns. The
burials at St. Michael's, Cornhill, for 1625, numbered 33; in
1624 they were 11, and in 1626 only 10. The death-rate in
the parish of St. James, Clerkenwell, for this year was
appalling: the burials numbered 1120. No fewer than 557
plague victims were buried at St. Margaret's, Westminster,
in the one month of September 1648.

Eleven years later came a fresh incursion of the plague
in London, when the general mortality was 10,400. Some of
the registers bear obvious witness to this epidemic, but it
would be tedious to give figures illustrative of this less fierce
epidemic of 1636. In 1637, in 1641, and again in 1647,
the registers give proof of minor attacks, when the London
deaths from the plague were comparatively heavy.

After this last date there came a lull of nearly twenty
years in the storm waves of this foul disease, which, in
contrast to the sweating sickness, was ever most destructive
in squalid, dirty neighbourhoods, and was so specially
prevalent among the lower orders that it was often called the
Poor's Plague. This long continued immunity from attack
caused even the usual sanitary precautions of those days to
be neglected, whilst a general carelessness and coarseness of
living characterised the earlier years of the restoration of the
monarchy. At length, in 1665, nature took her revenge in a
terrific onslaught on humanity, resulting in what will ever
be known as The Great Plague of London. The approach
of the storm was not without its heralds. A few isolated
cases of plague occurred in the Westminster parishes of St.
Giles and St. Martin in November 1664, and a few occurred
in the ensuing winter. The real outbreak began in May
1665, and it took about six months to travel from the

LONDONS
LAMENTATION.
Or a fit admonifhment for City and Countrey,

Wherein is defcribed certaine caufes of this affliction and vi-
fitation of the Plague, yeare 1641. which the Lord hath
been pleaf:d to inflict upon us, and withall what meanes
muft be ufed to the Lord, to gaine his mercy and favor,
with an excellent fpirituall medicine to be ufed
for the prefervative both of Body and Soule.

London, Printed by E. P. for Iohn Wright Iunior. 1641.

TITLE-PAGE OF "LONDON'S LAMENTATION,"

FIRST PRINTED IN 1641.

western suburbs of Westminster across the city to the eastern suburbs of Stepney. The mortality rose from 43 in May to 590 in June, to 6137 in July, to 17,036 in August, and to the appalling total of 31,159 in September, after which it began to decline. According to the bills of mortality, the total number of plague deaths in 1665 was 68,596. This fearful total would doubtless have been enormously increased, but it is estimated that about two-thirds of a population of 460,000 fled into the country to escape the contagion.

No thorough and reliable history of the Great Plague of London has yet been written. Trustworthy contemporary references and statements are to be found in the diaries of Evelyn, and of that cowardly self-lover, Pepys. As to Defoe's fascinating and apparently realistic *Journal of a Citizen*, it is but a highly imaginative work of fiction, based upon vague recollections and untrustworthy hearsay. It may be well to set forth a few facts gleaned from the parochial registers.

The first plague entry of 1665 in the register book of St. Paul's, Covent Garden, occurs on 12th April; it is distinguished by the letters *pla*. The future cases have, for the most part, the full word. The plague deaths during the year were 219, and were thus divided:—May, 1; June, 3; July, 17; August, 43; September, 97; October, 41; November, 11; and December, 3. There was a slight outbreak in this parish in the summer of 1666, when there were 8 fatal cases.

The register books of St. Margaret's, Westminster, show that the first burial after death from the plague in that parish occurred on 14th June, and from that date until the end of August there were upwards of 200 such interments. The plague-marked burials for September were 263, and for October, 147. In November the numbers dropped to 77, in December to 39, and in January, 1665–6, to 13. The total plague burials were 759, but the actual number of deaths was probably much in excess of this total; for there are many gaps left in the registers for both September and October, pointing to hasty and irregular interments, intended to be subsequently filled up.

Further to the west, the then sparsely populated but large parish of Kensington did not escape. The register for 1665 has 23 plague-marked entries.

The plague took over five weeks in moving from Westminster to the city parish of St. Olave, Hart Street, as shown by the following entry:—

"1665, 24 July. May, daughter of William Ramsey, on of the Drap's almesmen, and ye first reported to dye of ye plague in this p'rish since this visitac'on; and was buryed in ye new ch.yd."

Twelve days earlier, namely, on Wednesday, 12th July, there had been collected in the church of St. Olave

"Y^e some of thirty-eight shillings, being ye first day apoynted to be kept as a day of publique humiliac'on for averting ye plague of pestilence."

Between 24th July and 5th December 326 burial entries with the significant "P" prefixed to them, are to be noted in these registers.

The registers of St. Dunstan's for this terrible year record 856 burials, 568 of which are distinguished by the plague initial.

Among the registers of the smaller city parishes, St. Dionis, Backchurch, shows a mortality for this year of 75; St. Mary, Aldermary, 97; St. Nicholas, Acon, enters 27 interments distinguished by "Plague," "Plag," or "Pl." The parish of St. Thomas the Apostle gives a death-roll of 158 for 1665, whilst there were but 27 interments in 1664, and only 13 in 1666.

At St. Peter's, Cornhill, the total mortality for 1665 was 121, and the interments are for the most part distinguished by " Plague " or " Pl "; in 1666 there are only 16 burials registered.

The mortality was awful in the widespread parish of Stepney, to the east of the city; the deaths for the year actually numbered 6583, including 116 sextons and grave-diggers.

In concluding these references to plague entries in the London registers it may be remarked that no registers are more distinct in this matter than those of St. Olave's, Hart Street. Six distinct visitations of the plague appear in the books of that parish. (1) In 1563, 49 persons were buried in September, and 43 in October. (2) In 1578 the registers record the burial of 15 persons in September, 12 of whom died of the plague. Under 5th November occurs this entry :—

"Was buried Mr. John Hodgesonne woolwynder late church-warden of the p¹ who died before he had given up his accounts."

(3) The third visitation occurred in 1593. Three who died from the plague were buried "in one pit" on 19th August. Of one household, a son, a daughter, and three servants died within a few days. (4) This parish suffered severely from the plague in 1603-4, especially among infants and children ; 107 burials are recorded between 24th March 1603, and 30th January 1604. (5) The next plague year, 1625, was yet more fatal ; there were actually 229 interments in the four summer months of June, July, August, and September. (6) The references to the great plague fear of 1665, which only spared 4 sparsely populated parishes out of 130 in and around the city of London, have already been given.

Several other parishes, in the vicinity of London, in

addition to those already mentioned, afford record evidence of pestilence.

Thus the registers of Twickenham show that 67 persons died of the plague in 1605, and 24 in 1615.

Northampton, on the great north road from London, was for many centuries subject to a continuous stream of travellers passing to and fro, and hence was peculiarly liable to infection. In 1570 the plague broke out in the town in the autumn, and on 13th October the Assembly ordered all the infected houses to be marked on the doors with " Lord have mercye uppon us." The inscription was to be kept on the door for twenty days after any death, the visited inmates confined strictly to their houses, and victuals distributed at the public cost. This plague did not die out until the end of March 1579.

Northampton took stringent precautions to prevent the terrible plague that visited England at the time of the accession of James I entering the town, including the setting of day and night watchmen on the south and west roads outside the walls. But the sickness obtained foothold in September 1603, and after ceasing in 1604, broke out again yet more severely in October 1605, when nearly 500 perished. There was a still worse visitation in 1638, when the death-rate leapt up in all four parishes at an alarming rate. In the register-book of St. Sepulchre's for this year, the following entry occurs among the burials on 29th March :—" Att which time the sickness beegan." It had run its course by the end of the year, for on 1st January is entered :—" Att which time the Lord bee praised the sickness ceased." In this parish the deaths in 1638 were 114, though the average number for the adjacent five years was only 18.

The following table, compiled by the Rev. R. M. Serjeantson from the registers of the four Northampton parishes, shows the mortality during the visitations of 1578

1603, 1605, and 1638, together with the usual death average :—

	Deaths in 1578.	Average for 5 Years.	Deaths in 1603.	Deaths in 1605.	Average for 5 Years.	Deaths in 1638.	Average for 5 Years.
All Saints . . .	134	47	107	411	91	247	76
St. Giles . . .	21	10	20	123	22	185	21
St. Peter . . .	9	4	16	26	6	19	7
St. Sepulchre . .	16	7	88	65	20	114	18
Total . . .	180	68	231	625	139	565	122

In many cases *plague* is written before these burial entries; in other instances *p.* or *pest.* Northampton again suffered heavily from the plague in 1647, when "a new peste house remote from the towne" was wisely provided; but the registers for this period are either missing or defective.[1]

References to the spread of the plague into different parts of Northamptonshire are met with in various parish registers of the county. At Grendon, in 1603, "a stranger dyed in the hall close and there buried in regard of infeccon the xxth of November." The same register has twelve entries of death from the plague in 1605.

The register of St. Martin's, Stamford Baron, the parish of Stamford within the county of Northampton, contains evidence of the grievous character of the visitation of 1604. No fewer than 125 names are there entered "wch departed by the sicknes namely the plague"; included amongst them is one who was "a falconer of Burghley." It may here be mentioned that the same register gives sixteen deaths from the plague in 1642.

[1] The action of the Assembly or Town Council during all these epidemics, from 1578 to 1647, was for the most part vigorous and much in advance of what might have been expected. See *Northampton Borough Records* (by Rev. Dr. Cox), vol. ii. 233–40.

Another visitation was brought about in the far north of the county towards the close of 1606, when the dread infection was brought from London, as is set forth in the registers of St. John's, Peterborough :—

"1606, Dec. 16. Henry Renoulds was buryed Henry came from London, where he dwelt, sicke of the plague and being receyved by William Browne died in his house. The saide William soon after fell sicke of the plague and died and so did his sonne, his daughter, and his servant : only his wyfe and her mayde escaped with soars. The plague brought by this means to Peterburgh continuod there till September following."

When the plague was raging in the county town in 1638, it spread from Northampton to the retired village of Wold. Under that year occurs the register entry :—

"At this tyme the plague was in the towne : of wch there dyed 18, not such a moneth (April–May) to be seen in all this Booke, but it pleased Almightie God to turne from wrath to mercie so y^t there did no one dye for a long tyme after blesed be his name.

"1638, 24 Sept. Ann Rendall a poor woman who did attend on ye infected was buryed."

In the neighbouring parish of Holcot there was a grievous visitation in the same year; the register shows that the death rate, which averaged seven about that period, rose to sixty.

The Great Plague of London, 1664–5, was reflected in different parts of Northamptonshire. At Barton Seagrave, in 1665, seven members of the household of John Norton died of the plague; after the sixth entry follows :—

"God of his mercy sanctify this sad Providence and remove it fro among us if it bee thy will ! (Even now) Elizabeth Crue (nurse at John Norton's) dyed and was buryed Novemb 13th 1665. Note. Here through ye infinite (and never to be forgotten) mercy of O^r God ye plague was stayed."

In the small parish of Yardley Hastings, 60 burials from the plague are entered between 5th June and 3rd January,

1665. Then occurs, "Mary Brown died naturally not of this distemper."

Considering its breezy elevation, natural drainage, and great distance from all port contamination, the small county of Derby seems to have been exceptionally subject to plague visitation, according to register testimonies, during the sixteenth and seventeenth centuries. At a much earlier date, this county probably suffered more severely from the horrors of the Black Death of 1349 than any other part of the kingdom. The episcopal registers at Lichfield yield appalling proof of the deadly character of this scourge so far as the clergy were concerned. The Derbyshire benefices at that period subject to episcopal institution numbered 108. The average annual number of institutions to these benefices throughout the century was seven; in 1346 they numbered four, in 1347 two, and in 1348 eight; but in 1349 the number leapt up to sixty-three, and in the following year to forty-one. Seventy-seven beneficed priests of Derbyshire (more than two-thirds of the whole number) died in that one dread period, and twenty-two more resigned. Nor were the regular clergy more fortunate; the abbots of Beauchief, Dale, and Darley, the prior of Gresley, the prior of the Derby Dominicans, and the prioress of Kingsmead were among the victims. If death thus seized upon the beneficed clergy and on the superiors of religious houses, it is reasonable to suppose that the parochial chaplains, and the ordinary canons, monks, nuns, and friars, suffered at least as badly. It is by no means unlikely that the rest of the population died off in a like proportion, and that two-thirds of the inhabitants of this county were swept away within a twelvemonth.[1]

A highly interesting and exceptionally full fourteenth-

---

[1] See Preface to vol. iv. of Dr. Cox's *Churches of Derbyshire* for fuller particulars.

century chartulary of the chantries pertaining to the church of Crich, Derbyshire, shows the ravages that took place in 1349 in the single household of the Wakebridges of Wakebridge, one of the most wealthy and healthily situated in the whole county. The calendar of obits observed by the chantry priests of 1350 foundation shows that Sir William de Wakebridge, the founder, buried in 1349 a brother on 17th April, a sister-in-law on 28th May, a second brother on 15th June, a third brother on 11th July, his father and a sister on 5th August, and his wife and a second sister on 11th August.

The earliest parochial register of Derbyshire of a plague death occurs in the first register book of Darley Dale; this parish was visited by the plague in the spring of 1558.

"1557–8. Agnes Buxton dyed of ye plague and was buried the 1st March.
"1558. Alice Stafford dyed of ye plague and was buryed 14th April."

There are five other like entries during April.

During the years 1592–3, Derby suffered most grievously. The following entries occur in the first register book of All Saints :—

"1592, Sept. Ricus filius Willmi Sowter Sep 31 die ex peste. The Plauge began in Darby in the house of William Sowter bootcher, in the parishe of All Sts in Darby, Robertt Woode Ironmonger and Robertt Brookhouse ye Tanner beinge then bayliffes, and so continued in the Towne the space of 12 moneths at ye least as by the Register may appeare.
"1593, Oct. 29. About this tyme the plauge of pestilence, by the great mercy and goodness of almighty god, stayed past all expectacions of man, for it ceased upon a sodayne at what time it was dispersed in every corner of this whole parishe, there was not two houses together free from it, and yet the Lord had the angell stey as in David's tyme, his name be blessed for ytt. Edward Bennett, minister."

This register book shows how very destructive the plague was in the house where it first occurred. Richard Sowter's death on 31st September was followed by that of his mother, Alice, on 25th November, by his brother and sister, Edward and Maria, on 29th November, by his brother John on 5th December, and by his father, William, on 8th December. There are 255 entries of plague death in this parish from September 1592 to October 1593. The registers of St. Alkmund's record 91 plague deaths during the like period, and those of St. Michael's 21 ; whilst those of St. Peter's and St. Werburgh's, though not specifying the cause, record 50 and 57 deaths respectively, the average in each case for the five adjacent years being only five.

In 1637 there are 59 plague deaths entered in All Saints' registers and 9 in those of St Alkmund. The registers of St. Peter's record 16 deaths from the like cause in 1586, and 63 in 1645 ; in the latter year it is stated that "the plague was in Darby and the assizes kept in Fryers Close." Hutton, the entertaining but imaginative historian of Derby, gives a graphic account of the condition of Derby during the plague of 1665, which, he says, visited this town at the same time that it devastated London. Had he referred to the register books of the five old parishes of Derby, he would have been saved from this bad blunder ; the death rate for that year was normal throughout the town.

Chesterfield was severely visited in 1586–7. After a burial on 7th October, 1586, it is written in a later hand on the margin of the register—" Here began the great Plague in Chesterfield." From this date up to November 1587 the deaths very far exceeded the average. The visitation carried off whole households. Of a family named Harry, Humphrey and Robert, sons of Robert, were buried on 24th October, 1586; Robert himself, and Elizabeth his servant, on 30th October; Jane, Robert's wife, on 2nd November; John, son of Nicholas Harry, on 12th November; and Nicholas on 25th November.

The Chesterfield register for October 1603 has, in a parenthesis, the words, "Plague at Brimington." Brimington was then a township and chapelry of Chesterfield. In Dr Pegge's *Collections* at the College of Arms (vol. iv.) there is a reference to this severe visitation. He says that at that time "Goodacre bridge was pulled down to prevent communication, and never rebuilt"; the victims were buried at Brimington.

The same register book has a marginal note, after a burial on 27th February 1608–9, to the following effect:— "Here began the latter Plague in Chesterfield. 1 Plague in 1586." Judging, however, from the actual entries of burial, this visitation was not nearly so serious as its predecessor.

The township of Belper, Derbyshire, was a mere chapelry of the widespread parish of Duffield until the nineteenth century. The ground round the ancient thirteenth-century chapel was not consecrated for burial until 1793. But the chapel yard had been largely used for burial in a time of dire necessity at a much earlier date. In 1609 the plague so grievously afflicted the then small population of Belper, that between 1st May and 30th September 53 persons died of the plague and were interred by the chapel. The following Latin entry, giving their names, is taken from the Duffield register:—

"Insuper hoc anno 1609 a primo die Maii usque de ultimo Septembris omnes quorum nomina hic conscribuntur mortui sunt de Plaga apud Belpare et eorum corpora juxta capella ibm humantur. Videz. Ux. Johis Bullivant cum duobus pueris, Alicia Taylor, Elizabetha Berdesley, Willm Streyte, Willm Berdesley, Thomas Berdesley cum filiis suis, Hugo Ashberie et ejus filiis, Radus Martyn, Willm Martyn, Johes Jackson et ux. ejus cum duobus pueris, ux. Willm Berdesley cum Pedlere (*sic*), Alicia Berdesley, Thomas Robynson, Johes Nieson et ux. ejus, Anna Myllners, Vid. Collier cum puero, Thomas Belye et ux. ejus cum puero, mater Thome Berdesley cum

11

puero, ux. Willm Ryley, Johes Browne et ux. ejus, Johes Peate et ux. ejus cum duobus pueris, Thomas Birkynshawe cum famulo et puero, ux. Thome Banforth, ux. Anthonii Fletcher cum puero, Willm Clewes cum puero, Georgius Brinckshawe, Arthurus Cleton et ux. ejus, Willm Potter, Johes Hardwycke—in numero Quinquegint' tres."

This visitation of 1609 can also be traced, though to nothing like so grave an extent, in the registers of other parts of Derbyshire. Thus at Dronfield there is the entry of the death from plague of William Townsend, curate of Holmesfield, who was buried on 24th March, 1608–9, in the chapel-yard of that hamlet.

The famous story of the plague in the retired Derbyshire village of Eyam has been so graphically told in prose by William Wood in his *History of Eyam* (first published in 1843), which has passed through numerous editions, and has also been so well sung in the poetry of Mary Howitt, that only a brief register summary of this extraordinarily virulent attack need be here attempted. Eyam was a village of some 350 inhabitants in a hollow of the Derbyshire hills, with no resident doctor, but two ministers. The one was the rector, the Rev. William Mompesson, a young man of 27, with a wife and two children ; the other was the Rev. Thomas Stanley, a rector under the Commonwealth, ejected for non-conformity in 1662. Both of them played heroic parts during the epidemic.

The first victim was George Vicars, who is said to have received the fatal infection in a box of tailor's patterns from London. The register shows that he was buried on 7th September, 1665. The next victim was Edward Cooper, who was buried on 22nd September, and there were four other interments from the like cause later in the month. In October the numbers had grown to 23 ; the plague deaths during the next six months fluctuated from four to nine. The total of those who had perished from the pest up to the

MOMPESSON'S WELL, EYAM

beginning of June, 1666, was 77. This number out o
a population of about 350 was sufficiently grievous; but
the fury of the plague then broke out with renewed vigour,
claiming 19 victims in June, 56 in July, and 77 in August;
by the end of this last month nearly four-fifths of the inhabitants had been swept away.   During the latter part of June
the little churchyard perforce closed its gates; funeral rites
were no longer read, no one thought of coffin or shroud,
and the dead were hastily hidden out of sight in some
shallow grave or hole dug in the fields or in the gardens
round the cottages.   The plague then began to slacken, in
fact there were but few fresh victims to be found; nevertheless 24 died of the pest in September.   This left but a
total population of 45, and out of that small total 14 more
perished in the beginning of October.   The last victim was
buried on October 11, and then at last it might be said that
the plague ceased, after having slain fully five-sixths of the
inhabitants.

If it had not been for the authority of Mompesson, to
which the inhabitants bravely assented, the plague would in
all probability have spread to many of the surrounding
parishes.   A boundary line was drawn round the village,
about half a mile in circuit, and marked by various familiar
objects, beyond which no one was to go.   One of the August
victims was Catherine Mompesson, the rector's wife, but
the rector himself, as well as his maid-servant, escaped the
infection.   In 1669 Mompesson left Eyam for the rectory
of Eakring, Notts, where he married again and died in
1708.

Let the ground round the village be honoured and
hallowed, says the historian of Eyam, for there—

> "The dead are everywhere !
> The mountain rich ; the plain ; the woods profound ;
> All the lone dells, the fertile and the fair,
>   Are one vast burial ground."

One of these plague burial places, a quarter of a mile from the village, known as Riley Grave Stones, is on the steep slope of a hill in the middle of a field, and is surrounded by a stone wall. Here are various simple tombstones to the memory of the Hancock and Talbot families, who were laid to rest in shallow graves. These tombstones were renovated in 1890 by Sir H. J. Burford-Hancock, Governor of Gibraltar.

There are various known sites of plague burials in fields and gardens up and down England, but very few of them are marked by gravestones. Just over, however, the borders of Derbyshire, on the high ground in Cheshire, south of Lyme Park, and near to the noted pre-Conquest Bow Stones, is another group of tombmarked plague burials, the victims of an outbreak of 1646. Three of these gravestones are to as many members of the Blakewall family who died on 26th July, 1646. Two others are to John Hampson and his wife and three children, and to Elizabeth Hampson; the following couplet is on the last of these :—

"Think it not strange my bones ly here
Thine may ly thou knowest not where."

These inscriptions are set forth in Earwaker's *History of East Cheshire* (ii. 314), but we noticed, during a recent visit, that some of the lettering has disappeared. These graves are in the parish of Taxal; the registers between 1644 and 1651 are defective.

The Midland Counties have numerous register references to epidemics in addition to those given with some detail as to Northamptonshire and Derbyshire. The following must be taken as a selection :—

"Walsall, Staffordshire, was visited with the plague in 1603. The first death from this epidemic was one 'Richard Smyth that died of plague,' who was buried on 30th October 1603. In the following month there were four plague deaths; and in January, February, and March 1603–4, eleven such deaths are entered."

RILEY GRAVE STONES, EYAM

The registers of St. Chad's, Shrewsbury, contain the following entry:—

" 1650. June—The Plaige began in Shrowsbure the 12th June in Fronkwell at John Pounds hoose Thomas Heayes Esq[r] Maior of Shrowsbury."

The registers of Little Marlow, Buckinghamshire, have the following entry under the plague year of 1621:—

" Mary, the wife of William Borlase, July 18, a gratious ladye she was, dyed of the plague, as did 18 more."

At Stoke Pogis, for the same year, seven burials are entered as dying of the plague in June and July.

The registers of Lavendon, Bucks, show that the plague of 1665 raged in that parish with great severity; the number of burials that year were 66, whereas the average of the seven preceding years amounted only to ten.

The visitation of the plague at Newport Pagnell, Bucks, in 1666, was very terrible. The registers show that the burials for the whole of 1665 amounted to 37, but in 1666 the total was 697. The worst month was July, when 257 interments are recorded. A contemporary writer, in a letter of 20 August, 1666, said that " Newport Panell, tho a considerable markett towne is not left above betwixt 7 and 800 peoples."

It is stated in the registers of Ramsey, Hunts, that 400 people died of the plague in 1665. The infection is said to have come from London in some cloth for a new coat.

The registers of Durnford, Gloucestershire, show that there was a visitation in this parish in 1627, when the deaths, which had averaged six in the last ten years, increased to twenty-six. Three of the interments are described as *sepultus in campis*, and two as *sepultus in clauso ejus*.

At the end of the first volume of the registers of East Retford, Notts (1573–1653), is the following recipe for the plague :—

"In yᵉ time of a plague let yᵉ person either infected or fearfull of yᵉ infection take a penny worth of dragon water, a penworthe of oyle olive, Methradate 1ᵈ, and treacle 1ᵈ. Then take an onion, and fill it full of pepper when you scraped it, yᵘ roast it ; and after yᵗ put it to yᵉ liquor and strain and drink it in yᵉ morning, and if you take yᵉ same at night lay soap and bay salt to your feet and sweat upon it, and with God's blessing you shall recover.

"THO. GYLBY, Vic."

The registers of the north of England bear emphatic testimony to the fierceness of the attacks of pestilence both in the larger and smaller towns, as well as in certain villages.

The mortality in 1579 at Newcastle-on-Tyne was very great. The municipal authorities wrote to the bailiffs of Yarmouth that the plague had carried off about 2000 persons between May and Michaelmas, and they warned them to refrain from sending vessels for coal. In 1588–9 there was another attack of this terrible scourge, when between May of the former year to 1st Jan 1588–9, 1727 died, as recorded in the registers of St John's.

"Died in this moneth, december, Mʳ William Selbye maior, and John Wilson sheriffe, 11 persons in the plage ; so that in all which hath died before this daye, being the firste of Januarie, in this towne, it is counted by all the records, in number to be in all 1727 persons, wherof iij hundred and 40 persons in St John's ; 5 hundred and 9 persons at the chapell, iij hundred at Alhalowes, iiij hundred at St Andrews . . . and one hundred and iij persons at St Nicholas."

The disease was again rampant at Newcastle in 1597–8, at the time when it was also raging in Cumberland and Westmorland, as well as at Durham and Darlington. In

1604 there were 100 burials of the pest registered at All Saints, about 20 in 1609, and 160 between April and December 1610. The numbers of pest deaths also corresponded with those of All Saints during these years. In 1625 there was a severe but less fierce outbreak in Newcastle, Gateshead, and Barnard Castle.

After a pause of about ten years the plague returned with intensified virulence in 1636. Fenwick, the religious merchant of Newcastle of those days, wrote—" Hast thou forgot how lord God spake to thee in that great plague Anno 1636, when there died in half-a-yeare about seven thousand which made thee almost desolate, thy streets growne greene with grasse, thy treasure wasted, and thy trading departed as thou never yet recovered it."

Nor is there any exaggeration in this estimate; the actual registers of the town record 5552 deaths in some eight or nine months, and in these pestilences there were always very many deaths unregistered. The perfectly awful character of this visitation is obvious when it is recollected that the population of Newcastle at this date must have been under twenty thousand.

The registers of Ravenstonedale contain no express mention of the plague, but the presence of the epidemic in certain well-known plague years is amply shown by the burial registers. The mortality was abnormally high in 1579, 1588, and 1597; whilst in 1623 the death rate was grievous. The interments in the last of these years (and three months went unrecorded) numbered 48, which is 33 above the average of that period.

In 1589 the plague broke out in Durham. In the register of St. Oswald's, the first two pest entries relate to the family of Masterman :—

"Sept. 20. Robert Maysterman and hys wyffe Margarete Maysterman, of the plage.

" Sept. 20. Adam M'man and iiij of hys systeres buryed of ye plage ye 26, 27, 28, 29 of September."

Against fifteen interments during October and November is the word " plague " written.

There is the following reference to the 1603–4 plague at Durham in the registers of St Giles' of that city :—

" Anne Ourd, wyffe of Christopher Ourd, bur. 25 Jan.   So all the hole household dyed in the vicitacion at this time, and so ye plague ceased."

Under the year 1644 is the following entry in the register of Eaglescliffe, co. Durham :—

" In this yeare there died of the plauge in this towne one and twenty people ; they are not all buried in the churchyard, and are not in the Register."

Cumberland and Westmorland, though abounding in natural drainage, abundant water supply, and apparently with everything tending towards health, were as much devastated by pestilent epidemics as the overcrowded towns.

The Hawkshead registers have an entry, under November 10, 1597, of a " pestilent sickness " brought into the parish by one " George Barwicke," of which 38 of the inhabitants died.

Notes in the Penrith register state that the " Plague was in Penrith and Kendal in 1554," that there was "a sore plague in newcastle, durrome and Dunston in the yere of our lord god 1597," and that it raged in 1598 in Kendal, Penrith, Carlisle, Appleby, and other places in Cumberland and Westmorland. At Penrith it broke out on 22nd September 1597, and continued till 13th December 1598.

" 1597. 27th day of September Andrew Hodgson a foreigner was buried.   Here begonne the plague (God's punishment in Penrith).   All those that are noted with the P. dyed of the infection, and those noted with F. were buried on the fell."

On 27th May, there were 13 plague burials, on 11th August 17, and on 2nd September 22. The fateful letter P is appended to 608 interments, and of these 213 are also marked with F, denoting burial on the fell; but probably the registers do not include many buried in their own gardens and elsewhere. An old inscription in the church, renewed in recent years in brass, states that those that died of the plague in 1597–8 were :—

"Penrith 2260, Kendal 2500, Richmond 2200, and Carlile 1196."

It has been suggested that these numbers include all within the particular rural deaneries. The whole district was grievously visited at this period. At Greystoke the average mortality of the parish rose from 45 to 182 in 1597. The Edenhall register also shows a great mortality. Gosforth leapt up from a death average of 13 to 56 in 1596, and 116 in 1597; Kirk Oswald from 10 in 1597 to 51 in 1598; Crosthwaite from an average of about 30 to 267 in 1597, and 84 in 1598; and Kirkby Lonsdale from an average under 50 to 82 in 1597, and 110 in 1598.

It should also be mentioned that the Penrith registers show that the normal number of deaths in the sixteenth century was about 50; but that in 1556 and 1557 it rose to 105 and 196 respectively; whilst in 1587 and 1588 it rose to the still far graver rates of 203 and 592.

A few instances of the pestilence entries must be given from the registers of the great county of Yorkshire.

The presence of the plague at Kirkburton is clearly indicated, although the word does not occur. In 1557 from January to end of September there were 64 deaths, but in 1558, during the same months, there were 164 deaths.

Nor is there any explicit mention of plague in the registers of Howden; yet it is clear that the town suffered very severely in 1579. The deaths during May, June, and July in 1577 were 23, in the following year 25, and the like number in 1580; but in 1579 they leapt for that period to 127.

The great pestilence of 1603 spread northwards in 1604. It caused 3512 deaths in the city of York during the latter year, being most severe in August and September. The markets were stopped, the minster and minsteryard closed, and the infected sent to Hob Moor and Horsefair, where wooden booths were erected for their reception. The registers of St Martin's, Micklegate, show 9 deaths in 1602, and 11 in 1603; but the interments for 1604 amounted to 68.

The Patrington register for 1537 records 38 interments, 21 of which were *e peste aut suspecti.*

Two instances from the Lancashire registers, one town and the other country, must suffice to illustrate the plague entries of that county. The following occurs in the register of Whittington :—

"From 19th December, unto 4th November, 1617, it pleased God to visit Whittington with a contagious sickness, within which time there was sicke in this parish about two hundred, in which time there deceased [here follow their names, the average mortality for a year being under ten]."

The number of burials recorded in the registers of the parish church of Preston, from 11th of November 1630 to the like date 1631, is a little over eleven hundred; the average number of the burials for several previous years was about eighty per annum. A contemporary diary states that the plague in Preston and the immediate neighbourhood "so raged in 1630 that the town was depopulated and corn rotted upon the ground for want of reapers."

The piteous entries of the Cheshire register of Malpas, with regard to the visitation of 1625, are cited below. With regard to this county it may be further stated that between 9th October 1605 and 14th August 1606 the Stockport registers record the burials of fifty-one persons who died of the plague.

Although there were various outbreaks of pestilence in such places as Colchester, Harwich, Norwich, Yarmouth, Lynn, and Wisbeach, the Eastern Counties have fewer register records of plague, so far as our experience goes, than other parts of the kingdom. At Chipping Ongar, in 1574, the interment of

"Thomas, a stranger, Surgeon of London buried 28 July,"

and nine others during that year, are bracketed together as " Died of the Plague."

Within ten miles round Boston the plague prevailed during the latter part of Elizabeth's reign, as is shown by the registers of Leake Frampton, and Kirton.

An entry of the year 1592 in the register of Holt, Norfolk, records that

"A greate plage wch beganne the 4 of Auguste continnued unto yᵉ 26 of Feb. followinge."

The average annual burials at that parish were 6; but in those seven months they amounted to 64.

The plague of 1665 reached Ipswich in September. In the registers of St Nicholas, the first plague death is entered on 13th September. Seven more plague deaths are entered in that month, and fourteen more before the end of the year. In 1666 there were seven plague entries in the same registers.

Evidence can be obtained, though by no means always from the parochial registers, of plague attacks during the sixteenth and seventeenth centuries at almost every seaport of the kingdom, small or large; a fact which materially helps to prove that the true plague, unlike the sweating sickness, was not of indigenous development. The great ports of Southampton and Plymouth, as well as the smaller ports of Cornwall and the Bristol Channel, were all subject to these severe epidemics. The following are some of the less known register references to the plague of the south and west of England.

The register of Cranbrook, Kent, formerly an important centre of the woollen trade, half-way between Maidstone and the old Cinque Porte, contains a long entry relative to a late Elizabethan visitation :—

"In this year following, 1597, began the great plague in Cranbrook, the which continued from April the 7th aforesaid to July 13, 1598. 1st it was observed that before this infection that God, about a year or two before, took away by death many honest and good men and women. 2. That the judgment of God for sin was much before threatened, especially for that vice of Drunkeness which abounded here. 3. That this infection was in all quarters of this Parish except Hartly quarter. 4. That the same begun in the house of one Brighteling, out of which much thieving was committed, and that it ended in the house of one Henry Grynnock, who was a pott companion, and his wife noted much for incontinence, which both died excommunicated. 5. That this infection gott almost into all the Inns and Suckling Houses of the Town, places then of much misorder, so that God did seem to punish that himself which others did neglect and not regard. 6. Together with this infection there was a great dearth at the corne time, which was cause also of much wailing and sorrow. 7. This was most grievous unto me of all, that this judgment of God did not draw people unto repentance the more, but that many by it seemed the more hardened in their sin.

"Now also this year others of the plague who were buried near to their several dwellings, because they could get none to carry them into the Church, for it was the beginning of this infection, so that none would venture themselves. The certain day of their burials one could not learn."

The registers of All Saints, Maidstone, show that the

town suffered severely from the plague of 1603; the word "plague" is attached to no fewer than 136 names within nine months, though the round annual death-rate was under sixty.

The plague appeared in Chislehurst, Kent, in 1603; the deaths, which previously averaged about ten a year, reached a total in that year of sixty-three.

In 1603 there was a most grievous visitation of the plague at Dorking. There were 108 interments recorded in the parish registers; many were buried in gardens or fields.

There was also high mortality at Strood, Kent, in 1603; the registers show 44 burials during that year, though the average yearly mortality of the period was only fourteen. In May 1609

"Morgan his wife and 2 children the same weeke, all of the pestilence."

During the year 1550 no fewer than 70 persons were buried at Minehead, Somerset; the annual average of interments at that time was under 20. In 1597 there is an entry to the effect that "ye blouddye flux raged in this year"; there were 57 interments. The plague was bad again in 1645, when about five times the average number of burials took place. There was another visitation in 1652.

The adjoining town of Dunster suffered grievously from the plague in 1645. It was in May of that year that Charles I sent the Prince of Wales, then a boy of fifteen, to Dunster Castle "to encourage the new levies." The Prince had just been driven from Bristol by the plague, and the court was not aware, as Clarendon tells us, that it was raging just as hot in Dunster town immediately under the castle walls. Clarendon's statement is strikingly confirmed by the parish registers, which show that there were actually eighty interments in the single month of May.

There was most terrible mortality from the plague at

Totnes in 1590; the registers of that year yield the following evidence: July—out of 42 interments, 36 of plague; August—out of 81, 80; September—39, all of plague; October—37, all of plague; November—25, 24 of plague; December—19, all of plague. There were a few cases in January and one in February, yielding a total of 246 plague deaths. No sooner had the disease died out in Totnes than it began in Tiverton, where the registers show that the deaths from plague and other causes between March 1591 and March 1592 were 551, or about one in nine of the population.

Redruth, Cornwall, had a severe visitation in 1591–92. The register for 1591 notes that

"The Plage began Aug. 11."

A further entry on 11th November 1592 states that

"The Plage ceased."

Twenty-seven deaths are entered for the single month of June, whereas the annual death-rate about that period was under ten.

The Plymouth registers prove that the town endured a terrible plague visitation in 1626, when 1600 fell victims to the epidemic.

The plague broke out somewhat severely at Basingstoke, Hants, in 1666, in which year 46 burials are registered as its victims. But the number was higher than this, for the Churchwardens' Accounts state that "The plague broke out at Basingstoke in 1666, and there are upwards of eighty knells recorded."

The Godalming, Surrey, registers show that there were thirty-four deaths from the plague in that parish in 1666; some of the victims are entered as " buried in ye garden."

Two household plague tragedies demand distinct notice. In 1625 there was a grievous visitation of the plague at

Bradley, in Malpas parish, Cheshire. The sweeping out of the whole family of Dawson as recorded in the Malpas register is characterised by the dreadful and unique incident of a dying sufferer digging his own grave :—

"Thomas Jefferie, servant to Thomas Dawson, of Bradley, buryed the 10th daye of August, in the night, he died of the plague.

"Richard, the sonne of Thomas Dawson of Bradley (that dyed of the plague) buryed the 13th daye of August, in the night, 1625, nihil.

"Raffe Dawson, sonne of the aforesayed Thomas, came from London about 25th Jul last past, and beinge sicke of the plague dyed at his father's house, and soe infected the sayd house and was buryed, as is reported, neare unto his father's house.

"Thomas Dawson, of Bradley, died of the plague, and was buryed th' 16th daye of August at 3 of the clocke, after midnight, nihil.

"Elizabeth, the daughter of the aforesayed Thomas Dawson, died of the plague of pestilence, and was buryed the 20th daye August.

"Anne, the wyffe of John Dawson, sonne of the aforesayd Thomas Dawson, died of the plague of pestilence, and was buryed the 20th of August.

"Richarde Dawson (brother to the above named Thomas Dawson of Bradley) being sick of the plague and perceyving he must die at yt tyme, arose out of his bed, and made his grave, and causing his nefew, John Dawson, to cast some strawe into the grave, which was not farre from the house, and went and layed him down in the sayd grave, and caused clothes to be layd uppon, and soe dep'ted out of this world; this he did because he was a strong man and heavier than his said nefew and another wench were able to burye; he died about the 23d of August, 1625. Thus much he did I was credibly tould.

"John Dawson, sonne of the above named Thomas, came unto his father, when his father sent for him, beinge sicke, and haveing layd him down in a dich, died in it the 29th daye of August, 1625, in the night.

"Rose Smyth, servant of the above named Tho: Dawson, and last of yt household, died of plague, and was buryed by Wm Cooke the 5th daye of September near the sayd house."

The plague tragedy at Great Hampden is still more pathetic than that at Bradley, Cheshire, inasmuch as the register entries are written by the rector himself, the husband, father, cousin, or master of the victims. Robert Lenthall, a relative of the Speaker of that name, became rector of Great Hampden in 1643. By his wife Susanna, he had two children, Adrian and Sarah. Shortly after the plague horrors of 1647 Robert Lenthall left Great Hampden, married a second time, and died rector of Barnes, Surrey, in 1658.

"1647. N.B. My daughter Sarah Lenthall was buried ye eleventh day of August An: supra, she came fro' London to Wickham and on ye Saturday only to see us and so to returne ye morrow in ye afternoone to Wickham againe, but then fell sick and on Wednesday morning following being ye 11th of August about an houre before Sun rise dyed of ye sickness, and so in ye Evening we buried her in ye meade called ye Kitchenmeade by ye hedgeside as you go downe into it on yor left hand, a little below ye pond at ye enterance into ye meade; she was aged 14 yeares, eleven moneths and seaventeene dayes—had she lived to Bartholomew day she had bin full 15 yeares of age.

"Susanna Lenthall my wife dep'ted this life Thursday evening about 8 a clock ye 26 of August, she died of ye sicknes comfortably and in peace and was buried August ye 27 by hir daughter Sara.

"John Gardiner a child yt lived in my house died of ye sicknes and was buried August ye 29th.

"Adrian Lenthall my sonne a hopefull yong man and were one and twenty yeares of age dep'ted this life of ye sicknes, Thursday morning a little before day breake and was buried at ye head of his sister Sarah's grave ye same day, being ye 2d of Septemb.

"My cosen John Pickering a lad about 13 yeares of age, dying of ye sicknes, was buried the 25 of Septembr. 1647.
"ROBERT LENTHALL, Rector"

Small-pox is now and again named in parish registers.

" 1667 (*Alstonfield, Staffs*), April 13. Tho. and Eliz., 2 children of
Thos. Stones, jun^r, who died of the small poxe, and wer both
burried in one grave."

The small-pox broke out with much severity at Basingstoke in 1714, when the registers show that out of 76 burials
during that year 52 died from this malady; among the
victims was Mr. John Davies, the mayor. There was another
severe outbreak in this town in 1781.

" 1799 (*Sandon, Essex*). William the son of Samuel Raven, by
Sarah his wife, was half baptized at home (being ill and
apprehended in danger of catching the smallpox if brought
to the church), Nov. 20th 1798. Received into the congregation June 2d 1799."

Inoculation was introduced into England by Lady Mary
Wortley Montagu early in the eighteenth century, but it was
bitterly opposed for many years, especially by the clergy.
The following entries occur in the burial register of Long
Barton, Dorset :—

" 1770. June 7 James Noake ; June 28 Alice Noake his wife ; July
16 Robert Stayner, a child ; July 20 Charles Stayner, his
brother. NB. These four last dyed of the small pox, catch'd
in the natural way, and during James Noake's Distemper,
many children and grown persons in the Parish were innoculated
(the first time this Method was introduc'd here) and all did
well.
"Note that in the year 1776 the small Pox was very epidemi-
cal both at Sherborne and in the Country, when the Innoculation
of that Distemper was introduced a 2d time into the Parish, and
many Persons were innoculated here by the Sherborne Apoth-
ecaries, with good success, at 5s. 3d. a head."

It does not appear that inoculation was by any means
always successful; it was sometimes fatal. Two deaths
from small-pox are entered in this same Dorsetshire register
under 1780.

12

The Italian name of "influenza" for an epidemic ague first came into England in 1743, and the casual use of the term became more general during the epidemic of 1762. With the severe epidemic of 1782, the Italian title became a fairly settled term in this country and was formally adopted by the College of Physicians. In that year a swift brief wave of catarrhal fever swept over the British Isles. It was most prevalent in May, June, and July, and affected from three-fourths to four-fifths of the adult population, but with very few fatal results. As the mortal cases were so exceptional, it is not surprising to find this epidemic for the most part ignored in the registers. There is, however, one interesting reference to it in a Shropshire parish:—

"1782 (*Selattyn, Salop*). This year being remarkable for Cold and Wett about Springtime, Much against the Farmers Concerns in General, which bro't on an Disorder, of the nature of a violent Cold, which raged so general thro' both England and Wales and all European Countries, which in England was commonly called the Influenza, and which happily was not very mortal. There was scarcely one escaped this distemper."

In 1763 there were thirteen interments of infants at Albrighton, Salop. After the last of these entries, it is remarked in the register:—

"The Scarlet Fever carried off many Infants this year."

References to surgery in registers are highly exceptional. The following is the pathetic entry of an early instance of the serious operation of lithotomy made by the hand of the patient:—

"1630 (*Hunstanton, Norfolk*). Hoc anno vij die August Robtus Burward vicarius de Hunstanton versus Londinum iter arripuit, et post sex Hebdomodas in quibus Chirurgum ibi expectaverat, xxij die Octobris inter horas x et xj ante meridiem pro calculo in vesica incisus fuit par Mª Mullins; et admiranda Dei

misericordia bonitate et auxilio suffultus patienter admodum
sciosuram suetinuit; post xvj Hebdomodas feliciter fere
sanatur, et tandem xvj die Februarii felici ac prospero itinere
ad Hunstanton revertitur. Deo optimo maximo sunt gratiæ
ingentes. Amen."

The vicar did not, however, live for many months to
enjoy his restored health, for in the following year this entry
occurs in the register :—

"1631. Robertus Burward sepultus erat July 3d."

The custom of the royal touch for curing scrofula or the
King's Evil has been traced back to the times of Edward the
Confessor. *The Ceremonies for the Healing of them that be
diseased with the King's Evil, as they were practised in the
time of King Henry VII* were printed by Mr. Hills in 1686
for the use of James II "in his houshold and chappel." The
old Latin form of Prayers at the Healing continued to be
printed in the Latin version of the Prayer Book as late as 1759.
This practice of touching for the King's Evil was much
resorted to by Charles I; but it prevailed to a still more
astonishing extent after the Restoration. Between 1660 and
1682 no fewer than 92,107 persons, chiefly children, were
touched for this disease by Charles II. Certificates were
usually expected from the parish minister and wardens to the
effect that the person had not previously been touched.
Part of the ceremony consisted, according to the rubric, in
the King " crossing the sore of the sick person with an Angel
Noble ; and the sick person to have the same angel hanged
about his neck, and to wear it until he be full whole." The
temptation of obtaining a piece of gold caused not a few to
strive to be touched on various occasions.

The Merstham, Surrey, register contains the following
list of certificates granted by the rector and wardens
between 1673 and 1680 :—

To the Kings moſt Excellent Majeſty. _6_

The ·Humble

PETITION

Of divers hundreds

of the Kings poore Subjeɛts,

Affliɛted with that grievous Infirmitie,

Cᴀʟʟᴇᴅ

The Kings Evill.

Of which by his Majeſties abſence they
have no poſsibility of being cured, wanting all
meánes to gaine acceſſe to his Majeſty, by reaſon
of His abode at Oxꜰᴏʀᴅ

London, Printed for _John Wilkinſon._
Febr.20. Anno Dom, 1643. _1642_

"Certificate to his Ma^ty about touching for ye Evill signed by y^e Rector and Churchward: of Merstham.

"To Prudennye daugtre of Will: Lovell Octob: 6° (16)73.

"To Elizabeth Richardson daugter of Eliz. Richardson Widdow Mar. 9° 73.

"To Thomas Deane ye sonne of Sam: Deane, Nov. 8° 1674.

"To Nicholas Cooper ye sonne of John Cooper, Dec. 4° 1674.

"To George Palmer ye son of William Palmer Mar. 5° 1676-7 ye Father and his sonne Harry touched before.

"To John Stanley, Labourer, Feb. 27° 1677-8.

"To Matthew Harbour April 11° 1678.

"To Jane Buckner spinster April 6° 1680.

"RICH LEWIS, Curate"

There are similar entries in other registers of about this period, as at St. Mary's, Bridgwater. The applicants eventually became so numerous that Charles II issued a proclamation on 9th January 1683-4 appointing the times when the touch would be administered, insisting on each applicant bringing a certificate signed by his minister and one or both wardens "testifying according to the truth" that this was the first application, and ordering all ministers and wardens to keep a register of all certificates they shall from time to time give. In the Churchwardens' Accounts of Stanford-in-the-Vale and Marlborough are entries of payment for the King's declaration as to the Order of Touching.

After this proclamation entries as to certificates are naturally more frequent in the registers, from which the following are selected :—

"1684-5 (*Eccleston, Lancashire*), March 21. A Certificate given to John Brindle For being touched by his Majesty for ye K. Evil.

"1685-6 (*Ibid.*), March 31. A Certificate given to Jane Hawet of Writtington for being touched for ye Kings Evil.

"1685 (*Hambledon, Bucks*), 17 May. Mary Wallington had a certificate to goe before the King for a disease called the King's Evil.

At the Court at WHITEHALL

The Ninth of *January* 1 6 8 3.

Order of Councill Appointing ye times for ye Kings touching for ye Evill

Present

The Kings moſt Excellent Majeſty,

Lord Keeper	Earl of Huntingdon	Earl of Bathe	Mr. Secretary Jenkins
Lord Privy Seal	Earl of Bridgewater	Earl of Craven	Mr. Chancellour of the Exchequer
Duke of Ormond	Earl of Peterborrow	Earl of Nottingham	Mr. Chancellour of the Dutchy
Duke of Beaufort	Earl of Cheſterfield	Earl of Rocheſter	Lord Chief Juſtice Jeffryes
Earl of Oxford	Earl of Clarendon	Lord Biſhop of London	Mr. Godolphin.

26. Jan. 1683.

Hereas by the Grace and Bleſſing of God, the Kings and Queens of this Realm by many Ages paſt, have had the happineſs by their Sacred Touch, and Invocation of the Name of God, to cure thoſe who are afflicted with the Diſeaſe called the Kings-Evil ; And His Majeſty in no leſs meaſure than any of His Royal Predeceſſors having had good ſucceſs therein, and in His moſt Gracious and Pious diſpoſition, being as ready and willing as any King or Queen of this Realm ever was in any thing to relieve the diſtreſſes and neceſſities of His good Subjects ; Yet in His Princely Wiſdom foreſeeing that in this (as in all other things) Order is to be obſerved, and fit times are neceſſary to be appointed for the performing of this great work of Charity, His Majeſty was therefore this day pleaſed to Declare in Council His Royal Will and Pleaſure to be, That (in regard heretofore the uſual times of preſenting ſuch perſons for this purpoſe have been prefixed by His Royal Predeceſſors) the times of Publick Healings ſhall from henceforth be from the Feaſt of *All Saints,* commonly called *Alhallon-tide,* till a week before *Chriſtmas* : and after *Chriſtmas* until the Firſt day of *March,* and then to ceaſe till the *Paſſion Week,* being times moſt convenient both for the temperature of the ſeaſon, and in reſpect of Contagion which may happen in this near acceſs to His Majeſties Sacred Perſon. And when His Majeſty ſhall at any time think fit to go any Progreſs, He will be pleaſed to appoint ſuch other times for Healing as ſhall be moſt convenient : And His Majeſty doth hereby accordingly Order and Command, That from the time of Publiſhing this His Majeſties Order, none preſume to repair to His Majeſties Court to be Healed of the ſaid Diſeaſe, but onely at, or within the times for that purpoſe hereby appointed as aforeſaid. And His Majeſty was further pleaſed to Order, That all ſuch as hereafter ſhall come, or repair to the Court for this purpoſe, ſhall bring with them Certificates under the Hands and Seals of the Parſon, Vicar, or Miniſter, and of both or one of the Churchwardens of the reſpective Pariſhes where they dwell, and from whence they come, teſtifying according to the truth, That they have not at any time before been touched by His Majeſty to the intent to be healed of that Diſeaſe. And all Miniſters and Churchwardens are hereby required to be very careful to examine into the truth before they give ſuch Certificates, and alſo to keep a Regiſter of all Certificates they ſhall from time to time give. And to the end that all His Majeſties Loving Subjects may the better take knowledge of this His Majeſties Command, His Majeſty was pleaſed to Direct, That this His Order be Read publickly in all Pariſh-Churches, and then be affixt to ſome conſpicuous place there ; And that to that end the ſame be Printed, and a convenient Number of Copies ſent to the moſt Reverend Fathers in God, the Lord Arch Biſhop of *Canterbury,* and the Lord Arch Biſhop of *York,* who are to take care that the ſame be diſtributed to all Pariſhes within their reſpective Provinces.

PHI. LLOYD.

LONDON,

Printed by the Aſſigns of *John Bill* Deceas'd : And by *Henry Hills,* and *Thomas Newcomb,* Printers to the Kings moſt Excellent Majeſty. 1683

PROCLAMATION AS TO TIMES FOR "TOUCHING," 1683.

" 1686–7 (*Measham, Derbyshire*). Katherine Brooks that she might be touched for the King's Evil had certificate, March 2d 1686–7.

" 1767 (*Alrewas, Staffs*). Edward Hall, who was touched and cured by his Majesty King Charles II for the King's Evil, was buried Jan. 19th, aged 110 years."

The registers of Blakesley, Northants, mention that two persons went, in 1683, "to London to be touched of the King's evil."

In the second book of the registers of Hargrave, Northants (1683–1756), is written :—

" A Register containing the names of the Persons that have been touch'd by his Majesty to the intent to be healed of the Disease called the Kings Evil in the Parish of Hargrave."

This " register " contains, however, only two names whc were thus touched in February 1683–4, namely, Philip and Amy Cannard.

James II touched above 5000 persons during a single progress of the year 1687. William III positively refused to touch patients, the custom being distasteful to him on the score of expense as well as on that of superstition. His refusal was taken in certain quarters as a proof that he was no rightful King. Queen Anne's ministers thought it politic to revive the use, and the *Gazette* of 12th March 1712 officially announced the appointed time of touching. Dr. Johnson, when a child, was amongst those then touched by Queen Anne. The custom finally died out with the advent of George I, "who believed in little or nothing."

CHAPTER X

HISTORICAL

Arrival of King Philip—Marian burnings—Funeral of Mary Queen
of Scots—The Armada—Elizabethan martyrs—Levies on the
clergy—Border warfare—Historic entries at Youlgreave—
Victories of Van Tromp, 1639—Dewsbury registers—The Great
Civil War—Casualties in Northamptonshire, Derbyshire, etc.—
Register irregularities caused by the war—Tamworth registers
—The Protestation and the Covenant—The death of the
Protector and of his Relict—The Restoration—Rye House Plot
—Death of Charles II and accession of James II—Monmouth's
rebellion—The Prince of Orange

IF the vast store of national muniments at the Public
Record Office were to be destroyed and all libraries burnt,
the leading facts of English history since 1538 could
be gleaned from the parish records. Various interesting
incidents connected with the close of the reign of Henry VIII
and of the successive reigns of his three children have been
already set forth in the extracts from the Much Wenlock
registers.

Philip landed at Southampton in July 1554; the following
entry must refer to the later arrival at the Metropolis :—

" 1554 (*Trinity the Less, London*). Alice Meleche the daur of John
Meleche xyened being the daie that Kinge Phillipp came from
beyond the seas and landed att Greenwich att five o'clock att
night."

There are one or two register references to the cruel
burnings for religion under Queen Mary.

" 1556 (*All Saints, Derby*), Aug. 1. A poor blinde woman called
   Joan Waste of this parish, a martyr, burned in Windmill
   Pit.
" 1558 (*Richmond, Yorks*). Richard Snell b'rnt, bur. 9 Sept."

The funeral of Mary Queen of Scots secured an entry at
Peterborough :—

" 1587 (*Cathedral Church of Peterborough*). The Queene of Scots was
   most sumptuously buried in the cathedral church of Peterburgh,
   the first day of August, who was for her deserts beheaded at
   Fotheringay about St. Paules day before.
      " Anthony More, one of the children of the Queens Majesties
   kitchen, wch followed at the Funerall aforesaid of the Queen of
   Scots was buryed the iii day (of August)."

The Armada entered the Channel 19th July 1588 ; suffered
in a series of engagements during that month ; and retreated
northward in August and September, enduring much further
loss from storms.

" 1588 (*St. Oswald's, Durham*). Upon munday beinge the xijth day
   of August, the Right honorable earle of Huntington, lord presy-
   dent under O^r,most gracyous sufferayne lady quene elyzbethe,
   caused a generall muster to be upon spenymore of all persons
   within thage of xvj and lx yeares, onely within the bysshopryke,
   and no further, where weare assembled on Spenymore ye same
   day to ye full number of xl thowsande men, redy to serve
   hyr majesty when the shuld be called, whom god preserve
   longe to rayne over us, a mother in Israell.   Amen.
" 1588 (*Earl Framingham, Norfolk*). The 19 of Nov. was a day
   of Thanksgiving to God for the great and wonderful Overthrow
   of the Spanish Navy which came to fight the Pope's Battle
   against this Island for their Gospel, at which overthrow the
   very enemies were so astonished that some of them said Christ
   had become a Lutheran, and all that saw it did say that it was
   the Lord's Work, so this day was appointed by our Church to be
   spent throughout the realme, in preaching and praying, singing
   of psalms, and giving thanks for a thankful memorial of the
   Lord's merciful mercies yerelie."

In the spring of the year 1589, being the year after the destruction of the Armada, a boy was baptized at Dunster, on the Somerset coast, under the name *Victorie*.

The registers of St. Oswald's, Durham, contain a vehemently worded entry as to the butchery of four Roman Catholic priests in 1590 :—

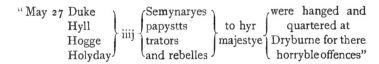

" May 27 Duke ⎫   ⎧Semynaryes⎫   ⎧were hanged and
        Hyll   ⎬ iiij ⎪papystts ⎬ to hyr ⎪   quartered at
        Hogge ⎪   ⎨trators   ⎪majestye⎨ Dryburne for there
        Holyday⎭   ⎩and rebelles⎭   ⎩ horryble offences"

It will scarcely be credited that the " horryble offences " of these four English priests consisted in the simple fact that, being subjects of the Queen and ordained priests of the Roman Church, they remained in their own country to minister to their co-religionists. This offence, under the Statute of 27 Elizabeth, subjected them to the disgusting capital penalties of high treason.[1]

The long-continued rebellion of the Earl of Tyrone in Ulster, towards the end of Elizabeth's reign, is mentioned in at least one English register :—

"1595 (*Aston-by-Birmingham*). This tyme there was a great goinge into Ireland against the Earl of Tyrone the clergey payed deerly. It cost the Vicar of Aston xx marks."

The petty raids of the Border warfare are well illustrated in the following graphic extracts of 1601–2 from the Penrith registers :—

"March 2d. About two of the Cloke at the fare end of Plumpton Wall in Bowman Gill was one James Atkinson of

---

[1] See Challoner's *Missionary Priests* (ed. 1878), i. 169–70. When dwelling on the scandals of the Marian persecutions, those under Elizabeth are usually forgotten by our historians. During the latter's reign 127 priests, 53 laymen, and 3 women suffered violent deaths solely for their religion : see an article in the *Church Quarterly Review*, vol. viii., on "The Elizabethan Martyrs."

Killington, a Carrier, in coming from Carlisle robed of three carriage horses and vij p. in moneye.

"March 18th. The night last was Branton and Gillisland spoiled by Scotts thiefs and their goods taken with prisoners. This tyme was great spoiling and robing in this countrie, especiallie in Cumberland, burning in Gillisland and other places.

"March 23d. At night was Richard Wood of Plumton spoiled by thiefs and he taken prisoner into Scotland. This tyme such watching in Penrith in the night as was not a hundreth yeres before, fiftie watchers neightlie.

"March 29th. This daye was Corbie spoiled by the Borderers, and one George Salkeld killed by them.

"April 3d was the Town dyke at the Overside of Penrith newly casten againe by the townsmen for the defence of the town and invasion of the Borderers who do threat the same.

"April 5th. At night was Casel Carrocke spoiled by the incurrate of pirates, borderers, thiefs, and murtherers."

The registers of Youlgreave, Derbyshire, contain a variety of historical notes as to the opening years of the seventeenth century.

"1601–2. Uppon the 8th day of this moneth of Februarii being Septuagessima was the conspiracy by the Earles of Essex, Rutland, and Southampton with their confederates in London.

"Upon the 19th day being thursday, Essex and Southampton were arraigned at Westminster and found guilty by the peiares of this land for high treason.

"The 25th day of the said moneth of Feb. being the first day of Lent, was Robert earle of Essex executed within the town of London.

"March 23. Our most gracious soveraigne Lady Elizabeth quene of Englande, France, and Ireland, departed this lyffe upon Wednesday, after she had reigned most peacablye 44 yeares, 4 moneths, 11 daies.

"1603, March 29. James King of Scotland was proclaimed Kinge of England, France and Ireland at Baunkewill (Bakewell) uppon Monday. Whom the Lord preserve.

　　　And a gallant King and Queen
　　　Was they and happy in their Reigns."

In May and June 1616, there are the entries in the register of St. Oswald's, Durham, of seven recusants (all women) choosing their abode in accordance with a persecuting statute of that period.

The following is an example:—

"Memorandum that I Margret Swinburne the wif of Thomas Swinburne Esquier of the parish of St. Oswaldes in the city of Durham have delivered my nam and presented myself accordinge to a statute provided for conffirminge of recusantes within the compas of five myles, and chuse for my aboad my now dwelling house in Elvet aforesaide.

"MARGRET SWINBURNE"

The clerk who entered the registers of Dewsbury for the month of February 1625–26 seems to have been anxious to air his learning and power of calculation. After writing in the margin that

"Ouse Bridge at Yorke was broken downe sixtie and tew years synce," he continues: "Februarye. Edmonde son of John Hage of Oscote baptised ye seconde day beinge Thursdaye and Candlemas daye 1625 and ye same Coronation daye of Kynge Charles An° Dni dicte: from ye worldes creation 5575 : Noahe floude 3919.

"James son of James Pickerde baptised yt day. Synce Yorke was built 2592 : and Yorke Minster built 697 : and Londoun was built 2734 : Caroli regis, etc., primo.

"A yonge childe being a daughter not baptised of Edwarde Walter and Marye Claytoun basseborne buried ye vjthe daye.

"An° Ætatis Caroli regis Novemb. 19–24. A conquesto Anglia 558 : and synce ye Israelites departed out of Egypte 3553.

"Myles Cooke and Issabell Nowell married ye xijth day beinge Sondaye Sexagesima or Sonday before Shrove Sondaye An° Dni 1625 : An° regis dni dicto primo : a mundi creatione 5575 : synce ye begininge of Quene Elizabethe her raigne 68."

The victories of Van Tromp obtain register notice. Van Tromp took two Spanish fleets, off the Downs, in 1639, namely, on 16th September and 21st October.

" 1639 (*Wadhurst, Sussex*). Exit annus 1639. This yeare was the great sea Battell (Van Tromp's action) neare unto Dover, betwixt the mighty Armado of Spaine riding near our Coasts neare Deale, and the Hollanders, wherein the mighty Armado, consisting of great shippes, was vanquished by the Hollanders. The winter was exceeding windy and tempestuous, and therefore there was much shipwreck."

The Great Civil War of the seventeenth century naturally left considerable traces of its ravages and disturbances among the entries of the parochial registers throughout the greater part of the kingdom, more particularly in the districts where the conflicts or skirmishes were the most constant.

The county of Northampton was specially involved in the strife. At the outbreak of hostilities between the King and the Parliament in 1642, Northampton was held as a garrison for the latter under Lord Brooke. In January 1642–43 the registers of St. Sepulchre's record the burial of "Robert Hutchins, a souldear." In May 1643 there is the burial entry of "A souldear who died out of goodman Hilton's house." In October of the same year there was a midnight skirmish of royalists under Prince Rupert before the north gate close to St. Sepulchre's. As a result there are five burial entries of slain soldiers. In the following year there are several like entries, particularly about the date of the battle of Cropredy Bridge, which was fought on 29th June. Sir William Waller, the Parliamentary general, marched to Towcester on 7th July, and arrived at Northampton on 4th July with 7000 horse and foot.

" 1644. A canoneere of Sr William Waller buried the 3d of July.

"A souldier buryed from Richard Letts, buryed the 11th day of July.

"Major Hobson was buryed from Valentine Roberts the 13th day of July.

" A souldier from Robert Harris was buryed the 18th day of July."

The decisive battle of Naseby was fought on 14th June 1645. On the following day " Robert Harris, souldier under Major Huntington," was buried at St. Sepulchre's. From that date up to the middle of July thirteen other soldiers found burial in this churchyard, several of whom were " unknown by name." An entry in the All Saints' register under date 29th June 1645 states that " This month thirty comon souldiers sepult. fuit." Doubtless many of the severely wounded at the great fight at Naseby were brought into Northampton and there died. Sir Edward Littleton, a devoted royalist, who was wounded and taken prisoner, was buried at St. Sepulchre's on 19th June, and Sir Thomas Dallison, an officer of Rupert's brigade, at St. Giles' on 20th June. The All Saints' registers record the burial of Captain Bush (an officer of Cromwell's own regiment of horse), and a cornet on 16th June. In the same registers are the burials of Captain Potter on 27th June, and of Captain Cooke on 29th June. Captain Potter was one of the two " Commissioners of Parliament residing in the Army "; Captain Cooke was " Commissary General of Horse provisions " in the Parliamentary army. In the letter of Mr. Thomas Herbert (the other Parliamentary Commissioner) to Mr. Speaker Lenthall describing the battle, the dangerously wounded condition of both these captains is mentioned.

In the course of the following July, Cornet David, two soldiers, and a " clarke of the band," were buried in All Saints' churchyard, and Captain Brampton Ferne at St. Sepulchre's.

The following are amongst other burial entries in different parts of the county of Northampton which were apparently due to the Civil War disturbances :—

Cotterstock	1643	Edward Spratton was buried the 2 day of Jeune, who was slain at Mr. Norton's gates the same day.
Helmdon	,,	Mr. Thorntone, a quarter-master of the Kinges Majestie⁵ armie was buried the firste daye of December.
Collyweston	1644	Gowen Barnes, a Drummer from London, White-chappell, buried May 18th.
Daventry	1644-5	March 18. Humfree Bayliss, Quarter Master to Sir Wm. Compton, buried.
Collyweston	1645	Thomas Boivill, a wounded souldier, dyed and was buried Sept 22.
Daventry	1645	Nov. 28. Edward Wilkesson a souldier, buried.
Fotheringhay	1646	Gulielmus Preston occicus a milite quodam, sepult. 29 November.
Etton	1648	Edward Rossiter by a shott from Woodecroft House received two wounds whereof he presently dyed June the 5 and on the 8th day of the same was buryed at Etton.

Between 1645 and 1650 William Ponder signs the Courteenhall, Northants, register as " Rector." This has been crossed out by a successor in every instance, and the word " Intruder" substituted.

Derbyshire was another midland county much involved in the turmoils of the Civil War period. The entries in the register of the great church of All Saints, Derby, are of much interest; partial and blundering quotations have been set forth in Burn's work :—

" 1642. The 22 of this August errectum fuit Notinghamie Vexillum
    Regale. Matt. xii. 25.
    Oct. Bat at Kinton (Edgehill) 23 day.
    Nov. Bat. at Branford (Brentford) 12 day.
" 1642-3, Jan. Bat at Swarston Bridge 5 day.
    ,,   Ashbie ye 17.
    Feb. 11. Sep. William Parker, souldier under Cap: Sanders.
    March. The 20th day ye Hon. Lord Brooke slaine at yᵉ
        Siege against Lichfield Close. It was yielded up
        5th day.
        Ye 19th day the battell at Stafford, E. of North-
        ampton was slaien.
" 1643, April. The 8 day Prince Rupert Besieged yᵉ Close at Lich-

field wch was valiently mentained till ye 21 and ye took ful quarters and with great honor marcht away.

June 4. The body of Lord Erle of Northampton formerly slayne at Stafford was now buried in the familie vault belonging to the Honble house of the Lord Cavendish Erle of Devon, wch there now lyeth Elizab. Countess Shreusbi and William Erle of Devon."

The Earl of Northampton was killed at the battle of Hopton Heath, near Stafford, 19th March 1643. The young Earl requested that he might have the dead body of his father, but it was refused. Sir John Gell's account of the transaction is as follows :—

"Within three days came a trumpeter to Colonel Gell, from my young Lord of Northampton for his father's dead body, whereupon he answered, if he would send him the drakes which they had gotten from their dragoons, and pay the chirurgeons for embalming him, he should have it ; but he returned him an answer, that he would doe neither th' one or th' other ; and soe Colonel Gell caused him to be carried in his company to Derby, and buried him in the Earl of Devonshire's sepulchre in All Hallow's Church."

The rector of Brailsford was another Derbyshire clergyman who used the parish register for brief memoranda as to the events of the times.

" 1648. Memorandum. C. R. began his R. 1625 March 27 ; set up his standard at Nottingham 22 Aug. 1642. Beheaded at Whitehall 1648, Jan. 30. L⁴ Capell, Baron of Hadham, beheaded at Westminster, March 9. A dear year; oatmeale in the north at 3d. per pound; wheate, Winchester measure, at 18d. a hoope, viz. at £2. 16. 6. per load.
" 1650. Memorandum.—Gen. Cromwell went into Scotland this year.
"Car. 2ᵈ coronatus Scotia Sconiæ juxta Johnston. Sermon preached by Mr. Robt. Douglas, minister at Edinburgh, moderator of ye Commission of ye generall assembly. 2 Kings ii. 12, 17.

"1651. Mr. Love ⎫ beheaded 22 August.
       Mr. Gibbons ⎭

The battell of Worcester 3 Sept.

James Stanley, E. of Darby, beheaded at Boulton in Lancestyre, and Captain John Benbow at Shrewsbury, 15 Oct. Sir Timothy Fetherston beheaded at Chester 22 Oct."

The register book of Coton-in-the-Elms, in the south of the county, has one remarkable entry as to the great strife :—

"In 1643 Philip Greensmith a soldier was executed upon a Tree at the green of Coton for deserting his colours, March 31st. The Tree dyed by degrees."

There were various troubles in Longford parish, about half-way between Derby and Ashborne, in 1645 :—

"The 14th day of August there were two soldiers killed, yᵉ one at Alkmanton pistolled with two bullets in at ye backe and out at ye belly, his name as it said was George Harris borne in Buckinghamshire in a towne called Grimston.

"At the same time was buried William Savage a souldier slaine at Hungrey Bentley hee was killed with a sword wherewith he had many thrusts, buried the said 14th of August.

"John Malley was attacked and had his house broken in sundry places by souldiers the first of November in the night, and because they could not get in and he would not yeild they shot him with a sluge into the head and soe died, and was buried the 2ᵈ day of November."

The following entries pertaining to the Parliamentary strife occur in the parish registers of North Wingfield :—

"1643, 13 Dec. Ann Clay, and John Platts two souldiers was buried.

"1644, 24 Aug. Thomas Slye being a parliament souldier was buried.

"1645, 6 Dec. Patrick Turrie a souldier being sleane was buried.

"1645–6, 23 Feb. Thomas Robin a souldier being a Scotish man was buried.

   ,, 8 March. . . . a souldier of the Scotts armie was buried."

13

North Wingfield is the adjacent parish to South Wingfield; the celebrated Wingfield Manor House, now a fine
ruin, stood in the latter parish. It was strongly fortified,
and formed a centre of petty warfare until dismantled by
order of the House of Commons in June 1646. It was
originally held by the Parliament, but in December 1643
was successfully stormed by the Royalists. It was
recaptured, after a long siege, by Sir John Gell for the
Commonwealth, in July 1644. In 1645–6 Derbyshire suffered
much from having the Scotch army quartered within its
limits, the inhabitants being bound to find them free quarters
and horses.

On 18th August 1648 came the rout of the great royalist
army of the Scots, under the Duke of Hamilton, at Preston.
The defeated cavalier forces disbanded themselves in Derbyshire, dispersing in various directions. Large numbers of the
infantry were arrested when vainly endeavouring to conceal
themselves amidst the hills and dales of the wild Peak
district. One of the most terrible episodes of the strife in
the Midlands was the sickening event in the church of
Chapel-en-le-Frith, which brought undying shame on all
concerned in this monstrous act of wanton overcrowding.
The incident is thus described in the parish register:—

"1648, Sept. 11. There came to this town of Scots army led by
   Duke Hambleton, and squandered by Colonell Lord Cromwell,
   sent hither prisoners from Stopford under the conduct of
   Marshall Edward Matthews, said told 1500 in number, put
   into ye church Sept. 14. They went away Sept. 30 following.
   There were buried of them before the rest went 44 prisoners,
   and more buried Oct. 2 who were not able to march, and the
   same day y^t died by the way before they come to Cheshire
   10 and more."

The register book of the old town of Bruton, Somerset,
contains the following rhymed account of the successful

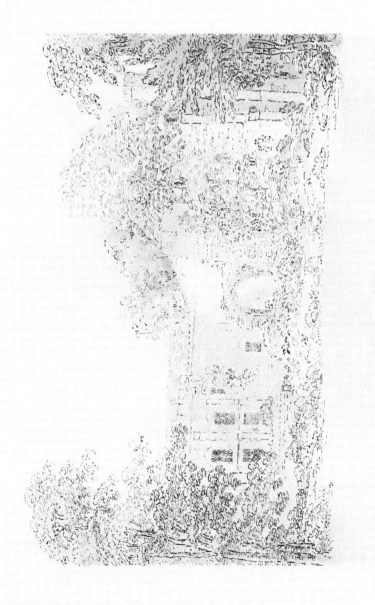

WINGFIELD MANOR HOUSE

(FROM A DRAWING BY COLONEL MACHELL, 6 AUGUST, 1755)

repulse of a Parliamentary force on 23rd February 1642-3. In honour of this event it was customary to ring the church bells on the eve of St. Matthias for at least a century after the restoration of the monarchy :—

> "All Praise and thanks to God still give ;
> For our deliverance Mathias Eve,
> By his great power wee put to flight,
> Our rageing foes that Thursday night,
> Who came to Plunder, Burne, and Slay
> And quite consume us ere the day.
> Thus he our feeble force supplide :
> In weakness most he's magnifide
> Serve god with fear, on him depend
> As then, soe ever, he will defend."

A few other historical references to the days of the Commonwealth struggle may be cited from other parts of the country. The East Riding parish of Burton Fleming has the following register entry in 1642-3 :—

"The Quene Majesty did lie at north burton with her army the 3ᵈ of March."

Queen Henrietta Maria landed at Bridlington Quay from Holland on 22nd February 1642-3, and from thence proceeded to York, where she arrived on 9th March.

Later references to the strife in Yorkshire of this year occur in the registers of St. Mary's, Beverley, for 1643 :—

"June 30. Our great scrimage in Beverley, and God gave us the victory at that tyme, ever blessed be God.

"July 30. Thirteen slaine men on ye King's party was buried.

> ˙ All our lives now at yᵉ stake,
> Lord deliver us, for Christ his sake.'

"1643 (*Allhallows, Bread Street, London*), the 6th of October was buried at Lawrence Poulteney's, Captain John Jackson. He died at Mr Gethint of his honourable wounds received at the fight of Newbury. Colonel Harvie, with his regiment of horse attending ; his troops, so near as they could to the place of his burial, and others his friends on foot, followed the bier. He died in the faith of the gospel. Received, 16s. 8d.

"1643 (*Whorlton, Durham*). Mary dau. of Jude Johnson bap. 4 Feb, w^h was the day y^t all men were warned to goe against ye Scotts and y^t day was ye heavens set on fire to warn all ye Country.

"1646 (*Bromfield, Salop*). About the midel of May nine Souldiers were buried.

"1648 (*Staindrop, Durham*). William Joplin, a souldier slaine at the seidge of Raby Castle, was buried in the church 27 Aug 1648. Mem. Many souldiers slaine before Raby Castle, which were buried in the parke and not registered.

"1648-9 (*Selattyn, Salop*). Charles the first, King of Great Brittain, France, and Ireland, Defender of the Faith, suffered Martyrdom upon a Scaffold before the gate of the Royall Palace of Whitehall in Westminster the thirtieth day of January. The memory of the just is blessed."

In reading or examining parochial registers, it is not infrequently found that they are defective or irregular from about 1642 until the establishment of civil registration in 1653. In several cases entries are made giving the reason for this irregularity, as is shown by the following extracts.

In the first register book of Glinton, Northants, occurs this entry :—

"Mr. Utting being Curate and Register in y^e time of Usurpation no notes is able to be found except this Regester is defective."

There are but few entries from 1642 to 1647 in the first register book of North Lydbury, Salop. After the year 1643 appears this memorandum :—

"These years being times of wars the Register was neglected." . . $\left.\begin{array}{c}1643\\1644\\1645\\1646\\1647\end{array}\right\}$

"*Kibworth*, co. *Leicester*. Ano Dni 1641. Know all men, that the reason why little or nothing is registered from this year 1641 until the year 1649, was the civil wars between King Charles and his Parliament, which put all into a confusion till then; and neither minister nor people could quietly stay at home for one party or the other.

" 1643 (*Burton Latimer, Northants*). The three yeares following were most of them lost in the tyme of the warre; w^t could be found was incerted as appeares. Michael Swinson being then clerke (as hee saith) lost the notes of the names wch hee had taken in paper, so that they could not be ingrafted. As of Baptizings, so of marriages and burials.''

There is something pathetic in the terms of the brief entry amid the registers of St. Bridget's, Chester—

" 1643. Here the Register is defective till 1653. The tymes were such——"

A great contrast in length is afforded by the explanatory note in the registers of Maids Moreton, Bucks :—

" A.D. 1642. This year the worst of Parliaments wickedly rebelling against the best of Princes King Charles 1 ; the kingdom underwent most sad affliction, especially churches, whilst they pretended reformation, were everywhere robbed and ruined by the Rebells. In this Church of Moreton the windows were broken, a costly desk in the form of a spread eagle gilt, on which we used to lay Bp. Jewel's works, doomed to perish as an abominable idoll ; the Cross (which, with its fall, had like to have broke out the brains of him who did it) cut off the steeple by the soldiers at the command of one called Colonel Purefoy of Warwickshire. He carried away what he could, and, among other things, the Register was hid ; and for that cause is not absolutely perfect for divers years, tho' I have used my best intelligence to record as many particulars as I could come by."

" 1644 (*Croston, Lancashire*). From May 20 till Feb 2 this boke hath bee neclected by reason of wars.

" 1648 (*Shipton, Salop*). From the yeare of our Lord God 1644 unto the yeare of our Lord God 1648 This Register Booke was taken out of Shipton church and was not to be found: the Chest wherein it was kept being Broken up by souldiers, whereby it cometh to passe that all Burings Weaddings and all Children that were Baptized betwixt the yeare 1644 and 1648 in the parish of Shipton were not herein registed."

The Tamworth parish registers have a variety of entries relative to the great strife, and to the consequent change in matters ecclesiastical :—

"June, 1643. Towards the latter end of this month the towne and castle of Tamworth were taken in from the enemye by the Parlements for us under the command of Coll : W. Purefrey.

"September, 1643. About the begining of this moneth Mr Theoph. Lord was called to bee the preacher at Tamworth both by the Governor and Towne but was forbid to doe any servise publikely excepting preaching as his duty.

"May, 1644. About the latter end of this moneth of May the honorable Comittee of Safety for the county of Warw: at Coventry sitting fixed Theophi Lord the preacher to supply the whole duty of the min^r in Tamworth the former man that challenged the place to be his goeing away about 2 months before, and never acquainting the Towne.

"19 June, 1646. Buried the Body of Henry son of Tho : Piccard of Camb: an infant, his father Thom : was slaine by the enemy in Litchfield close about March last."

The closing incidents of the life of the ill-fated Charles are thus noted in the registers of Carisbrooke, Isle of Wight :—

"1648. The 6th day of September. King Charles went from the Castell to Newport to treat, and the last day of November he went from Newport to Hurste Castle to presonn cared away by to tropes of horse."

The Protestation and the Covenant were two entirely separate matters, not infrequently confused by local historians and register students. Signatures to both of these formal declarations are now and again found in registers or among parish documents.

The Protestation, an idea of Pym's, was an undertaking to defend the "True Reformed Protestant Religion," etc., i 6   a Solemn   4 3

LEAGVE AND COVENANT,

for Reformation, and defence of
Religion, the Honour and happinesse
of the King, and the Peace and safety of the
three kingdoms of

ENGLAND, SCOTLAND, and IRELAND.

We Noblemen, Barons, knights, Gentlemen, Citizens, Burgesses, Ministers of the Gospel, and Commons of all sorts in the Kingdoms of England, Scotland, and Ireland, by the Providence of God living under one King, and being of one reformed Religion, having before our eyes the Glory of God, and the advancement of the Kingdome of our Lord and Saviour Jesus Christ, the Honour and happinesse of the Kings Majesty and his posterity, and the true publique Liberty, Safety, and Peace of the Kingdoms, wherein every ones private Condition is included, and calling to minde the treacherous and bloody Plots, Conspiracies, Attempts, and Practices of the Enemies of God, against the true Religion, and professors thereof, in all places, especially in these three kingdoms ever since the Reformation of Religion, and how much their rage, power and presumption are of late, and at this time increased and exercised, whereof the deplorable state of the Church and kingdom of Ireland, the distressed estate of the Church and kingdom of England, and the dangerous State of the Church and kingdom of Scotland, are present and publique Testimonies. We have now at last (after other means of Supplication, Remonstrance, Protestations, and Sufferings) for the preservation of our selves and our Religion, from utter Ruine and Destruction, according to the commendable practice of these kingdoms in former times, and the Example of Gods People in other Nations, after mature deliberation, resolved and determined to enter into a mutuall and solemn League and Covenant, wherein we all subscribe, and each one of us for himselfe, with our hands lifted up to the most high God, do sweare;

MArch 22   1643

THE SOLEMN LEAGUE AND COVENANT—PREAMBLE

taken by the Lords and Commons in May 1641, and sent out for signature throughout the country. It seems, however, to have been only signed to any great extent in those parishes where the minister or squire, or both, were of pronounced Puritan tendencies.

The Covenant was a solemn league, originated in Scotland in 1638, to oppose the projects of the king, and adopted in a modified form as a treaty between England and Scotland by the Parliaments of the former on 25th September 1643. It consisted of six articles, mainly designed for the preservation of the reformed church in Scotland and for the reformation of religion in England and Ireland (including the extirpation of both popery and prelacy), and also for maintaining the liberties of Parliament. It was ordered to be signed by all over eighteen years of age, and the names of those who refused to be reported to Parliament.

A full record of the wordy Protestation occurs in the register of Appleby Magna in the midst of the entries of 1648. To it is prefixed a list of 144 names, beginning with those of Sir William Joanes Knt, and Thomas Mould, rector :—

"The Protestation made by the house of Parliament to be taken of everyone from the age of 16 years and upwards. Anno Dom. 1641, Feb. 27, I A.B. doe, in the presince of Almighty God, promise vow and protest to maintaine and defend, as farre as lawfully I may, with my life power and estate of the true reformed Protestant religion expressed in the doctrine of the Church of England, against all Popery and Popish innovations, within this Realme contrary to the said doctrine. And according to the duty of my Allegiance his Majesties Royal Person Honor and Estate, As also the power and priveledge of Parliament the lawful rights and liberties of the subject, and every person that maketh his protestation, in whatsoever he shall doe in the lawful pursuance of the same, And to my power and as farre as lawfully I may, I will oppose and by all good ways and means endeavour to bring to condigne punishment all such as shall either by force, practice, counsells, plotts, conspiracies or otherwise doe anything to the contrary of anything in this present protestation contained, and further that I shall in all just and honourable wayes endeavour to preserve the union and peace between the three kingdoms of England Scotland and Ireland, and neither for hope, feare, nor other respect shall relinquish this promise, vow, and protestation."

The register book of Great Doddington, Northants, has an entry to this effect :—

"We whose names are underwritten have made the Protestation framed and made by the House of Commons. Antho. Warters cler."

Then follow seven written names and forty-nine marks.

At East Haddon, in the same county, are exactly one hundred signatures or marks appended in the register to the following declaration :—

"The Prokylation made by the Parliament the third of May anno domini 1641 was taken and made by all us whose names and marks are here under written and set doune (as was presented and thought fit May twentie fift Anno predicto) the twentie of June eodem Anno Domini 1641."

The earliest register book of Pentrich, Derbyshire, contains 180 signatures and marks appended to this Protestation, extending over six pages. The Kedleston registers of the same county contain 36 signatures to the like protest ; though in this latter case it was not read and signed until July 1644.

As to the Covenant, it was insisted on by civil and military authorities rather than by the ministers, and hence the names who signed it are seldom met with in registers. At Cherry Burton, Yorks, there is a registry entry of November 1646 to the effect that

"All these tooke the Scottish Covenant ; under Mr. Tho. Micclethwayte."

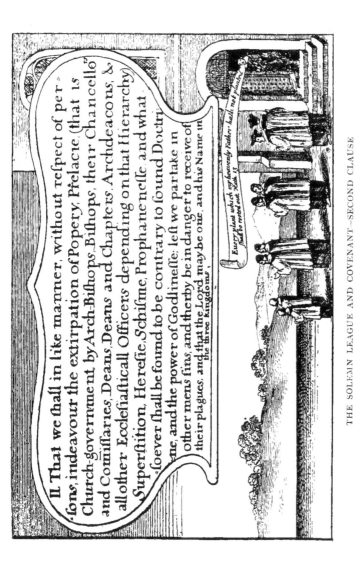

II. That we shall in like manner, without respect of persons, indeavour the extirpation of Popery, Prelacie, (that is Church-government by Arch-Bishops, Bishops, their Chancello͞rs and Comīssaries, Deans, Deans and Chapters, Archdeacons, & all other Ecclesiasticall Officers depending on that Hierarchy) Superstition, Heresie, Schisme, Prophanenesse, and what soever shall be found to be contrary to sound Doctrine, and the power of Godlinesse: lest we partake in other mens sins, and therby be in danger to receive of their plagues, and that the Lord may be one, and his Name in the three kingdoms;

Every plant which my heavenly Father hath not planted shall be rooted out. Matth. 15

THE SOLEMN LEAGUE AND COVENANT—SECOND CLAUSE

Fifty-six names are appended.

The death of the Protector and of his Relict both obtained register notice.

A Yorkshire parish register may be cited, from among several others, as containing a precise record of the Protector's death :—

> "1658 (*Hackness, Yorks*). His Highness the Lord Protector dyed the 3 day of September. And Lord Richard his sonn was proclaimed in his stead in London on Saturday being the next day, and in Yorke and Hull upon the Tewsday then followinge."

As a sequel to this, the actual registry entry of the burial of Cromwell's widow may be cited :—

> "1665 (*Norborough, N'hants*). Elizabeth, the relict of Oliver Cromwell, sometime Pro : of England, was buried Nov. 19."

Elizabeth Cromwell died at the house of her son-in-law, John Cleypole, of Norborough, who was Master of the Horse to the Protector, and a member of his short-lived House of Lords. Cleypole was responsible for the mutilation of the Norborough register book, from which the entries between 1613 and 1646 have been torn out, as is recorded in the following memorandum :—

> "The reason of this defect in the register was because one Mr. John Cleypole, a factious gentleman, then living in the parish of Northborough, caused the register to be taken away from mee, John Stoughton, then rector, for which I was by the Ecclesiastical Court then holden at St. Martin's adjudged for satisfaction the sum of £2. 10s."

John Stoughton was rector from 1659 until his death on 15th March 1695–6.

The exuberant royalty occasionally displayed in registers at the time of the Restoration has now and again a suspiciously time-serving flavour about it. For instance, the initials appended to the following outburst in the register

book of Barton Seagrave, Northants, show that it was
written by one William Henchman, who could not have
been a churchman, and who had been content to accept
the living at the hands of schismatics in 1657!

"Memorandum in perpetuum. King Charles yᵉ second (after
twelve years exile) was (by a miracle of mercy) restored unto his
three kingdoms (his undoubted right) May 29, 1660. Soli Deo
gloria. W. H."

The following, from the register of St. Chad's, Shrewsbury, has a more genuine ring :—

"1660, May 1. King Charles the second entered London one ye
29 of this instant May after 16 yeares exile and in the 12 yeare
of his raine it being the day one wich he was borne and the
30 yeare of his age which day is yearly to be observed in memory
of his Majestie's happie restoration whom god grant long to
raine. A blessing to his Church and victorious over his
enemies.
"1661 (*Tamworth*), April 23. Coronation of our Dread Soveraigne
Lord Charles the Second of England, Scotland, France, and
Ireland, King Defender of the Faith whom God long preserve."

The register of Portsmouth parish has an elaborate
and illuminated entry of the marriage of Charles II
with "the most illustrious Princesse Dona Catarina, Infanta
of Portugall." They were married at Portsmouth by the
Bishop of London on 22nd May 1662.

John Wiseman, vicar of Rowington, Warwickshire,
ejected during the Commonwealth, on returning to his
benefice in the autumn of 1662, wrote in the registers :—

"By usurped Authority these many yeares wasted wrongfully out
of my liveinge."

After entering a baptism on March 14th 1662–3, he added :—

"Thus farr for halfe a yeare upon my returning to my place
againe wrote by me
"JOHN WISEMAN, Vicar of Rowington"

The Rye House Plot is commemorated in the following entry:—

" 1683 (*Bamburgh, Northumberland*), September 9, being ye thanksgiving day for ye preservation of our gracious king his dearest brother from ye bloody conspiracy of ye fanaticks and non-conforming ministers now in hold as being of ye conspiritors. . . ."

There is at least one ill-judged register panegyric on Charles II, the most selfish and sensual of our kings; it is set forth in the parochial records of Chapel-en-le-Frith:—

" Upon Friday, ye sixth day of this month, did our most gracious and sovereign Lord King Charles ye 2^a of ever-blessed memory depart this life, having reigned six and thirtie years and a weeke, to ye getting himself great honour and love, both in foreign parts and at home, for he very much endeavoured ye establishment of peace, justice, and piety, and by his wisdom was much prevalent therein. England did (as indeed there was great cause) very much bewail and lament ye death and loss of soe gracious a king. After his death ye Imperial Crowne of England did lineally descend to his royale Highness James, Duke of York and Albaine, brother to ye late King, who was crowned King of England, etc., upon St. George's day being 23^d of April, 1685."

The Duke of Monmouth's rebellion of 1685 has left its stamp on the parish registers of Taunton, where he was proclaimed King on 20th of June. He was defeated at Sedgemoor, near Bridgwater, on 6th July, and beheaded on Tower Hill on 15th July. Judge Jeffreys began his infamous "Bloody Assize" at Taunton in the following August. The registers of St. Mary Magdalene's were much interrupted by the rebellion during June. Two soldiers were buried in July 1685; "a King's soldier" and "two Rebel soldiers" in August; in September four rebels were executed, six rebel soldiers and one king's soldier buried; and in October, November, and December, and up to April 1686, are numerous like entries.

In the burial register of the parish of St. James, Taunton, the following entries occur under 1685 :—

"July 9 was buried John Gotnell, executed for treason against his majesty.

"The same day was buried John Birges, executed for treason against his majesty.

"The 9 day, was executed John Grinslade, for treason against his majesty, but buried the 10 day of July, in the year 1685."

These entries are followed by those of six others executed on 9th of July, but buried on the 10th. These nine persons were probably part of the nineteen executed by Colonel Kirke on the Cornhill, under martial law, on his arrival from Sedgemoor on Thursday, the 9th July.

Judge Jeffreys caused nineteen others to be executed on 30th September 1685. The burials of two of these are entered in the registers of St. James' on 1st of October, and of one on 2nd of October.

The advent of the Prince of Orange also obtained register notice :—

"1688 (*Wadhurst, Sussex*), Nov 4. The Prince of Orange invaded England and landed at Torbay nigh to Dartmouth.

"Feb. 13th. William and Mary were proclaimed King and Queen of England : a thanksgiving day for deliverance from papacy and arbitrary power."

The following is the last historical entry for which space can be found :—

"1697 (*St. Mary Magdalene, Canterbury*), October ye . . . the Peace betwixt England and France was proclaimed with drums and trumpet. Ed. Beverton Mayor."

CHAPTER XI

STORMS, FROSTS, AND FIRES

Storm of 1606-7—The Snowstorm of 1614-15—Later seventeenth century storms—The frost of 1683-4—"The great storm" of 1703—A late snowstorm—Aurora Borealis of 1716 — Earthquakes — Other eighteenth-century storms — The Cherry Burton register — Eclipses — Comets — Fires — The Great Fire of London

STORMS, frosts, fires, and other unusual natural occurrences, such as eclipses, comets, and meteors, are occasionally recorded in parish registers. The following are selected examples :—

" 1606-7 (*Barnstaple, Devon*). In the 20th day of Januarie there was suche a mightie storme and tempeste from the river of Barnstaple with the comminge of the tyde, that y^t caused much lose of goods and howses to the valewe of towe thousand pownds, besyde the death of one James Froste, and towe of his children, the which his howse fell downe upon them and killed them. This storme began at 3 of clocke in the morninge and continued tyll 12 of clock of same daye. Per me Robte Langdon, Clarcke, teste.

" 1606-7 (*Ibid.*). In the year of o^r Lord God 1607, in Januarie, the river of Barnstaple was so frozen that manye hundred people did walke over hande in hande from the Bridge unto Castell Rocke with staves in ther hands as safe as they could go on the drye grounde, being ye very same moneth the floud was.

" teste ROBTE LANGDON, Clarck of Barum

" 1607 (*Boughton, Northants*). This yeare (1607) on the tuesday in Whitson weeke there fell such a hayle storme that it brake the strawe of the rye then growinge in the bridge Fielde that it coulde not growe to the greate losse of all the inhabitants and did little hurt in any fielde but this, the hailstones were generally 3 inches about, some cornerde and some flatt like fygges. God grant us repentance."

Towards the end of January 1614–15 there began a series of heavy snowstorms throughout England, which continued, without any long pauses, until the middle of March. The fullest and most remarkable of the register entries of this series of storms are those of Yorkshire and Derbyshire.

In the register book of Beeston-next-Mileham, Norfolk, there is a very long entry recording this great snow, which began on 21st of January 1614–15, and did not begin to melt away until the 16th of the following March. Three men were found dead in the open fields.

"(*Framlingham, Suffolk*). The 21st of Januarie Ano 1614 ther was sutch a Water at the Mill Bridge as the like was never scene in any man's time then lyveynge, and the next daye began the great Snowe, wch laye full seaven weekes."

"(*Almandbury, York*). In this year 1614–15 so great a fall of snow as was not known in the memory of any living; far exceeding that in 1540 in magnitude and duration; in which many travellers as well as inhabitants at Saddleworth perished."

"(*Alstonfield, Staffs*), Jan 20: 1614–15. The great Snow began to fall, and so continued increaseing the most dayes until the 12 of March."

"(*Morley, Derbyshire*), March 12 (1614–15), ye great snow broke wch had continewed from Friday seaven weakes before.

"Note. This yeare after the great Snowe followed a great Drought which continued the most part of Soumer."

"(*Youlgreave, Derbyshire*).—*A Memoriall of the Great Snow*

Beginninge   This year 1614–5 Jan. 16 began the greatest
Jan. 16.   snow snow (sic) which ever fell uppon the earth,
               within man's memorye. It covered the earth
An elne deep   fyve quarters deep upon the playne. And for
uppon the   heaps or drifts of snow, they were very deep; so
playne ground. that passengers both horse and foot, passed

over gates, hedges and walles. It fell at 10
severall tymes and the last was the greatest, to
the greate admiration and feare of all the land,

East, West, for it came from the fowre p^{ts} of the world, so
North, South. that all cuntryes were full, yea the South p^{te} as
March 12. well as these mountaynes. It continued by
daily encreasing until the 12th day of March
(without the sight of any earth, eyther uppon
hilles or valleyes) uppon w^h day (being the
Sabboth. Lorde's Daye) it began to decreasse ; and so by
little and little consumed and wasted away, till
End 28 Maii. the eight and twentyth day of May for then all
the heapes or drifts of snow were consumed,
except one uppon Kinder's Scowt, w^h lay till
Witson week and after."

" Hynderances and Losses in this Peake Cūtry by the
Snowe Abovesayd

" 1. It hyndered the seed tyme.   A very cold spring.

" 2. It consumed much fodder (multitude of sheep, cause, continuance of cold wether).

" 3. And many wanted fewell ; otherwyse few were smothered in
the fall or drownded in the passage ; in regard the floods of water
were not great though many.

'The Name of our Lord be Praysed.'

"The spring was so cold and so late that much cattell was in
very great daunger and some dyed.

" There also fell ten lesse snowes in Aprill, some a foote deep,
some lesse, but none continued long.   Uppon May day, in the
morning, instead of fetching fflowers, the youthes brought in flakes
of snow, w^h lay above a foot deep uppon the moores and mountaynes.
All these aforesayd snows vanished away and thoed with little or no
rayne."

" 1615—A Dry Summer

" There was no rayne fell uppon the earth from the 25th day
of March until the 2nd day of May, and there then was no shower ;
after which there fell none tyll the 18th day of June, an then there
fell another ; after y^t there fell none at all tyll the 4th day of August,
after which tyme there was sufficient rayne uppon the earth ; so
that the greattest p^t of this land, specially the south p^{ts} were burnt

upp, both corne and hay. An ordinary Sumer load of hay was at 2 *li.* and little or none to be got for money.

" This pᵗ of the peake was very sore burnt upp, only Lanki-shyre and Cheshyre had rayne ynough all the Sumer ; and both corne and hay sufficient.

" There was very little rayne fell the last winter, but snow onely."

Other storms of the seventeenth century are occasion-ally commemorated.

" 1617 (*Etton, Northants*). About the 25 of February it began and continued snowing until the sixth day at night of March. And the summer before was great store of Rayne and floode.

"H. MAPLESDEN, Curate "

The registers of Castle Church, Stafford, have the follow-ing entry under 1621 :—

" The windy Thursday was 21 March 1593, and the windy Monday was 28 Jan. 1627."

" 1655 (*Howden, Yorks*). This yeare in ye Moneth of August fell a great Raine wherr in some places the waters exceeded their Boundes swept away much Hay some Corne, and other Hay corrupted by the unseasonable Season (yᵉ like scarce memor-able). It enlarged the price of Corne yet in mercie ye Lord comunicates above our deserts his Blessings towards us.

" 1655 (*Ibid.*). In yᵉ moneth (December) ye River Ouze was (in some places) soe frozen yt at Langrick and also betweene Aersmouth and Booth people went over on yᵉ Ice yet not much Snow.

" 1660 (*Hackness, Yorks*). Be it remembered that the Eight day of December in the Eveninge aboute Fower or five of the Clocke there began to arise a great storme of winde and raine and Mr. Chapman and myselfe were comeinge from Scarbr. then but the storme was soe forceable that we were faine to turne backe and lye at Scarbr. that night, but the storme of the winde did waxe more forceable in soe much that it unbuyred many houses of Thatch, blew downe many windmills and Trees in Orchards and other places and continued untill abowte one of the Clocke in the night. It may well be called the greate windy Satterday night for noe man liveinge never sawe such a winde many hay

Stackes and Corne Stackes I beleive were blowne downe at that time.   JOHN RICH

" 1662 (*Tasley, Salop*), Dec. 16. John son of John Craffe and Ann, of the p. of Morvell, was bap. here, there being a great flood that day, soe that they could not goe to their parish Church.

" 1673 (*St. Werburgh's, Derby*), July 19th, being Sabbath day at night, there was a great Floud. The water was two Foot high in the middle ally, it weare masured, so that it came into Cheasts and wett all the writings. Such a Flood was not known in our agge before.

" 1676–7 (*Darley Dale, Derbyshire*). A great frost which began at Martimas 1676 and continued till January 3, 1677. Ye Derwent was actually frozen, and att ye dissolving of the frost a great flood, and incredible quantities of ice was brought on the water banks into tollerable inclosed grounds, and up to the churchyard steps.

"THOMAS MOSSLEY, Rector "

The frost of 1683–84 was one of terrible severity; the forest trees were split; most of the hollies were killed; myriads of birds perished; and the Thames was frozen over from December to 4th of February.

" 1683 (*Wing, Rutland*). This yeare the longest and the sharpest frost that ever was knowne. All things whatever that had any moistnes in them were frozen both within dores and without for a long while together.

" *Ubley, Somerset.* In the yeare 1683 was a mighty great frost, the like was not seene in England for many ages. It came upon a very deep snow, which fell immediately after Christmas, and it continued untill Ladyday. The ground was not open nor the snowe cleane gone off the earth in thirteene weeks. Somm of the snow remained at mindipe (Mendips) till midsummer. It was soe deepe and driven with the winde against the hedges and stiles, that the next morning after it fell men could not goe to their grounds to serve their cattell without great danger of being buried, for it was above head and shoulders in many places and some it did burie—did betooken the burieing of many more which came to pass before the end of the yeare; but in a few days the frost came soe fearce, that people did goe

14

upon the top of it over wals and stiles as on levell ground, not seeing hardly where they was, and many men was forced to keep their cattell untill the last, in the same ground they was in at first, because they could not drive them to any other place, and did hew the ice every day for water, by reason of the sharpness of the frost and the deepness of the snow. Som that was travelling on mindipe did travell till they could travell no longer, and then lye down and dye, but mortality did prevail most among them that could travell worst, the sharpness of the season tooke off the most parte of them that was aged and of them that was under infirmities, the people did die so fast that it was the greatest parte of their work (which was appointed to doe that worke) to burie the dead; it being a day's work for two men, or two days' work for one man to make a grave. It was almost as hard a work to hew a grave out in the earth, as in the rock, the frost was a foot and halfe and two foot deepe in the dry earth, and where there was moisture and watter did runn, the ice was a yard or fower foot thick, in soe much that ye people did keepe market on the River at London: 'God doth scatter his ice like morsels, man cannot abide his cold.' Psalme 147, 17.

"1683–4 (*Holy Rood, Southampton*). This yeare was a great Frost, which began before Christmasse, soe that ye 3rd and 4th dayes of this month February ye River of Southampton was frossen all over and covered with ice from Calshott Castle to Redbridge, and Tho: Martaine ma^r of a vessell went upon ye ice from Beray near Marshwood to Milbrook-point. And ye river at Ichen Ferry was so frossen over that severall persons went from Beauvais Hill to Bitterne Farme, forwards and backwards. "1683 (*Barrow, Derbyshire*). Mem^d that the great frost begun in November, and lasted about 13 weeks, ending in February."

The following comprehensive entry as to the storms of the end of the seventeenth and beginning of the eighteenth century occurs in the register of Donington, Shropshire :—

"1696, Feb. 7th. Wee had then a most Violent Storm or rather a Sort of Hurricane, wch blew West and N. West; it blew down 2 Barns at ye parsonage of Donington and did great spoyls in most Towns of England, the Cathedral of St. Chad at Lichfield received great Damage, neare 1000 £ loss; 3 young men were

killed at Pepperhill by the Falling Chymneys, and many lost
their Lives in other places.

" 1700, Feb. 5th and 6th. Wee had great Winds, and very violent
from ye same quarter, wch did much Damage.   Ye like again
on Xmas Day, 1701, which also did much hurt."

The Great Storm of November 26–27, 1703, which devastated England, destroying the Eddystone lighthouse and
doing incalculable damage in a few hours, is commemorated
in several registers.   We can only quote from two :—

" 1703 (*St. Mary Magdalene, Canterbury*). Memorandum : That in
ye yeare 1703 there hapened in ye month of November on
ye 26 day a mighty dreadful tempestious wind which there has
not bin ye like in oure age.

" 1703 (*St. Oswald, Durham*). Mem^d that on ye 27th Nov 1703
was ye greatest hurricane and storme that ever was known in
England ; many churches and houses were extreamley shattered
and thousands of trees blown down ; thirteen or more of her
Majestyes men of war were cast away and above two thousand
seamen perished in them.   N.B. the Storme came no further
north than Yarmouth."

There was an exceptionally late and heavy fall of snow
in many parts of England in 1713 :—

" 1713 (*Lowick, Northants*), April 13 being ye Munday after Easter
week there fell a great snow and lay all night and hung on y^e
trees next day as at X'mas."

The celebrated Aurora Borealis of March 1716 extended
from the west of Ireland to the confines of Russia.

" 1715–16 (*Chapel-en-le-Frith, Derbyshire*), Feb. 1. On that day there
was an extreme wind.   It blew the weathercock off the steeple
and brake it in pieces, and a great Ash down in the Churchyard ; with vast great loss to most people in their houses, some
being blown downe.

    "Upon the 30th day of March, 1716, between the hours
of nine and twelve at night, there appeared in North and
Northwest a strange sort of light in the air ; it streamed up

like unto long picks, of a large bigness, some black, some the colours of the rainbow, some a whitish colour, and at last it broke into flashes like lightening or smoke, as if it had been smoke of guns, as fast as you could clap your hands, very terrible to behold. It lasted so for the space of an hour, and then turned to streams again. It happened to be so the year before within one day of the same time of month, but was no lightning at that tyme, but was far lighter the year before, for there were several who could read in a book at that time of night. I have seen it myself several nights besides, but not so violent as it was these two nights, but could never hear from any what the cause could be."

Earthquakes are occasionally named :—

" 1727 (*St. Pancras, Exeter*). On the 19th of Jully between foure and five of the clocke in the morning, all the houses in Exeter did shake with an Earthquake that people shake in their beds from one side to the other, and was al over England, and in some places beyond sea, but doed but little damage : tis of a certain truth.

" 1750 (*Rothwell, Northants*). On Sunday Sept. 30th We were terribly alarmed with a violent shock of an earthquake. It was felt at this Town about half an hour past twelve at noon. I was at that time administering the Holy Sacrament, and was with the whole Congregation in the greatest surprise. Its first approach was heard like a mighty wind, or rather the driving of many coaches. The motion was from S.W. to N.E. The continuance was as near as I could judge about half a minute and was very dreadful and awful. The earth was sensibly perceived to heave under our feet. The church tottered to its Foundation, and the east window shook most violently, as if it was all coming down and from the Roof, which we thought was falling on us, we heard dreadful crackings three or four times as if great prodigious weights were flung upon it. In Fear and Trembling we expected instant Death either by being crushed under the ruins of the church or else that we should have been swallowed up alive : but as Almighty God directed, no harm happened unto us. They who were in the Churches or Houses were more sensibly affected and felt it most than those who were walking. It

was felt in the Neighbouring Towns of Northamptonshire and
Leicestershire.　　　　　　　　Thomas Barrett, Vicar "

The following are among other eighteenth-century storms
named in registers :—

"1746 (*Hunton, Kent*). On Midsummer day this year happened
the greatest storm of Thunder and Lightening Wind and Rain
yt was ever known in the memory of man.
"1749 (*Baslow, Derbyshire*), Augt. 22d. The same night was the
most terrible for lightning, thunder, and rain there was ever
known in this age.
"1763 (*Hunton, Kent*). On nineteenth day of August this year
happened a much greater storm of Thunder Wind Hail and
Rain than in the year forty six. The hailstones bein Six and
Seven Inches round.
"1767 (*Askham, Westmoreland*). Memorandum that in the night
between Jan. yᵉ 10th and 11th there happened the greatest
fall of snow I ever remember; the snow was so deep that I
could not go to Church, Jan. the 11th being Sunday, an
accident that never happened to me before in the course of
my ministry, and I am now in the forty-eightte of it.
　　　　　　　　　"William M'Iver, vicar of Askham
"1795 (*Prees, Salop*), February. The largest Flood and the severest
Frost that has been ever known by the oldest inhabitant,
Mr. Morleton." [The great frost of 1794–5 lasted from
24 Dec. to 24 Feb.]
"1807 (*Eaton-under-Heywood, Salop*), 22nd July. A most awful
and tremendous storm of Thunder, Lightning, Hail and Rain.
Hail fell in this neighbourhood 4 to 5 inches in length
resembling broken ragged Ice. The wheat cut off at the
heads, windows destroyed, everywhere the Hail could reach.
Fruit and Gardens nearly destroyed. In short—It was an
awful visitation; may it ever be remembered in this neighbourhood.　　　Rd. Fleming A.B., at that period Curate "

The Cherry Burton, E. R. Yorks registers contain
several noteworthy entries towards the close of the seventeenth century :—

"1684. On the 12 of November were seene two sunns in the

Firmam^t betwixt twelve and one of the clock att Bps Burton.

"1687-8. Memorandum upon Sunday Febr: 12th there happened about halfe a quarter before foure in ye afternoone, after sermon, a sudden violent pulsation, or as it were a Mighty Thump in ye earth tht is a kind of earthquake, tht resembled the report of a cannon, wth some noise before and after, and causing the earth and the buildings thereon to shake, but it lasted but a moment in this place. Ita testor. Cherryburton, Febr: 12, 1687.   JOHN JOHNSON R^r *ibid.*

"1692. Decemb. 8th (which was the day of ye Death of the second squire) about 2 a clocke in ye night was a violent Tempest of Wind whc overthrew ye Chantry Helmes and the Chymnez of ye Lodging parlour of the parsonage house, whc was rectifyed the July following.   JOHN JOHNSON Rector

"1696. In February or March were seene Two sons in ye morning Tide by 2 Inhabitants."

Eclipses are occasionally mentioned in registers :—

"1597 (*St. Nicholas, Newcastle*). Darke Satterday was 25 Feb. 1597.

"1652 (*Brignal, Yorkshire*), Mar. 29. The darke Monday the sunn beinge eclipsed 10 in 12—that is ten parts in twelve darkened, so that th day seemed as twilight.

"1699 (*St. Andrew, Newcastle*), Sep. 13. The Sun and the Mune was in the clips betwixt nin and ten in the morning and was darkish about three quarters of a hour."

The mention of Comets or Meteors also occurs from time to time, of which the following entries are examples :—

"1618 (*Morley, Derbyshire*). Memorand. that this yeare Novemb. the 25th and for three weekes after, the blazing starre appeared in the East and did retrograde. January the 11th the Whitehall was burned and Queen Anne died the spring followinge.

"1662 (*Hackness, Yorks*). Be it remembered that on Thursday the xxxth of October I went to my doore aboute brake a day and to my thinkeinge y^t did lighten and I looked towarde the weste and there I beheld a Blazeinge Starr that blazed out with a longe fiery blazeing streame and somewhat thicke and broade at the end thereof and continued not longe but wasted away.   JOHN RICHARDSON

"(*Crowhurst, Sussex*). A Blazeing starre appeared in ye Kgdom in ye yeare 1680, it did first shew itselfe 10th of December y^t yeare 80 which did stream from ye South west to ye middle of ye heavn broader y^n a Raine Bow by farre and continued till ye latter end of February."

The following are a few of the register entries relative to disasters by fire :—

"1612 (*Barnstaple, Devon*). In the yere of O^r Lorde God 1612, in the 5th day of the monethe of Auguste was the towne of Teverton burned the second tyme with fyer to the number of 260 dwellynge houses. Mr. Pentecost Doddridge, Mayor of Barnstaple.   ROBT. LANGDON, Clarcke

"1615 (*Howden, Yorks*). Pity y^t sad accident upon Saturday the fift of this moneth happened at Fockerthrop in ye house of Francis Blancherd, husbandman, being himselfe his wife and two sons at Holden Market one at home and some neighbour servant came to fetch fire (ye wind southward), it seemed some sparke scattered in ye dunghill kindled in ye straw ascended the barne and dwelling house being remote from help, it consumed there his substance (oh hevie returne) the Lord in mercie divert the judgements our sins soe much deserve.

"1647 (*Bruton, Somerset*) :—

> By furious flames this 13th day of August
> Brewton was like to be consumed to dust,
> But God in mercy quenched the flames indeed
> As then, so always hees our help at need.

"1665 (*Newport, Salop*). Memorandum that on Friday in the afternoone, beinge the 19 day of May, Anno 1665, happened a sudden furyous fire, which began in the house of Richard Shelton, a smith, then livinge at the Chitlop, which by Saturday noone following were burned out of habitation about 162 families, besides the better part of 10 more houses puld to pieces and much prejudiced. Tho. Munk. Newport sin no more, lest a worst punishment befall the. The losse to Newport wase 30,000 pounds.   T. MILLINGTON "

There is an incidental reference to the Great Fire of London in the registers of All Hallows, Bread Street :—

"1667, June 19, was born and christened Michael, Son of Michael and Phebe Pyndar; but, by reason of the dreadful fire, was born in Coleman Street, in Sir William Bateman's House, where many of this parish for some time inhabited."

It would appear from this entry that Sir William Bateman was one of the many charitably disposed citizens who put his mansion at the disposal of the houseless.

The church of St. Dionis Backchurch was one of the many destroyed by the fire. The following are two of several records of interment in the ruins :—

"1667–8, Jan. 10. Mr. Francis Tryon was buried in the ruins of the chansel. Mrs. Martha Bennett, wife of Mr. John Bennett, Pewterer, that dwelt in the parish at the time of the great fire, dyed the seaventeenth day of May, and was buried in the ruines of the Chansell the twentieth day of May.

"Mr. Thomas Stenhouse, Apothecary, an Inhabitant in the Parish at the time of the said fire, dyed the thirteenth day of June, and was buried in the ruines of the Church, in the body or middle part of the Church the fourteenth day of June.

"1729 (*Bozeat, Northants*). Be it known to succeeding ages that Tuesday the ninth day of September Anno 1729 a suddain and violent fire broke out in the Parish of Bozeat about two of the clock afternoon, at one Widow Keech's, who was baking upon the hearth in a poor house amongst the churchyard houses, which in the space of three or four hours (with a strong wind) consumed fourty one Dwelling houses, besides all outbuildings (not five shillings worth of useful Timber saved). Four farms were burnt with full crops of Harvest and great quantitys of Household Goods. The Bell-frames were twice on Fire. The whole loss amounting to near Four Thousand Pounds. Blessed be God there were no lives lost, nor anybody hurt amidst so great danger. And whereas the Vicarage House was burnt with the Register Book, Thomas Drake, present a new one."

CHAPTER XII

OLLA PODRIDA

Penance for incontinency and slander—Penance for marrying
deceased wife's sister—Tollesbury font inscription—Flesh
in Lent—Butchers' recognisances—Number of communicants
— Altar wine — Benefit of clergy — Witches — Gipsies —
Parochial whippings—Records of exhibitions—Tithing notes

UNDER this heading are gathered together a considerable variety of subjects which occur with greater or less
frequency in parish registers, but which could not
readily be included in any of the previous chapters.

Penance of a public character by no means came to an
end with the Reformation. Its prevalence during Elizabethan,
Stuart, and post-Restoration times depended largely on the
vigour with which the archdeacon and his officials carried
on their duties. For the most part the archidiaconal courts
were held with regularity, and the churchwardens urged to
make due presentments. On conviction for divers of the
less serious offences, such as non-payment of tithes or Easter
dues, or for the non-observance of Sundays or Saints' Days,
offenders were admonished, and if obstinate excommunicated; but in such cases absolution and discharge could
usually be obtained on payment of a fine. In proved cases
of slander and of incontinence, humiliating public penances
were, however, as a rule exacted. The ordinary penance for
such offences was the standing in church during service time
(and occasionally also in the market-place) and reciting a

form of confession. In the eighteenth century the custom prevailed in London diocese, and probably elsewhere, of penance for slander taking place in the vestry, immediately after morning prayer, when the offender confessed and asked pardon of the slandered person in the presence of minister and wardens and a select number of other witnesses. The white-sheet penance before the whole congregation was reserved for incontinence. Among the later Essex cases of this form of penance of which records remain, may be mentioned Danbury, 1731; Boreham, 1755; and Coggeshall, 1764.[1]

It is satisfactory to find, as the result of considerable research, that men as well as women underwent, from time to time, the sheet penance for incontinence. It is of no small interest to note that a man did public penance in Ashingdon church, Essex, in 1717, for the now *civilly* legalised sin of marrying his deceased wife's sister.

The following are a few of the more remarkable register entries as to penance.

John Browne for incontinency was ordered, on 14th February 1572-3:—

"On the next marquet day at Aveley in the countie of Essex to stand in the same marquet in a whitt shete and a rodd in his hand penitently and to desire the people to pray for him."

"1597 (*Croydon, Surrey*). Margaret Sherioux was buried 23d June. She was enjoined to stand iij market days in the town and iij Sabeathe dayes in the church, in a white sheete, with a paper on her back and bosom, showing her sinne. . . . She stood one Saturday and one Sunday and died the nexte.

"1677 (*Scotter, Lincoln*), May 27. Johanna Johnson absolved from the sentence of excommunication and did her penance yt day and the 29th of May following for committing fornication with one Rob[t] Knight of Morton in the parish of Gainsburgh.

"1682 (*Cherry Burton, Yorks*). Anne Baker did pennance March

---

[1] See Dr. Cox's "Ecclesiastical History of Essex," in *Vict. Co. Hist. of Essex*, vol. ii. pp. 41-2, 75, etc.

26: publickly. The said Anne Baker layd a Foundation of the Towne Stocks which was seven pounds payd by John Findon of Hutton Cranswicke, who was supposed to have gott the said Anne Baker with child, and was fined seven pound by Mr. John Ertoffe and Mr. Toby Hodson, Justices.

" 1699 (*Culworth, N'hants*). Memorandum. Upon ye 25 of Febr. Marg* Tyler of this Parish did perform penance according to y* following order.

An Order of Penance

to be performed by Margaret Tyler of Culworth in y* County of Northton as follows :—

" The s*d Marg. Tyler shall upon y* Sunday next after y* divine service stand before y* minister's Reading Desk appareld in a white sheet from head to foot and in y* presence of y* congregation there assembled make her confession as follows :—Good People, I confess I have grievously offended Almighty God by falling into ye foul sin of Fornication and thereby given an evil example to my neighbours for wch I am most heartyly sorry and do earnestly beg pardon of Almighty God and of all others that I have offended by this my evil example and I do promise (by y* grace of God) never to offend in y* like again. And I do also promise before God and this congregation to live herafter more soberly and godly in all other respects as a good Christian ought to do. And that I may perform my vows and promises made before this congregation, I do most earnestly desire y** prayers."

On Sunday, 6th April, John Bradley and May White performed public penance in the same church, and an entry is made in the register that the order and the certificate were the same as in the case of Margaret Tyler.

" 1717 (*Sutton Vallence, Kent*), Nov. 25. Eliz. Stace did public penance for ye foul sin of adultery committed with Tho. Hutchins jun*, in Sutton Vallence church, as did Anne Hynde for y* foul sin of fornication committed with Tho. Daws.   SA. PRAT, Vicar

" 1725 (*Roxby, Lincoln*). Memorandum. Michael Kirby and Dixon Ukel had two bastard children, one in 1725, y* other in 1727, for which they did publik Penance in our P'ish Church Feb. y* 25th, 1727, for adultery.

"1728 (*Uxbridge, Middlesex*). N.B. On July 7, Unity Winch did penance at morning service for May 26. [On the 26 of May is an entry of the baptism of the illegitimate child of Unity Winch.]

"1740 (*North Aston, Oxon*). Memorandum that Mr. Cooper sent in a form of penance by Mr. Wakefield, of Deddington, that Catherine King should do penance in ye Parish Church of North Ashton, ye sixth day of March, and accordingly she did. Witness, William Vaughan, Vicar. Charles May, John Baillis, Churchwardens.

"1785 (*Caundle Bishop, Dorset*). On Sunday, the 23 day of October, Susannah Philips, who lives near Colonel Bridge in this parish of Bishop's Caundle, did Penance in this Church, by standing during the whole time of Divine Service near the Reading Desk, in a white Linen Sheet, and immediately after the Second Lesson repeating words after the Minister to the following effect. . . ."

[The words are not given; the baptismal register records the baptism on 21st March 1788, of "Job, bastard son of Susana Philips."]

As to nineteenth-century instances of white-sheet penance up to about 1850, see Vaux's *Church Folk-lore* (1899), pp. 173–8.

The inscription on the font of Tollesbury, Essex, affords remarkable evidence of the heavy fine of £5 paid by way of penance to avoid prosecution in the ecclesiastical courts.

The small octagonal font of this church bears round the margin of the bowl, in very distinct lettering, what is surely the quaintest font inscription in all Christendom :—

> "Good people all I pray take care,
> That in ye church you do not swear,
> As this man did." .

An entry under the baptisms in the parish register explains this strange distich :—

"1718, August 30th. Elizabeth, daughter of Robert and Eliza Wood, being ye first childe whom was baptized in the New Font which was bought out of five pounds paid by John Norman, who some few months before came drunk into the church and cursed and talked loud in the time of Divine service, to prevent his being prosecuted for which he paid by agreement the above said five pounds. Note that the wise rhymes on the font were put there by the sole order of Robert Joyce then churchwarden."

"The Table of the Vigils, Fasts, and Days of Abstinence," together with "The days of Fasting or Abstinence," including all the Fridays in the year, as set forth in the Book of Common Prayer, are well known. But the great majority of even well-informed people appear to be ignorant of the way in which these tables were enlarged and strengthened by Act of Parliament in 1562 (5 Eliz. cap. v, secs. 14 to 23). By this Act persons were forbidden to eat flesh not only on Fridays, and at such seasons as the "Embering Days" and Lent, but also on Wednesdays and Saturdays. Offenders were liable to a fine of £3 or three months' imprisonment, and any householder permitting flesh-eating on his premises to a fine of 40s. The fines were to be divided into three parts : one for the crown, another for the informer, and the remaining third for the use of the parish wardens. Provision was made whereby dispensations could be granted to any one of the rank of a lord of parliament for 26s. 8d., to a knight or his wife for 13s. 4d., and to all others for 6s. 8d. Licences to eat certain white meats could be granted by curates to sick parishioners ; 4d. was to be paid to the curate, and he was to enter the licence in the church book. If such a licence was granted to one not genuinely sick, the minister was liable to a fine of five marks.

Butchers were bound under recognisances not to kill, dress, or permit to be eaten any flesh in Lent, on any fish-days appointed by law to be observed, or on any Fridays. A proclamation to this effect was issued as late as 29th January 1660 by Charles II. But from Elizabeth's days onward certain butchers obtained licences to kill for the sick and infirm in large towns.

The legal obligation, as distinct from that of the Church, of abstaining from meat was enforced by various statutes. In 1687 abstinence from meat was enjoined during Lent by royal proclamation, but it was advertised in the *London Gazette* that an office was opened in St. Paul's Churchyard where licences to eat flesh in any part of England could be obtained on condition of giving alms to the poor! After the revolutions of 1688 these statutes remained a dead letter, but they were not repealed until 1863.

It will be noticed that several of the following register extracts are of the year 1632–33, when Laud's vigorous actions doubtless drew attention, *inter alia*, to the statute of 1560.

On the fly-leaf of the first register of St. Margaret's, Westminster, entry is made of licences to eat meat during Lent 1568, 1569, and 1570,[1] and of licences to butchers to kill.

"Lycens gyven and made of whom and to whom for eatyng of flesh in yᵉ tyme of Sycknes yᵉ vj day of March 1568.
    1. Fyrst Wyllyam Stanton Nedborow yᵉ xxvjth of February.
    2. It. Wylliam Worlye, yoman of yᵉ garde yᵉ ijᵈ of Marche.
    3. It. Thomas Lyghton gentylman iijᵈ of marche.
    4. It. Lawrence Griffyn the vjth daye of marche aᵒ p'dicto.
    5. It. to Thomas Payne one of yᵉ garde yᵉ xijth daye of March.
    6. It. to Margerye Spenser, wyffet to Willm Spenser yᵉ ijᵈ of Marche.
    7. It. to Richarde Jordan yᵉ xxth daye of marche a Lycens.
"Lycense gyven for eating of Fleshe in the tyme of Sycknes the vijth daye of February aᵒ 1569.
    First Ralfe Cannocke a license to kill from my lord keeper the vijth daie of Februarie.
    It. Richard Hodges licensed by my lord of Canterbury ye ixth Februarie.

[1] Cited from Burke's *Key to Parish Registers*.

It. Willm Moore and Elizabeth his wief ye xvijth of Februarie.

It. Robt Bowmont and Agnes his wief ye xvth of Februarie.

It. of Willm Smethe the xvijth of Februarie.

It. of Willm Clerke the xxth of Februarie.

It. of Margaret Stynte the xxij of Februarie.

It. of John Thrushe the vth of Marche.

It. of Willm Maddocke the viijth of Marche.

Barnes A lycense to kill from my lord of Leicester the laste daye of Januarie 1569.

It. Willm Lyngard the xiijth daie of marche.

It. Rychard Preist the xxth daie of marche.

"Licens gyven to eate fleshe in tyme of sicknes for this lent tyme A° 1570.

Mystres Margaret Staunton licensed by the phisition and the Curate the xxijth daie of Februarie.

Mr. Richard Preist and his wief are licensed to eate fleshe by my lord of Canterbury the iiij day of Marche 1570.

Richard Jordayne licensed by the Curate the ij^d of Marche.

Ralfe Cannock licensed by my lord keeper the iiijth of Marche.

John Barnes licensed to kill fleshe by therle of Lecester the iiijth of Marche an° predicte.

betterys Hutton licensed by the Curate the xiijth of Marche.

Elizabeth Bacheler lycensed by the Curate the xjth of Marche.

Willm Hudson and Agnes his wief licensed the xvjth of Marche.

"1590 (*Colly Weston, N'hants*). Zecharie Hunt the parson of Colliweston made a lycence to Mr. Roger Dale Gentleman and to Elizabeth his wife and to Mr. Frauncis Bullington to eate flesh for the time of lent for Wednesdays, Fridaies, saterdaies and other fasting dayes during the time of their sicknesses and diseases according to the statute in y^t case provided dated the xxij of March.

"1591 (*Westerham, Kent*), 11 March. Memorand that Thom Ringe Curate of Westerham grants to John Daulinge sen^r Gent a lycense to eat Fleshe for viij days by reason of his sickness and impotency.

"1618 (*St. Mary's, Leicester*). License to Lady Barbara Hastings to eat Flesh in Lent on account of her great age.

"1619 (*Newington, Surrey*). I, James Fludd D.D., and Parson of the Church of St. Mary, Newington, do give license to Mrs. Anna Jones of Newington, the wyfe of Evan Jones, Gent., being

notoriously sick, to eat flesh this time of Lent during
the time of sickness only, according to law in that
case provided; videl. in the 5 Eliz. and 1 Jacob. c. 29,
provided alwaies that during the time of her sickness she
eat no beef, veall, porke, mutton, or bacon. In witness
whereof we have hereunto set our hand and seal. Dated 8
March.

" 1632 (*Boughton-under-Blean, Kent*). M^d that upon ixth of August
was granted a licence to Dame Elizab: Routh wife of
Sir John Routh of this pish in respect of her sicknesse and
bodilie infirmitie to eat flesh according to a statute made to
that purpose in quinto Elizabethe."

The register book of North Curry, Somerset, records
a licence "to eat flesh this Lente" granted in 1632–33 by
the vicar to Mrs. Johan Conock, "a gentlewoman of about
90 years of age."

" 1633 (*Wedmore, Somerset*), March 1. Whereas upon my own
certaine knowledge my wife lying now in childbed is very weak
and sicke, and by eating of fish she may very much if not
altogither endanger her life : I Martin Law being Vicar of the
said parish of Wedmore doe as in me lyeth lycence and
authorise her to eate flesh according to the forme and effect of
the Statute in that case provided.

" 1633 (*Bromfield, Salop*), Mar. 22. A license for eating of fleashe
granted to Sr Charles Foxe Kt, and registered Mar. 29.
His testibus, Wm. Jennings gar^r, John Wigley.

" 1633 (*Gayton, N'hants*). Mem^d that upon the 22d of March
Anno dom 1632 was a license granted by me John Marks,
Parson of Gaiton, to the Lady Marie Samwell, in respect of the
weakenes of her body and present sicknes, to eate flesh for
the space of eight dayes. And the same againe renewed
March the 30th 1633.

" 1633 (*St. Alkmund's, Derby*), 19 March. Whereas Katherine
ye wyfe of Nathanael Bate of Little Chester, being great with
child (and by reason of health) infirm and weak, and therefore not
able to feed upon fish meats without apparent damage (as I am
credibly informed) I doe therefore by these presents permitt (so
farr forth as by the statutes of the kingdom I may) unto y^e
said Katherine Bate to provide for herself, and to feed upon

such flesh meatts, as by the said statute are licensed, in this case during all ye time of her sicknesse and noe longer. In witnesse whereof I have hereunto set my hand. H. Coke, Minister and Preacher of the Word of God in the Parish of St. Alkmund's aforesaid. Test. Thomas Nash.''

During this same Lent the vicar of St. Alkmund's granted another licence to

"John Bullock, of Darleigh Abbey Esquier, something diseased and for ye present not safe to feed upon fishe, to feed upon flesh meate according to the direction of his phisition."

Nicholas Andrewes, vicar of Godalming, granted a licence in February 1639 to Frances Porter,

"who now lyeth in childbedd sick to eat flesh for and during ye time of her present sickness."

The following is an undated entry in the register book of Knodishall, Suffolk ; it is probably of the year 1632–33 :—

"Whereas Mr. Arthur Jenney, Esq., of Knotshall, & his wife Anne beinge trubled wth sicknes, he wth ye Tissecke [consumption] & she beinge bige wth child, soe that they are not able to eate salte fishes continually, I, James Johnson, Minister of ye parishe a bove sayd, accordinge to ye statute in tht cause pvided, have granted them to eate some fleshe for ye recoverie of there health, wch libertie was granted to them ye beginge of Lent. If sayd not yet recovered, the: desier to have ye same libertie continued to them still wch. I willingly doe conferme with ye assisstance of one of ye Churchwardnes as ye statute directeth mee, March 10th.
"James Johnson, Minister
"Henry Mawlinge, Churchwardinge"

It is not often in registers that we find any reference to the number of either Celebrations or Communicants, though information on both these points can occasionally be gleaned from Churchwarden Accounts.

In the register, however, of St. Michael le Belfry, York,

15

there are four pages of Elizabethan date yielding interesting particulars. These passages, which extend from 1572 to 1578, are thus prefaced :—

"The number of communycantes at penthicoste, 1572, w'thin the p'ishe church of St. Michaels als Befram, examyned before, according to L. Archbushope of York his graces enjunctyons in that behalf commanded.

"In p'mis Mr. will'm Allen et uxor, Item gartred hall, Vidua Faile et Edmonnde Fale, uxor smyth, Mr. James Stocke et uxor, Martyne Wayte."

There were also Celebrations that year on the feast of St. John Baptist, with 12 communicants; on the Sunday before Michaelmas, with 12; on Sunday, 9th November, with 7; on Christmas Day, with 26; on "Newyeares Day," with 12 ; and on the Purification, with 16. There are seven Celebrations entered for 1573, five for 1574, two for 1575, and two each for 1576, 1577, and 1578. In all these cases the names of the communicants are entered. It is scarcely possible to think that these lists are complete, for in no single year is an Easter Communion recorded.

"1620 (*Bakewell, Derbyshire*). The whole number of Communicants at Morning Prayer first on Easter Day 282. Eodem die at yᵉ latter Prayer 132 : Total, 419.

"1682 (*Hillingdon, Middlesex*). This year on Easter Day and Low Sunday 300 persons received the Comunion, alarmed to their duty by an order from Henry, Lord Bishop of London."

In the reign of Queen Anne, the Holy Communion was administered six times a year at North Wingfield, Derbyshire—namely, on Palm Sunday, Good Friday, Easter Day, Midsummer, Michaelmas, and on the Sunday before Christmas Day. The actual amount collected at each Communion is sometimes entered in the register; the total for a year and a half only amounted to £1, 16s. 1d.

The following unhappy entry at the end of a register

book of Clunbury, Salop, helps to explain the large amount of wine occasionally provided for the Communion :—

"Mr. Parry has agreed with the Parishioners of Clunbury to take instead of the spare wine at the Sacrament ten quart Pottles of good Port wine annually to be delivered to him in every year at Easter—the Parish Clerk to have the Pottles.

"Easter Day, 1808"

The singular custom, known as Benefit of Clergy, whereby not a few lives were mercifully saved at a period when capital punishment was hideously common, is too well known to require any explanation. A remarkable instance has been already cited in the third chapter, wherein a lad of eighteen, in 1541, failed to escape the gallows for thieving; for, though he pleaded privilege of clergy, it was found he could not read. The following is another register entry, which shows how three condemned prisoners were saved by a knowledge of letters :—

"1601 (*Penrith*), Jan. 27. A Jayle deliverie at Carliell when 7 prisoners condemned, whereoff foure were executed at Herrabie, viz: Ebbies Arch and Arche Armestrone als Wiskrills, Scottsmen, one Burthorne and one Nicolson, and three saved by the booke."

That dark page in the story of English superstition, when witchcraft was believed to be a reality, demanding the severest punishment, receives abundant illustration in parochial registers. In mediæval days witchcraft was regarded as an offence against the Church, and was only punishable by the ecclesiastical courts; but the superstition throve amazingly in post-Reformation days. The first penal statute against witches was in 1541, but it was repealed under Edward VI. Early in Elizabeth's reign public opinion was roused against witches by the strenuous preaching of Bishop Jewell, with the result that a new and severer statute became law in 1564, and was rigidly enforced, under which many hundreds of imaginary witches suffered death. Eleven witches and wizards were executed at Lancaster in 1612, and several more condemned to the pillory. Nine women were the victims of this cruel law at Leicester in 1616. It was not, however, until the days of the Commonwealth that the full rage of ignorant fury against witches broke out; in Suffolk alone during a single year sixty persons were hung for witchcraft. Between 1649 and 1685 there were over three hundred trials of witches throughout England. After the revolution of 1688 the superstition began to steadily lose ground, but as late as 1716 Mrs. Hicks and her daughter, a child of nine, were actually hung at Huntingdon "for raising a storm of wind by pulling off their stockings, and making a lather of soap in a basin in league with the devil"! The odious Elizabethan statute was not repealed until 1736.

It should be noted that the Church did not surrender her claim to deal with witchcraft in consequence of statutory enactments.

In the parish register of Hart, Durham, there is a curious entry, under 20th July 1582, as to the action taken by the Chancellor of the diocese against Allison Lawe, of Hart. She was declared to be "a notorious sorceror and enchanter," and was sentenced to do penance once in the market-place at Durham, "with a papir on her head," once in Hart church, and once in the church of Norton.

The following occur among other register entries relative to witches and witchcraft :—

"1602 (*Howden, Yorks*). Eliz. a wich died at Knedlington xx° August.

"1630 (*St. Mary's, Reading*), Jan. 10. Bur Kattren Roose, apprehended for a wich.

"1650 (*St. Andrew's, Newcastle*), 21 August. Thes partes her under named were executed in the Town Mor for wiches. Mathew

THE FRONTISPIECE OF MATTHEW HOPKINS' "DISCOVERY OF WITCHES,"
1644

Bonmer, Isabel Brown, Margrit Maddeson, Ann Watson, Ellenor Henderson, Ellenor Rogers, Elsabeth Dobson, Mrs. Ellsabeth Anderson, Jane Hunter, Jane Koupling, Margrit Brown, Margrit Moffit, Kattren Welsh, Aylles Hume, and Marie Pootes. The same day, prisoners executed on the town mor belonging to the hy Kastel were hanged nine thieves, and Jane Martin for a wich, the myllers wif of Chattin.

"1691 (*Holy Island*). Bur 16 July William Cleugh bewitched to death.

"1699 (*Coggeshall, Essex*), Dec. 27. The Widow Comon, that was counted a witch, was buried."

The death of this poor creature was probably the result of the repeated gross violence to which she had been subjected. The following occurs in Archdeacon Bufton's diary :—

"1699, July 13. The widow Comon was put into the river to see if she would sink, because she was suspected to be a witch, and she did not sink but swim."

This cruelty was repeated twice again ere the month closed, namely, on July 19th and 24th, with the like result in each case.

An Act was passed in 1530 "concerning Outlandish People calling themselves Egyptians . . . using no craft for merchandise, but deceiving people, that they by Palmistry can tell men's and women's fortunes and so cheat people of their money and commit many heinous felonies and robberies." It was therefore enacted that such persons should be henceforth excluded from the realm, and that those already here should depart within sixteen days or forfeit their goods. In 1554 a further Act was passed making it felony for a gipsy to remain in the kingdom after twenty days from the proclamation of the Act ; but a proviso was made for such "Egyptians as shall leave that naughty idle and ungodly life," and serve some honest householder. A statute of Elizabeth, 1563, was most cruelly severe ; by its provisions it became a capital felony "to continue for one month in any company or fellowship of vagabonds commonly called Egyptians." This law was not repealed until 1783, when it was rightly styled "a law of excessive severity."

"1592 (*St. Nicholas, Durham*), 8 Aug. Simson, Arington, Fether-stone, Fenwicke, and Lancaster, were hanged for being Egyptians."

It is pleasant to find that the registers bear testimony to the fact that not a few of the clergy were more merciful than the law, and were ready to administer Christian rites to these wandering "Egyptians."

"1564 (*Lanchester, Durham*). William the son of an Egiptian bap. 19 Feb.

"1576 (*Swainswick, Somerset*). John Phillip, the sonn of John Phillip, an Egiptian, was heere baptized the 10th daie of Maie.

"1581 (*Loughborough, Leicestershire*). Margaret Bannister, Daughter of William Bannister, going after the manner of roguish Aegyptians, was baptized the 2d of April.

"1687 (*Camberwell*). Robert Hern and Elizabeth Bozwell, King and Queen of the Gipsies, bur. 2 June.

"1696 (*Haughton, Staffs*), May 8. Thomas Lovell and Hannah Blewitt, gypsies, married.

"1702 (*Chapel-en-le-Frith, Derbyshire*). A poor traveller, who went under the name of an Egiptian, was buried in the churchyard 20 April."

Parochial whipping was occasionally, inappropriately enough, entered in the registers instead of in the Church-wardens' Accounts. Thus in the first register book of Askham, Westmoreland, between a baptism and a marriage, is entered, under the year 1610:—

"October the 3d day was John Hurst and Jane Wachell two poor travellers whiped."

The following are some later entries in the church registers of a like character:—

" 1621 (*Stokeley, Yorks*). John nipplaye a vagrant and a wandring begger of a lowe stature brown headed and somewhat bleare eyed aged about fiftye years was this xiiij day of Apryll openlye whipped at Stokesley for a wandringe begger and misdeymeaninge him self in his wandringe accordinge to the lawe.

THE WHIPPING POST AND STOCKS, ALDBURY, HERTS.

" 1633 (*Wadhurst, Sussex*), 11th June. Anne Diplock was whipped for a rogue.

10th Dec. John Palmer and Alice his wife were whipped for rogues.

23d Dec. Thomasina Hemming, John Ballard, Margery Oiles, Robert Spray, and John Sargent whipped.

" 1637 (*Bakewell, Derbyshire*), 6 Nov. Thomas Tomlinson and Dorothy his wyfe of Wakefield or thereabout were taken begging at Bakewell, and whipped according to ye law, and he sent home.

" 1672 (*Croft, Yorks*). Jane Bultrey, of Darlington, was seet in the Stoxe at Crofte and was whipt out of the Towne the 3 day of Jan.

" 1698 (*Brentford, Middlesex*), 26 Feb. Alice and Elizabeth Picker-

ing, wandering children, were whipped according to Law, and
sent with a Pass to Shrewsbury, the place where they were born.
" 1698 (*Mentmore, Bucks*). Mem^d A Beggar woman of Slapton whipt
at Mentmore 5 July."

The Mansfield church registers are disgraced by a
variety of these entries, signed by John Firth, vicar. It
is difficult to understand how a clergyman possessed of a
spark of humanity could bring himself to write out the
account in God's House of the shameless flogging of two
children in 1693. There are entries of the whipping of a
man and a woman in 1680, in 1681, and in 1683. In the
last of these years it is mentioned that the woman was 22
and black-haired, whilst the man was "aged." There are
various other cases, but they culminate with the following :—

"5 Dec. 1693. John Walker and Elizabeth Walker, two sturdy
vagrant beggars, one of about 15 and the other about 13 yeares
old were openly whipped at Mansfield for wandering beggars."

Records of local exhibitions sometimes occur in old
register books, of which two examples are appended :—

" 1568 (*St. Nicholas, Durham*). Mem^d that a certain Italian brought
into the cittie of Durham the 11th day of June a very great
strange and monstrous serpent in length sixteene feete, in
quantitie and dimensions greater than a horse ; which was
taken and killed by speciall pollicie in Athiopia within the
Turk's Dominions. But before it was killed it had devoured
(as it is credibly thought) more than 1000 persons, and destroyed a whole country.
" *St. Mary Magdalene, Canterbury*, December the 6, 1687. Then
the lion was baited to death in the White Hart Yarde by dogges."

Tithing notes of considerable interest are occasionally
entered in registers, usually on fly-leaves at the end of the
volumes. They are of value as illustrating the considerable
diversity of custom when tithes were paid in kind. Space
can only be found for one such entry, but it is the fullest

and most interesting that has come to our notice. It occurs
in the parish register of Whilton, Northants, and is one of
the very numerous extracts kindly supplied by the Rev^d R.
M. Serjeantson :—

" *The tithe of Sheep*. On new years day make a tale of the sheep.
Take every tenth fleece of what they shear of that number. In
what they have sold out of it before shearing take a halfpenny a
sheep. The same take for all they buy in after new years day.
If the Person has ten sheep on new years day and they come to
seven by the time of shearing give him three half-pence and take a
Fleece. Out of ten fleeces he who pays Tithe chuses two and the
Parson has his choice out of the rest. The same method is to be
observed with respect to the Tithe of Lambs which is to be taken
the nineteenth day of April.

" *Of Pigs*. If there are seven, one is due, but then the Parson
must pay three half-pence; if there are but six, they pay six half-
pence; if there are twelve they pay a Pig and two halfpence. But
the Parson is bound to keep a Boar.

" *Of Calves*. If they have seven from new years day the Parson
must have one, paying three halfpence. And as many halfpence
are due to the Parson as they have calves under seven. They
must keep the Tithe calf three weeks.

" *Of Cows*. Take the Tithe of milk from the 19th of April counting
the twentieth day the first of the ten: take it morning and night: leave
off taking when the first shock of corn is cut : begin again to take it
ten days after Harvest ends and continue to do so till new years day.

" N.B. The Parish is bound to keep one Bull and the Parson
another, who if he pleases may keep a Breeder besides his Bull.

" *Of Hay*. Take the tenth cock of Hay and the seventh at last. All
Farm land pays Tithe ; all sow meadow and Whittom meadow : as
also Duglake and Househorn, the Mill and all belonging to it.
The Farm land is to be known by the Farm Balks. The Town land
pays threepence a yard Land called Hay-silver.

" *Of Corn*. Take the 10th sheaf or cock of graine, Beans and Pease,
and the seventh at last. Chuse your sheaf out of the First Shock,
but take in the same place out of every shock in that land.

" N.B. The two mills pay three shillings and four pence a year
each.   JOHN SPATEMAN, Rector
                              " 10 *June* 1741"

CHAPTER XIII

THE DATES AND CONDITIONS OF THE REGISTERS

The Blue Book Returns of 1833—Numerous blunders—Mediæval
death registers—Parish registers prior to 1538—The numbers
of 1538–39 registers—Transcripts ordered in 1597 and in
1603—Grievous defects of Bishops' Transcripts exposed in
1800—Act of 1812—Returns of 1831—Transcripts of the
peculiars of Lichfield and Southwell—Careless loss of registers, instanced in Kent and Bucks—Irregularities of entry—
Trades and occupations in London, Chesham, Lancashire,
etc. — "Sir" signifying priest — Puritan names — Similar
names in one family—Double names—Contracted form of
entry — Birth registers — Printed registers — Nonconformist
and Huguenot registers

OFFICIAL inquiries were made of all the clergy in
1831, as to the exact date, condition, and number of
the parish registers in their custody. An abstract
of their replies was published in a Blue Book issued in 1833.
It is not generally known that the returns themselves, with
which are frequently included fuller statements from the
clergy, are extant at the British Museum in eight great
folio volumes, beginning Add. MS 9,355. The dates of the
registers given in this Blue Book and in the original returns
are, however, by no means to be trusted; our own experience, extending over fully forty years, is that at least
one in five is quite wrong. In some cases registers have
been lost or stolen since that date, but in far more instances
the clergy, through ignorance or carelessness, blundered in
filling up their returns, occasionally assigning an extra-

vagantly early date to the first entry, and still oftener overlooking older pages that had been wrongly bound up, or forgetting that in many instances the extant registers of baptisms, marriages, and deaths did not synchronise.

According to the Parish Register Abstract of 1833 there were

40 registers beginning prior to 1538

772	,,	,, in	1538
1822	,,	,, ,,	1538–58
2448	,,	,, ,,	1558–1603
969	,,	,, ,,	1603–1650
2757	,,	,, ,,	1650–1700
1476	,,	,, ,,	1700–1750

There were also between 600 and 700 of later dates.

As to the registers said to begin prior to Cromwell's order of 1538, the large majority of the forty set forth in the Blue Book prove on investigation to be but moonshine. Several of the careless blunders made in 1831 and published in 1833 continue to be printed in recent directories and even in more important diocesan calendars or returns. Misreadings of the figure seven account for several errors. Thus in the case of Penkevil, Cornwall, the initial date of 1516, as usually set forth, proves to be 1576, and that of Sinnington, Yorks, 1577 instead of 1517; whilst at West Thorney, Sussex, the register was made to begin in 1530 instead of in 1570. Still more extravagant mistakes, which elude explanation, are occasionally made at the present time, of which a single example must suffice. The registers of Skeffington, Leicestershire, were quite recently asserted and reasserted to begin in 1514; but a special journey of investigation, undertaken for the purposes of this book, proved that they do not begin until 1590! In another country parish, which shall be nameless, the custodian charged 3s. 6d. for his search to ascertain the initial entry, and a subsequent personal visit showed that he was forty years wrong in his written and signed assertion !

There are, however, beyond doubt certain parochial registers which begin before 1538, but less than half the number named in the 1833 Blue Book. To account for this, it must be remembered that there is a fair amount of evidence to show that some of the mediæval clergy of England were, at all events, in the habit of keeping fitful and informal registers, particularly of deaths, long before the sixteenth century. Thus in the highly interesting fourteenth-century chartulary of the chantries of Crich, Derbyshire, there are entries of the exact death-days of various members of the Wakebridge family and their connections from 1344 to 1368 inserted in the calendar.[1] The twelfth-century obituary of the priory of Cistercian nuns at Wintney, Hants, printed by Hearne in 1729, abounds in entries of the death-days not only of prioresses and sisters of the convent, but also of a variety of benefactors both lay and clerical. There are also two most notable and exceptionally full obituaries, extending far beyond the actual monastery, in connection with the Derbyshire Abbey of White Canons at Beauchief.[2] The records of a serious dispute between the parishioners of St. Helen's, Abingdon, and the ancient Benedictine abbey of that town, which came to a head in 1396, incidentally show that an exact register of the sixty-seven persons buried in the new cemetery of St. Helen's from its opening in 1391 had been duly kept.[3]

There can be little doubt that the more careful and methodical of England's parish priests would, if only for their own satisfaction and information, keep occasional

[1] Harl. MS. 3669. See Dr. Cox's *Churches of Derbyshire*, iv. 36–47.
[2] See *Vict. Co. Hist. of Derbyshire*, vol. ii. 68.
[3] *Vict. Co. Hist. of Berks*, vol. ii. 56-7.

records, however casually entered, of the various offices of the church as affecting individual parishioners. Hence it came about that in a few cases, when Cromwell's order came forth in 1538, the parish priest thought well to transcribe at the beginning of the newly ordered official register some of the recent entries from his parochial notebook. Of such definite transcripts, extending back for some years, there are six instances extant, and it is quite probable that there were more in the original paper register books of 1538, but such extraneous and unofficial matter would naturally be omitted for brevity's sake by the transcribers on to parchment at the end of the century.

By far the most remarkable of these early instances is that of Tipton, Staffordshire. This register actually begins on 20th of December 1513, on which day a baptism was entered, and another in March 1513–14. Six baptisms are entered under 1514, ten under 1515, eleven under 1516, three under 1517, ten under 1518, and six under 1519. As to marriages, there were three in 1514, two in 1516, and five in 1517.

The second earliest parish registers are those of Altham, Lancashire. The oldest register consists of eight leaves of parchment; the top of the first page is so blackened with gall as to be quite illegible, but the date 1518 is supplied in a comparatively modern hand, and there seems no reason to doubt its accuracy. On the second page occurs the date 1519, and on the third page 1520. The entries run on consecutively up to 1525. On the next batch of nine leaves the dates 1527 and 1533 can be plainly read. The regular register does not begin until 1596.[1]

The register book of Perlethorpe, Notts, begins :—

"The Register of all suche as have bynne Christened, maryed

---

[1] From information kindly supplied by the vicar, the Rev. H. H. Whittaker.

and buryed, in the parish of Parlthorp Thow'sbye since the yeare of our Lord 1528."

The entries for 1528 and 1529 are now illegible.[1] For 1530, 1531, 1534, 1536, and 1537 there are two entries, and three each for the years 1532, 1533, and 1535.

The registers of Carburton, Notts, begin :—

"The register book of Carburton, as have been Christened maried and bured in the parish of Carburton since the beginning of the yeare of our lord god and the five hundred twentie and Eight."

There is an entry of a baptism, a marriage, and a burial under 1528, none in 1532, one each in 1529, 1531, and 1536, and two each in 1530, 1533, 1534, 1535, and 1537.

The word "since" at the head of both of these registers shows that the entries were a compilation, and not entered year by year.

At Elsworth, Cambridgeshire, the registers also begin in 1528, when three baptisms are recorded, and there are about ten other entries prior to 1538.

In the case of Ashperton, Herefordshire, there is at least one yet earlier entry, namely, of the year 1521, but in a later handwriting than the rest of the beginning of the register. Between 1530 and 1538 there are several other entries.

Burn (1862) cites a marriage entry of 1534, and two baptisms of 1537 out of the register of Stoke Hammond, Bucks. Wolverton register, Bucks, begins with an entry of November 1535, and contains twenty-four entries prior to 1538. A recent letter of the rector of Kirton, Notts, also gives 1535 as the beginning of that register. Burn cites Goodworth Clatford as containing an entry of 1536, but no entry earlier than 1538 can now be found, and this is probably a misread-

[1] The Perlethorpe and Carburton registers were printed by Dr. Marshall in 1887–88. The writer of this book saw these registers in 1869, when several entries now faded were legible.

The Register booke of Tipton was
made the 20 day of December 1513

Joane the daughter of Thomas Whitehowse baptized 20 December 1513
Thomas the sonne of Richard Toole baptized the 30 of Februarie 1513
Elizabeth the daughter of Phillip Oliver baptized the 16 march 1513

Anno Dom 1514

Richard ye sonne of Edward Watson was baptized the 16 of April 1514
Joane ye daughter of Richard Bee was baptized the 16 of August 1514
William ye sonne of Richard Mople was baptized the 10 of Octob: 1514
William ye sonne of Thomas Bradley was baptized the 16 of Januarye 1514
Edward the sonne of Hugh Nitingale baptized ye 16 of Jannu: 1514
John ye sonne of Richard Meurke was baptized ye 26 of Jannuarii 1514

Anno Dom 1515

John ye sonne of John Mason was Baptised the 30 of march 1515
Elizabeth ye daughter of Thomas Hollihrad was baptized ye 22 of May 1515
Isabell ye daughter of Edward Watson was bapt: 10 day of June
Simon ye sonne of John Rawinson was baphio 28 of October
William ye sonne of Tho: Fellow was bapt: 5 day of December
Elizabeth ye daughter of Robert Ward was bapt: 1 day of Jann:
Elizabeth ye daughter of Richard Roe was bapt: 18 of February
Annes ye daughter of James Brome bapt: 20 day of Jann:
Joane ye daughter of Tho: Roe bapt: 10 day of —
John ye sonne of Tho: Smarte bapt: 4 day of march

Anno Dom 1516

Jane ye daughter of Rich: Poole bapt: 23 of Aprill
Elizabeth ye daughter of Kate Bradley bapt: 5 of June
Richard ye sonne of Rich: Mason bapt: 10 day of June
William ye sonne of William Wharwood bapt: 20 of June
Tho: ye sonne John Scripion bapt: 1 day of July
Humfrey ye sonne of Will: Rattley 13 day of July
Margaret ye daughter of Henne Molle bapt: 1 day of September
Joane ye daughter of Hugh Nighhingale bapt: 25 day of December
Dorathie ye daughter of Rich: Wallows bapt: 4 day Jann:
Mari ye daughter of John Roberts bapt: 3 day of —
Richard ye sonne of Edward Jordine bapt: 24 day of march

Anno Dom 1517

FACSIMILE OF FIRST PAGE OF TIPTON REGISTER, 1513
(KINDLY LENT BY MR. A. M. BURKE)

ing. The register of West Clandon, Surrey, begins in 1536, and has nine entries prior to 1538 (Burn). Parkham, Devon, has four marriages and two burials of the year 1537. The registers of Kingsbury, Warwickshire; Snaith, Yorks; and Somersal Herbert, Derbyshire, are also known to the present writer to begin in 1537, and this is also said to be the case with regard to the registers of Eling, Hunts; Fairstead, Essex; and Shrawley, Worcestershire.

Burn also sets forth 63 entries between 1535 and the end of 1537 which occur in a small folio paper book of St. James, Garlick Hythe, London; he states that "it is not the original, but a transcript (made probably in 1597) of apparently a genuine Register."

This analysis reduces the forty registers of the 1833 return alleged to be prior to 1538 to eighteen, and this list ought possibly to be reduced by one or two.[1]

There is, alas, no doubt whatever that there has been shocking carelessness with regard to the safe custody of parish registers since the 1831 return was compiled. There were at that time 772 registers beginning in 1538: there are now, we believe, 656 (see Appendix II.). Allowing for mistakes in the exact figures of both these summaries, it appears tolerably clear that about a hundred of our earliest registers have disappeared in the course of some eighty years. There are also a considerable number of registers whose first entry is in 1539; but they may as a rule be fairly considered as complying with Cromwell's order, for that order was dated 29th September 1538, and did not reach many an out-of-the-way parish for several weeks; and there would certainly be many sparsely populated parishes wherein there was no event demanding registry entering until 1539 was reached. There are 205 extant registers which begin in 1539 (Appendix III.),

[1] *Fraser's Magazine* for September 1861 has a blundering article wherein the names of forty-nine parishes are set forth as having registers prior to 1538!

so that the total of registers beginning at the earliest ordered date (including the sixteen prior to 1538), which can now be consulted, amounts to 877.

By a Constitution of Convocation in the year 1597, transcripts of parish registers, as has been already noted in the first chapter, were ordered to be forwarded to the bishop of the diocese. Subsequent ordinances were made as to their punctual transmission. The Canons of 1603 provided for the annual forwarding to the bishop's registry of a copy of the registers, signed by the minister and wardens. This was an admirable provision, so that in the event of fire or other destructive accident in the parish another copy would supply satisfactory evidence. It was also intended to act as a check on any alteration, erasure, or forgery of the original.

The great defect of this canon was the neglect to attach any fees for the transcript, either to the parish officials in making the copy and transmitting it, or to the bishop's officials for their safe storage and arrangement. The result has been such a scandal that Mr. Chester Waters was amply warranted in writing, in 1883, that "the bishop's transcripts, which ought to have formed an invaluable department of the public records, present a lamentable picture of episcopal negligence, parochial parsimony, and official rapacity.''

The report of the Committee on Public Records, issued in 1800, revealed a grievous condition of affairs. For instance, there were 142 parishes in Surrey, but the registry at Winchester had only 20 registers for all these parishes from 1597 to 1800. Each of these parishes ought to have annually sent a copy of its register for over two centuries, so that for this one county there was an actual deficiency of 28,206 transcripts! Salisbury, with 434 parishes, was in the habit of receiving only 9 or 10 transcripts a year, and not a finger was raised by bishop or registrar to secure obedience.

In Rochester diocese, at that date, only 7 parishes out of 95 were sending in their transcripts. The registrar of London diocese had the impertinence to send the following certificate to the Commissioners:—" I hereby certify that it is not the custom within the Diocese of London for any return to be made to the Bishop's Registry of either Burials or Baptisms "!

A table was compiled from these 1800 returns in Grimaldi's *Origines Genealogicæ*, from which it appears that the condition of affairs in several dioceses was much better than in those already cited. Thus, in Hereford, the whole of the parishes (323) were at that time making their annual returns, but there were none older than 1660.

The Act of 1812 made further stringent provisions to try and compel the sending in of the transcripts and their due custody, but with indifferent results. In 1831 a Parliamentary Return was made by the several dioceses in answer to inquiries whether the directions of the Act of 1812 had been complied with in various particulars, more especially as to what transcripts had been sent in since 1813, and whether they were kept in security from fire. A table compiled from this return (Burn's *Parish Registers*, 2d Edit. 1862, p. 203), shows the imperfect and insecure state of the transcripts at that date. In London diocese there were 192 defaulting parishes, in Bath and Wells 139, and in Lincoln 103. In twelve dioceses it was admitted that the returns were "subject to fire." Only one bishop (Lichfield) complied with the direction of the Act and made a Survey and Report!

In Mr. Phillimore's *How to Write the History of a Family* (1887) is a useful table of Bishop's Transcripts compiled from the two already mentioned, and giving a certain amount of extra information. In a few dioceses, the extant transcripts have of late years been well arranged, notably those
16

of Worcester, and to a considerable extent of Lincoln. Gross as has been the carelessness with regard to diocesan transcripts, it has been exceeded by the carelessness as to the actual parochial registers.   At the present time the transcripts considerably antedate the registers in not a few cases, not infrequently indeed by as much as a century (see Appendix).

In addition to the transcripts of registers which are in the keeping of diocesan officials, there were a certain number of parishes which never transmitted the copies into episcopal hands, inasmuch as they were "peculiars" attached to certain special ecclesiastical jurisdictions, and outside the control of the diocesan.   There are a few cases where transcripts of such parish registers are still extant and in separate control.

Dr. Cox, when cataloguing the muniments of the Dean and Chapter of Lichfield in 1881-3, found a large number of the registrar transcripts of the decanal or capitular peculiars scattered about in a variety of receptacles.   These separate parchment sheets were collected and arranged in parcels according to the respective parishes or chapelries.   The earlier of these transcripts were probably lost in the times of the Commonwealth struggle.   The large majority of them begin about 1660.   They all terminate in 1812, for the Registration Act of that year put an end to such returns being made to Chapter authorities.   The following is a list of these Lichfield peculiar transcripts, with the inclusive years, but it must be remembered that there are various missing years in all these fifty-four cases save three :—

Acton Trussell, 1659-1812; Alrewas, 1664-1812; Arley, 1673-1812; Armitage, 1623-1812; Ashford, 1669-1812; Bakewell, 1614-1812; Baston, 1662-1812; Bedwall, 1678-1812; Berkswell, 1662-1812; Bishop's Wellington, 1614-1812; Breaston, 1717-1812; Buxton, 1721-1812; Becley, 1639-

1812; Cannock, 1659–1812; Chadshunt and Gaydon, 1660–
1812; Chapel-en-le-Frith, 1659–1812; Chorlton, 1690–1706;
Chelmorton, 1663–1812; Colwich, 1659–1812 (*perfect*); Culver-
hall, 1791–1807; Edgbaston, 1678–1812; Edingale, 1669–
1812; Fairfield, 1663–1812; Farewell, 1663–1812; Fradswell,
1666–1812; Harborne, 1660–1802; High Offley, 1659–1812;
Hints, 1659–1812; Hope, 1661–1812; King's Bromley, 1632–
1812; Kniveton, 1675–1812 (*perfect*); Longdon, 1663–1812;
Longstone, 1666–1812; Long Eaton, 1672–1810; Mavesyn
Ridware, 1663–1812; Monyash, 1672–1812; Norton, 1659–
1862; Pipe Ridware, 1659–1812; Prees, 1669–1812; Risley,
1717–1812; Rugeley, 1659–1812; Sawley, 1672–1810;
Sheldon, 1675–1810; Smethwick, 1774–1812; Stafford, St.
Chad's, 1636–1804; Tachbrook, 1666–1810; Taddington,
1677–1812; Tideswell, 1671–1812; Tipton, 1672–1812;
Welford, 1638–1810; Whittington, 1663–1812; Whixall,
1756–1812 (*perfect*); Wilne, 1675–1812; Wormhill, 1686–
1812.[1]

In eight of these parishes, namely, Armitage, Ashford,
Cannock, Chadshunt, Fairfield, Farewell, Longdon, and
Monyash, the transcripts go further back than the extant
registers.

At Southwell Minster there are still retained a considerable number of transcripts which were sent in to that centre
from the various peculiars of that important collegiate foundation.   They are in a fragmentary state, and those that are
of seventeenth-century date have been printed (*Thoroton
Society, Record Ser.* i. 1903).   The following are the isolated
yearly returns still extant:—Beckingham, 1634, 1637, 1641;
Bleasby, 1633; Blidworth, 1638; Calverton, 1617, 1623;
Caunton,* 1614, 1619, 1628, 1641; Cropwell Bishop, 1638,
1641; Darlton, 1622, 1633, 1641; Dunham,* 1641; Edingsley,

---

[1] For missing years, see *Catalogue of Capitular Muniments of Lichfield,*
1886, pp. 82–3.

1638 ; Farnsfield, 1623 ; Halam, 1622, 1637 ; Halloughton, 1622, 1633, 1641 ; Holme, 1623, 1625, 1628, 1638, 1641 ; Kirklington, 1622, 1638 ; Morton,* 1622–3 ; North Muskham, 1623, 1633, 1638 ; South Muskham, 1623 ; Norwell,* 1638, 1641 ; Oxton, 1622 ; Ragnall,* 1623 ; Southwell, 1633, 1641 ; Upton,* 1633, 1638 ; Woodborough, 1623, 1627, 1637–8, 1640.   In the nine parishes, out of these twenty-four, which are marked with an asterisk, the transcripts are of earlier date than the extant parish registers.

The pitiful carelessness shown by the clerical custodians of parish registers in the past, and their loss in comparatively recent days, can be proved in every diocese and county.   It must suffice to draw attention to two strong proofs of this on a large scale.

Among the manuscripts of the Society of Antiquaries is a volume (No. clxxx.) containing a considerable number of genealogical or family extracts from various Kent parishes, which were transcribed in the year 1726.   It is stated in each case when the register began, and it appears that out of these twenty-six parishes, eight have since lost their first register book, which covered in each case about a century, beginning in the reign of Elizabeth.   The parishes are those of Capel, Ditton, Horton Kirby, Leigh, Luddesdown, Nettlestead, Sele, and Stock.

Not only were losses and destruction of parish registers frequent throughout the eighteenth and early part of the nineteenth century, but this gross indifference as to their custody continued for some time after the official returns of 1831 were compiled—thus disproving the expectation that the issue of that important Blue Book would naturally check an admitted evil.   Take, for instance, the county of Buckingham. Lipscombe's good history of that shire, issued in 1847, shows, when compared with present returns, that no small number of early register books disappeared during the second half of the nineteenth century. First register books, mostly of sixteenth century date, have been lost, since Lipscombe wrote, in the parishes of Beaconsfield, Bow Brickhill, Broughton, Chetwode, Denham, Foxcote, Haddenham, Great Linford, North Marston, Olney, Shenley, and Wyrardisbury.

It is by no means unusual to find gaps and irregularities in the continuity of registers at times other than the great Civil War, to which attention has already been called at some length. The following entry accounts for one of these breaks.

At the archidiaconal visitation at Northampton, on 10th October 1577, it was presented that the vicar of St. Sepulchre's

"will not kepe the booke of christenyngs weddings and buryenges because the churchwardens will not bringe the names of them y^t be christened wedded and buried and because they will not bringe him the booke and putt it unto his hands."

The archdeacon ordered the vicars to duly keep the register for the future. A reference to St. Sepulchre's registers shows a gap from 1574 to 1577.

Irrespective of the incalculable value of registers for genealogical and legal purposes, and the historical and entertaining information contained in their manifold notes, it will also be found that the dryest of them, which may lack even a line of interpolation or a single descriptive passage from beginning to end, will often yield no small amount of local knowledge to the intelligent inquirer, particularly as to the past trades and occupations of special localities.

The London registers are of particular interest in this respect, and afford abundant proof of how particular trades pervaded special localities in the sixteenth century. Thus, the registers of St. Mary Woolnoth show that this was the quarter of the city where the goldsmiths congregated. Three out of five infants baptized in this parish in 1538 were the children of goldsmiths. In 1539 eight such children were baptized, in 1540 nine, in 1541 six, and in 1542 ten.

So far as the occupation of those registered are concerned, one of the most interesting and varied of the city parishes is that of St. Mary's, Aldermary, where tailors and skinners largely predominated. The following occur between the years 1558 and 1594:—

Merchant tailors, 128	Baker, 1
Skinners, 63	Chandler, 1
Clothmakers, 35	Bowyer, 1
Draper, 19	Clarke (parish), 1
Dyer, 7	Cloakmaker, 1
Shoemaker, 7	Cordwainer, 1
Taylor, 6	Fustian dyer, 1
Gentleman, 5	Gentlewoman, 1
Haberdasher, 5	Grocer, 1
Barber surgeon, 4	Husbandman, 1
Physician, 4	Innholder, 1
Cobbler, 3	Minister, 1
Mercer, 3	Parson, 1
Scrivener, 3	Sergeant, 1
Barber, 2	Silkman, 1
Cook, 2	Silkweaver, 1
Embroiderer, 2	Shearman, 1
Knight, 2	Vintner, 1
Pewterer, 2	Yeoman, 1
Sexton, 2	

The trades or occupations of those entered in the register book of the small town of Chesham, Bucks, extending from 1538 to 1636, are frequently given. Shoemakers then, as now, after setting aside servants and labourers, were the most numerous, obtaining their leather from local tanners and curriers. The glovers, no longer extant at Chesham, were also numerous three centuries' ago, and next to them the tailors and weavers. The woodenware industry (the turners, shovelmakers, and trenchermakers of the register) is still one of the most important in the little town, but dyers, tanners, curriers, and cutlers have passed away. The following list of trades or occupations of the parishioners set forth in the register book is taken from Mr. Pegge's annotated transcript published in 1904 :—

Shoemaker, 23	Cutler, 3	Carter, 1
Tailor, 19	Dyer, 3	Clothworker, 1
Weaver, 19	Joiner, 3	Cooper, 1
Glover, 17	Mason, 3	Haberdasher, 1
Wheelwright, 15	Schoolmaster, 3	Innholder, 1
Tanner, 12	Bailiff, 2	Ironmonger, 1
Smith, 11	Banker, 2	Mercer, 1
Butcher, 7	Currier, 2	Pedlar, 1
Carpenter, 7	Glazier, 2	Physician, 1
Malster, 7	Meretrix, 2	Ropemaker, 1
Miller, 7	Midwife, 2	Salter, 1
Collarmaker, 6	Painter, 2	Sawyer, 1
Tilemaker, 6	Pinner, 2	Tinker, 1
Turner, 6	Ploughwright, 2	Trenchmaker, 1
Potter, 5	Sayer, 2	Vintner, 1
Shoemaker, 5	Brewer, 2	
Baker, 4	Bricklayer, 1	

Among the less common trade names in the early registers of Mitcham, Surrey, may be mentioned boddice maker, pumpmaker, tobacco-pipe maker, jacksmith, and ashman.

The following are among the occupations attached to burials in the sixteenth-century registers of Chesterfield : alderman, apprentice, armiger, bailiff, bellfounder, brazier, cardemaker, clericus, clothweaver, coverlett maker, deacon, fishmonger, generosus, gentlewoman, horseryder, miles, musicus, parson, peregrinus, pædigogus, pottigary, predicator, presbyter, pentionarius, sirgean, tanner, and vicar.

The vicar of Holy Cross, Canterbury, from 1698 to 1707, invariably entered the trade or occupation of those who were buried. The following are the heads of this singularly

varied list: alehouse keeper, barber, bayly, beggar, blacksmith, brewer, bricklayer, broomeman, butcher, carpenter,
carrier, chirurgeon, clerk, cobbler, collarmaker, comber,
cordwinder, counsellor, doctor, dyer, featherbed-driver,[1]
fellmonger, flaxdresser, fruiterer, fuller, gaol-keeper, gardener,
gentleman, glazier, glover, gluemaker, grocer, hemp-
dresser, hostler, huntsman, husbandman, innholder, joiner,
keeper, labourer, lay clerk, malster, mason, miller, milliner,
millwright, minister, nurse, merchant, officer, paper-
maker, parish clerk, postman, potter, salesman, saltfish-man,
sawyer, seaman, seamstress, sexton, shoemaker, shearman,
silkweaver, soldier, solicitor, spinner or spinster, tailor,
tanner, tinker, turner, upholsterer, victualler, washerwoman,
wheelwright, wigmaker, weaver, woolcomber, and woollen
draper.

In a good essay on the general characteristics of the
parochial registers of Lancashire, and of the varied information that may be gleaned from them, which appeared in
Memorials of Old Lancashire (1909), Mr. Brierley says:—

"Many glimpses of the trades practised in the various
parishes are furnished by the registers. In Wigan we find
"'panner' and 'peroterea,' in Walton 'furrier,' in Liverpool
'dishthrower,' in Ormskirk 'glasseman,' in Eccleston 'dryster,'
in Poulton and Cockerham 'saltweller,' in Croston 'salter,'
'spooner,' 'buttoner,' and 'glover,' in Upholland 'glover'
and 'potter,' in Eccles 'ymbroderer,' in Ribchester 'coatman'
and 'siever,' in Cartmel 'hammerman,' 'paperman,' and
'woodcutter.' Of these trades, it is feared that all but the
occupations of the 'boatman,' for the ferry at Ribchester, and
the 'woodcutters' of the Cartmel district, who still supply

---

[1] "A word of explanation may not be out of place about the featherbed-
driver. A driver of feathers or down placed them in a machine which, by a
current of air, drove off the lightest to one end, and collected them by
themselves." Hence, in *Othello* (Act 1, sc. 3) occurs, "My thrice-driven bed of
down."

the wood for the charcoal burning, have disappeared. The registers are wonderfully rich in trade names which have become obsolete or obsolescent. Such are 'crateman,' 'jersey comber,' 'dauber' (plasterer), 'mugman,' 'bonker' (bleacher), 'shearman,' 'corviser' (shoemaker), 'fletcher' (arrowmaker) 'pedder' (the true form of pedlar), 'thrower' (twister), 'blowman' (iron-smelter), and 'fusterer' (saddletree maker)."

"Lancashire, too, according to the registers, seems to have been famous of old for its musical tendencies, for not only de we find a 'piper' mentioned in almost every register—in Poulton described as a 'droner'—but Chipping, in addition, boasted a 'trumpeter,' Eccleston a 'blind harper,' Middleton a 'drummer,' Croston, Cockerham, and Cartmel a 'fiddler,' Culcheth a 'bagpipe player,' and Wood Plympton a 'musicus.'"

The remarkable light thrown upon the development of copper mining by a German company in the High Furness district towards the close of the sixteenth century by the Coniston parish register has recently been noted by that careful northern antiquary, Professor Collingwood (*Memorials of Old Lancashire*, 1909). In the last years of that century a company of Germans, already domiciled at Keswick for a generation, began to work copper mines at Coniston, carrying the ore on pack-horses to their Keswick smelting house. Their names and the outlines of their history are to be found in the now printed registers of Coniston and Hawkshead. These registers show that the Germans lived chiefly at Monk Coniston, that they attended Coniston church, but were buried at Hawkshead; that they married into the best yeomen families of the dales, and evidently intended to settle in the country of their adoption.

"The principal family names of these Germans at Coniston were Clocker, Colter, Moser, Godmunt, Suckmantle, Stoneparker, Ritseler, Phemcke, Plauntziner, and

Puthparker ; at least these are the forms into which their names were turned by the pen of the village clerk. Puthparker, in a more early form, was Pughbarger, probably for Puchberger; there were three Balthazars and three Symons in different generations of this family . . . Symon Puchberger was buried in the church at Hawkshead on 25th January 1640–1. The eldest Balthazar (as the registers tell us) was nicknamed ' Towsie,' which gives us a picture of the ' towzled ' old German, or rather Austrian, for Puchberg is an Austrian village not far from the great mining centre of Eisenerz, in Styria, where perhaps the Puchbergers served their apprenticeship to the trade already long established in the Erzberg, which was then, and still is, one of the wonders of the Alps—a mountain of solid iron ore. Plauntziver may imply origin from Planitzing, near Bozen, in the Tyrol; a Steinberg is near Innsbruck; Klocher and Moser are not uncommon names in the Tyrol; and as their chief came from Augsburg, it is likely that some of the men were drawn from the old mining districts of the Eastern Alps. But it is curious to find the ' Black Brothers of Styria,' of Ruskin's early fairy tale, domiciled so long before him in his own township, and to think of the romantic blend of German and Anglicised Norse that peopled the dales three hundred years ago. It is to the mixture of races that much of the strong, intelligent character of the dalesfolk is owing."

A title which is not infrequently found in early registers is likely to confuse those who are not used to mediæval phraseology. " Syr," or " Sir," was prefixed or attached to the names of such priests as had not graduated at either of the Universities. It used to be said in old days that there were only three " Syrs "—" Syr Kynge," " Syr Knyghte," and " Syr Prieste."

Between 1539 and 1553 this title of respect occurs with

some frequency in the registers of St. Margaret's, West-minster. The use of the term died out early in the reign of Elizabeth. It is to be found in the register of Minehead, Somerset :—

"1548. Sir John Richards sometymes Vicar of this parish bur. March 8."

The following instances occur in the Kidderminster registers :—

"1541, Oct iiij. buried of Sr John Barret preist.
      ,,   ,, xv.   ,,   Sr Nicholas write, preist.
"1542, Aug xxv. buried Sr Thomas Alchurch, prst.
"1543, April xx. buried Sir. Philip Pardoe, preist.
      ,,   Feb xix. buried Sir James Pirry, preist.
"1550, Mar xxx. buried Sr William Thomyns, preist late Vicar of Kitherminster.
"1553, August the xxiij day was christned Alexander the sonne of Sir William Spittle, preist."

There are also various like entries in the first register book of St. Dionis, Backchurch :—

"1547, Oct 27. Syr Thomas Powell pryste buried.
"1548, July 13. Syr Robert Johnson, parson of St. Margarettes, old fysh strete buried.
      ,,   July 15. Syr Thomas Barefoote, parson of thys parishe buried.
"1549, April 29. Syr William Erith, parson of S. Dennis p'ishe and Christiane Poole was maryed.
"1565 (*Ibid.*) Oct 18. Syr Peter Haryson, pryste and physysyon and sometyme parson of Crown land over in hamshire, in the Countye of Southamton."

Another late entry of this kind occurs in the Harbledown register, Kent :—

"1562, Mar. 13. Sᵣ Robert Mobery p'son preste of Hambledown bur."

It is commonly supposed that the giving of Puritan

names to children was a particular characteristic of the days of the Commonwealth. But a study of registers quite upsets this view, and proves that such names were for the most part given at earlier periods when Puritanism began to be aggressive. An examination of upwards of forty parish registers between 1640 and 1660, in a single county, merely reveals one name of this character. The elaborate godly names of some of Cromwell's troopers were, however, usually names assumed in adult life, and were not bestowed on them in baptism. The following are a few examples culled from baptismal registers :—

Evangelist (Shoreditch)	1563	Be Faithful (All Sts., N'ton)	1601
Deliverance (All Sts., N'ton)	1589	Free Gift (Chiddingley)	1616
Comfort (All Sts., N'ton)	1592	Repentance (St. Sepulchre's, N'ton,	1617
Joy Agayne (Daventry)	1594	Sighe (All Sts., N'ton)	1630
Know God (E. Haddon)	1597	Faintnot (Chiddingley)	1631
Repente (St. Dunstan West)	1599	Obedience (Wing, Rutland)	1656

Perhaps the most astonishing registered name is that of Shadrach Meshach Abednego, conferred in baptism, 3rd December 1777, on the son of Shadrach Meshach Abednego Smith, and Martha his wife, in the church of All Saints, Northampton.

The confusing custom of calling children of a family by the same name was by no means uncommon in the middle ages. Of this there are various proofs in pedigrees and genealogical notes of days prior to parochial registration. Lady Alice Tyrell, of Herons, who died in 1422, left four sons, two of whom were named William, and the other two John. Protector Somerset had three sons named Edward, all of whom were living at the same time. In the register of Beby, Leicestershire, are the following entries :—

"1539, Aug. 29. John and John Sicke, the children of Christopher and Anne, were baptized.

"Item, 31 Aug. The same John and John were buried."

Burn cites the following sentence from the burial entry

of Mary Topp, in the register of Stockton, Wilts, but omits the date:—

"Tres filias reliquit superstites Johannem Seniorem juvenem Johannem Juniorem adolescentem, et Edwardum puerulum."

In the early Elizabethan Survey of the Earl of Pembroke's manor in Wilts, etc., three brothers of the same name were sons of Janet Dight, widow, and the reversion of her holding went to "*Johanni primogenito, Johanni secundogenito, et Johanni tertiogenito, filiis suis*"; in another case three brothers are described as "John senior, John medius, and John junior."

The question of the early occurrence of more than one Christian name, and the time when such an occurrence became common, has often been discussed, more especially in the columns of *Notes and Queries*. It is usually stated that Henry Algernon, fifth Earl of Northumberland, who was born on 13th January 1477–8, is the earliest English instance of a two-fold baptismal name; the double name appears on his garter plate in St. George's Chapel, Windsor. Fuller, the church historian, mentions that Queen Mary gave her own name in addition to their own christian name to her godsons, so that they were called Anthony-Maria, Edward-Maria, etc.

Instances of double names were exceedingly rare during the reigns of Elizabeth and James I. Camden, the antiquary, says, on this subject:—

"I can only remember now his Majesty, who was named Charles James, and the Prince his sonne Henry Frederic; and among private men, Thos. Maria Wingfield and Sir Thomas Posthumus Hobby."

Anthony Ashley Cooper, the first Earl of Shrewsbury, who was born in 1621, is a notable exception. In the latter part of the seventeenth century the custom came more into vogue, but very slowly. Thus the registers of Tamworth have an entry in 1680 of the baptism of Robert, the son of Thomas Dooley Gyp ; and at Harlington, Beds, there is the entry of one Anna Letitia Wingate in 1686. Broadly speaking, however, the average register contains no double names until the nineteenth century is reached. In the last half of that century the custom of two or more Christian names set in with such general determination that nowadays it is a distinct exception to find anyone, no matter what the position, bearing only a single name.

We suppose Mr. Chester Waters was in earnest in citing the following baptism as recorded in the parish register of Burbage, Wilts :—

"1781. Charles Caractacus Ostorius Maximilian Gustavus Adolphus, son of Charles Stone, tailor, bapt. 29 April."

Up to 1812, when it was provided that all registers were to be kept after a set pattern, it was usual in not a few parishes to adopt labour-saving expedients in making the entries. One of the commonest forms of abbreviation was to use the initial letters b., m., and s., for baptism, marriage, and burial (sepulture). It remained for the vicar of Carburton, Notts, to adopt the following hieroglyphics :—

"Note, Since 1729 the Christenings, Burials, and Marriages are Set together and are distinguished by these marks, viz. † before Xtnings, ☺ a Deaths head before Burials, and a pair of Claspers ⋈ before marriages."

Reference has been made in the first chapter to the registration acts of William and Mary for the definite entry of the births of children who were not baptised, or at all events, not baptised in church, and to the general lack of obedience to these directions. It is quite exceptional to find any register entries of this nature.

Stitched into the first volume of the registers of St.

Mary's, Reading (which begin in 1538), are several lists of entries on leaves of paper thus headed :—

" The By-Register according to Actt of Parllement for Byrthe of those that are not baptised by the Minister of the Parish in the yeare of our Lord, 1695." There are five entries for 1696, eight for 1697, and twelve for 1698. They average about ten down to 1706, and then speedily lessen. The entries end in 1754, many of the later years having no entry, and several only one.

There is more evidence of compliance with these Acts in the north of England than elsewhere. The four following examples all occur in Northumberland.

The parish registers of Warkworth supply birth lists of a few *Liberi Dissentientium Ecclesiæ Anglicanæ* from 1723 to 1824 ; the three last cases are stated to have been baptized in the dissenting chapel.

In the register books of Elsdon, Northumberland, there is a record of " The Births of Dissenters Children as attested by their Parents." The entries begin in 1734, and occur somewhat fitfully down to 1819 ; they seldom number more than one a year.

Among the registers of Edlingham is a list of " The Dissenters Children as they were given in by their Parents." It extends from 1733 to 1812. They are distinguished by the capital letters D. or P., the latter, we suppose, for Presbyterian, and the former for other forms of dissent. The highest number thus registered in any year was in 1744, when there are nine entries ; they average about three a year.

The registers of Eglingham, also in the same county, include a record of baptisms of dissenters, headed " Chrisings not chrisened in the Church." It begins in 1696 with six of such entries ; they numbered thirteen in 1697, seven in 1698, eight in 1699, fifteen in 1700, sixteen in 1701, and three in 1702. These are followed by two or three entries under the years 1744, 1747, 1748, 1749, 1759, 1761, 1769, and 1770.

In the second register book of Moulton, Northants, which begins in 1689, is a short list of unbaptized children, or rather of families none of whose children were baptized. Eleven families are named ; they clearly belonged to a small Baptist community in the parish.

On one of the fly-leaves of the third volume of the registers of North Wingfield, Derbyshire, is the following list of births of unbaptized Quakers:—

"Tupton. Sarah d. of George and Ellen Wright, born 6 May 1698.

,, George s. of George and Ellen Wright, born 1 Nov. 1700.

" Pilsley. George s. of George and Ellen Turpin, born 1 April 1701.

,, Hannah d. of Thomas and Hannah Lynam, born 4 April 1702.

" Tupton. Margret d. of Nicholas and Hannah Turner, born 27 Sept. 1702.

" Pilsley. William s. of George and Ellen Turpin, born 17 Nov. 1703.

" Tupton. Hannah d. of George and . . . Ashley, born 17 Nov. 1704.

,, Katherin d. of Nicholas and Hannah Turner, born 21 Sept. 1705.

,, Daniel s. of George and Ellen Turpin, born 29 Jan. 1705."

The register entries of Atworth, Wilts, continue to record far more births than baptisms for some little time after the Restoration of 1660. From 1697 to 1704 there are entries in a separate place in the register book of the births of "Annabaptistes and Quakers." The last dissenter's birth we noticed was in 1710.

As to the highly commendable habit of printing carefully

compiled transcripts of registers, which has increased by
rapid strides during recent years, the first instance of which
we are aware is that of the registers of Durnford, Wilts, from
1574 to 1650, ten copies of which were printed in 1824 by
Sir Thomas Phillipps.

The Harleian Society began printing a parish register
series in 1876, and have now issued thirty-seven volumes.
The Parish Register Society began work in 1896, and have
already issued upwards of sixty volumes. Special societies
for the register printing of the counties of Lancashire, Yorkshire, Shropshire, Durham and Northumberland, Staffordshire, and Surrey have also done much excellent work. Other
societies for printing only the marriage registers have been
formed in the counties of Buckingham, Cambridge, Cornwall, Derby, Dorset, Gloucester, Hants, Hertford, Norfolk,
Nottingham, Somerset, Warwick, and Worcester; but these
are of limited value, and that only to mere genealogists;
they will prove, we fear, an impediment to the far more
desirable issue of complete registers. Many other excellent transcripts of whole registers have been issued by
individuals, notably by Mr. F. A. Crisp, and by Mr. J. M.
Cowper for Canterbury and the district.

The result of it all is that there are now (July 1909) about
600 parish registers in print in a fairly perfect state, the
large majority of them covering the period from their
beginning up to 1812, when official registration was imposed.
These are set forth in an alphabetical list in Appendix IV,
and for its comparative completeness we are greatly indebted
to the admirable *Key to the Ancient Parish Registers of England* (1908), by Mr. A. M. Burke.

This book is concerned in the main with Parish Registers,
in accordance with its title, but a very brief space may as
well be given to Nonconformist Registers. Those who
are desirous of information under this head should consult

17

a Blue Book, issued in 1841, entitled *Lists of Non-parochial Registers and Records in the custody of the Registrar-General* (Somerset House), wherein a county classification is observed; also a *Report on Non-parochial Registers*, issued in 1857, wherein are enumerated those registers of the sects that are still in private custody.

In a very few cases Nonconformist Registers have been printed. The register of Dukinfield Chapel, Cheshire, from 1677 to 1713, was printed by Mr. J. P. Earwaker in 1887; it contains some interesting extraneous notes, such as the death of Queen Mary from small-pox on 28th December 1696. The Shropshire Parish Register Society printed in 1903 ten registers of Dissenters from different parts of the county, the earliest being that of the Society of Friends, Shrewsbury, which begins in 1657.

The Huguenot Society, founded in 1885, has published several volumes of the valuable registers of Protestant refugees.

The registers of the Walloon church of Norwich were printed in 1887-88 (vol. i. parts 1 and 2), and arranged alphabetically. The baptisms extend from 22nd June 1595 to 22nd June 1754; the marriages from 21st October 1599 to 12th May 1611; the banns (*annonces*) from 23rd September 1628 to 4th June 1691.

The registers of the Walloon church of Southampton were printed in 1890 (vol. iv.). The *Admissions à la Ste-Cène* extend from 1568 to 1665; the baptisms from 1567 to 1779; the marriages from 1567 to 1753; and the deaths from 1567 to 1722. This congregation suffered appallingly from the plague in 1583, when there were upwards of 70 victims. The registers show yet more awful results in 1604, when the deaths in June and July amounted to 122, though the average death-rate of the Walloons for the whole year of that period only amounted to six,

The registers of the Walloon church of Canterbury were printed in 1891-98 (vol. v., three parts), under the editorship of Mr. Hovenden. The baptisms date from 1581 to 1837 ; the marriages from 1590 to 1747 ; and the deaths from 1581 to 1745. There are also entries of marriage contracts from 1580 to 1680.

The registers of the French church of Threadneedle Street, London, were printed in 1896–1906 (vols. ix., xiii., xvi.). The entries of baptisms and marriages extend from 1600 to 1714.

The registers of the Church of La Patente, Spitalfields, were printed in 1898 (vol. xi.). The baptisms extend from 1689 to 1785, and the marriages from 1689 to 1753.

The register of baptisms at the Dutch church at Colchester was printed in 1905 (vol. xii.) ; they date from 1645 to 1728.

The register of baptisms at the French church at Thorney, Cambridgeshire, was printed in 1903 (vol. xvii.) ; they date from 1654 to 1727.

APPENDIX I

A LIST OF SOME BISHOPS' TRANSCRIPTS WHOSE DATES ARE OLDER THAN THE PARISH REGISTERS[1]

Parish.	Register Date.	Transcript Date.
Abberton, Worcester . .	1661	1608
Abbots Bickington .	1716	1609
Abbots Morton . .	1728	1611
Abbotsham	1653	1597
Abington, Great	1664	1608
Abington, Little . . .	1687	1623
Abington Pigotts	1653	1599
Alfrick	1656	1611
Anstey, West	1653	1608
Ashford, Devon . .	1700	1596
Ashprington . . .	1607	1597﹡
Ashreigney	1653	1698
Bampton . . .	1653	1609
Barnet, Chipping . .	1678	1569
Barton (Camb.) . . .	1688	1600
Beaford . . .	1653	1598
Beaworthy . . .	1758	1602
Berry Pomeroy . . .	1602	1596
Bigbury	1678	1613
Bondleigh	1734	1607
Bow (Devon) . . .	1604	1597
Bradstone	1654	1611
Brampford-Speke	1739	1601
Bredicot . . .	1702	1609
Bredons'-Norton	1734	1612
Bricklehampton	1756	1617
Brinkley	1684	1600
Broadwas	1676	1612
Broome	1674	1613
Broughton-Hackett	1761	1609
Bushey	1684	1581
Caddington	1681	1597
Caldecot	1662	1611

[1] This list is largely taken from Mr. A. M. Burke's invaluable *Key to Parish Registers* (1908), and from a Supplement to the same (1909); it is only intended to supply examples of the value of the transcripts, and is very far from being complete.

Parish.	Register Date.	Transcript Date.
Cambridge (St. Andrew the Great) . .	1635	1605
Carleton (Cambs.)	1725	1602
Caxton	1741	1602
Chatteris	1613	1604
Chettisham	1701	1599
Cotheridge	1653	1611
Coughton	1673	1616
Coveney	1676	1600
Cutsdean	1696	1634
Daylesford	1674	1624
Doddington (Camb.) . . .	1681	1600
Dormston	1716	1612
Doverdale	1755	1612
Earls Cronor	1647	1612
Eckington	1678	1612
Eldersfield	1718	1612
Elmley Castle . . .	1665	1612
Eltisley	1653	1599
Ettington . . .	1661	1621
Fleet	1652	1561
Flyford Favel.	1679	1613
Flyford Gratton	1676	1612
Gamlingay	1698	1601
Girton (Cambs.) . . .	1629	1599
Grafton Temple . .	1695	1612
Gransden, Little	1730	1606
Graveley (Cambs.) . .	1642	1599
Hampton-in-Arden . .	1666	1615
Harleton	1636	1599
Harston (Cambs.)	1686	1599
Haslingfield	1709	1599
Himbleton	1713	1611
Histon	1655	1599
Horningsey	1628	1600
Huddington	1695	1612
Inkberrow	1675	1613
Keal East	1708	1562
Kempsey	1688	1608
Kingston (Cambs.) . .	1654	1589
Litlington	1642	1598
Littleport . . .	1753	1599
Littleton, North . . .	1661	1611
Longdon (Staffs.) . . .	1681	1663
Lulsley	1754	1622
Madresfield	1742	1611
Manea	1708	1645
Meldreth	1681	1599
Milton (Cambs.) . .	1693	1600
Mitton, Lower . . .	1693	1603
Monyash	1707	1672
Morden Steeple	1675	1599
Morton Bagot . . .	1663	1614
Naunton Beauchamp . .	1696	1611
Newton (nr. Wisbeach) . . .	1653	1599

Parish.	Register Date.	Transcript Date.
Norton Lindsey	1742	1607
Oddingley	1661	1611
Offley, High	1689	1659
Oldberrow	1649	1613
Parson-Drove	...	1607
Pedworth	1693	1607
Peopleton	1632	1612
Piddle, Wyre	1670	1605
Powick	1662	1611
Preston-Bagot	1677	1612
Queenhill	1733	1608
Rampton (Cambs.)	1674	1599
Rickmansworth	1653	1570
Rushock	1661	1608
Salwarpe	1666	1613
Sawston	1640	1599
Sheldon	1745	1675
Shelford, Little . . .	1686	1600
Slimbridge	1635	1571
Spernall	1676	1612
Stapleford (Cambs.) . . .	1707	1599
Stow (Cambs.)	1650	1600
Studley	1663	1613
Suckley	1695	1613
Sulhampstead-Banister . . .	1654	1613
Tadlow	1653	1638
Thetford (Cambs.)	1654	1599
Tibberton	1680	1612
Trumpington	1671	1599
Walden	1653	1581
Warwick, St. Mary . . .	1651	1611
Waterbeach	1653	1600
Welland	1670	1608
Wellow (Notts)	1703	1626
Wentworth (Cambs.) . . .	1754	1600
Whaddon (Cambs.) . . .	1692	1606
Whittlesey, St. Andrew . . .	1653	1622
Wichenford	1690	1599
Wick, nr. Pershore	1695	1608
Wickham, West (Cambs.) . . .	1682	1599
Wilburton	1739	1599
Witcham	1633	1607
Witchford	1725	1599
Wolford	1654	1612
Wolverton	1680	1614
Worcester, St. Andrew . . .	1656	1612
,, St. Clement . . .	1694	1609

APPENDIX II

LIST OF PARISH REGISTERS BEGINNING IN 1538

Abbots Langley, Herts
Abingdon, St. Helen, Berks
    ,,   St. Nicholas, Berks
Adelstrop, Glouc.
Adstock, Bucks
Akenham, Suffolk
Aldborough, York
Aldringham, Suffolk
Alford, Linc.
Alfriston, Sussex
Alkborough, Linc.
Almer, Dorset
Alstonfield, Staffs
Arlesley, Beds
Arrington, Cambs
Ashbourne, Derby
Ashill, Norfolk
Ashperton, Herefords
Ashton Steeple, Wilts
Askham, Notts
Aston Steeple, Oxon
Audley, Staffs
Avenham, Notts
Avonwick, Yorks
Awre, Glouc.
Baddow, Great, Essex
Badingham, Suffolk
Badminton, Glouc.
Badsey, Worc.
Balderton, Notts
Bale, Norfolk
Balstonborough, Som.
Bampton, Oxon
Bardsey, York
Bardwell, Suffolk
Barford, Warw.
Barkham, Berks
Barking, Suffolk
Barkway, Herts
Barnes, Surrey
Barney, Norfolk
Barningham, Suffolk
Barningham, Little, Norfolk
Barningham-Norwood, Norfolk
Barnstaple, Devon
Barrington, Cambs
Barrowby, Lincoln
Bayford, Herts
Beckenham, Kent
Beddington, Surrey

Bedfield, Suffolk
Bedingfield, Suffolk
Bedwin, Great, Wilts
Beeby, Leic.
Beeley, Derby
Bees, St., Cumberland
Beeston, Norfolk
Beeston, St. Lawrence, Norfolk
Belaugh, Norfolk
Belbroughton, Worc.
Belchamp, St. Paul, Essex
Belton, Leicester
    ,,   Lincoln
Bengworth, Worc.
Berkhamsted, Great, Herts
Berners-Roding, Essex
Bernington, Herts
Bessingham, Norfolk
Betley, Staff
Biddenden, Kent
Binfield, Berks
Birdham, Sussex
Bishops Tachbrook, Warwick
Blackawton, Devon
Blakeney, Norfolk
Blakesley, Northants
Bletchingley, Surrey
Blithfield, Staffs
Blockley, Worc.
Bluntisham, Hunts
Bolingbroke, Linc.
Bothamsall, Notts
Bovey Tracey, Devon
Boxted, Suffolk
Bradeley, Staffs
Bradenham, West, Norfolk
Bradfield, St. Clare, Suffolk
Bradfield-Combust, Suffolk
Brancaster, Norfolk
Braunston, Northants
Braunton, Devon
Brenzett, Kent
Brereton, Chester
Bretforton, Worc.
Bridford, Devon
Bristol, Christ Church
    ,,   St. Nicholas
Broadchalke, Wilts
Broadhembury, Devon
Brodsworth, York

Bromley, Little, Essex
Bromyard, Hereford
Broome, Norfolk
Broughton, Lincoln
,, Church, Derby
Buckenham, New, Norfolk
Buckland, St. Mary, Som.
,, Monachorum, Devon
,, West, Som.
Bucklebury, Berks
Buckminster, Leic.
Budeaux, St., Devon
Bungay, St. Mary, Suffolk
Bures, Suffolk
Burgh-in-the-Marsh, Lincoln
Burlingham, St. Andrews, Norfolk
Burnham-Westgate, Norfolk
Burton, Cheshire
Burton Latimer, Northants
Burton-Fleming, York
Bury St. Edmunds, St. Mary, Suffolk
Bushley, Worcester
Calne, Wilts
Camborne, Cornwall
Cambridge, St. Michael
Canfield, Gt., Essex
Canterbury, St. George
Cantley, York
Capel, St. Mary, Suffolk
Carleton-in-Craven, York
Carlton, Suffolk
Carshalton, Surrey
Castor, Northants
Cawston, Norfolk
Chaceley, Worc.
Chaddesley Corbett, Worc.
Chaddleworth, Berks
Chailey, Sussex
Chalgrove, Oxon
Chalton, Hants
Chalvington, Sussex
Charles, Devon
Charlton Kings, Glouc.
Cheam, Surrey
Chedburgh, Surrey
Chelmsford, Essex
Chelsfield, Kent
Cherington, Warwick
Cheriton Bishop, Devon
Chesham, Bucks
Chesterton, Warwick
Chettle, Dorset
Chetton, Salop
Childerditch, Essex
Chislet, Kent
Churchstow, Devon
Clacton, Little, Essex
Claines, Worc.

Clayhanger, Devon
Claypole, Lincoln
Cley-next-the-Sea, Norfolk
Clifford-Chambers, Glouc.
Clifton, Beds
,, Glouc.
Coleshill, Warwick
Colkirk, Norfolk
Colyton, Devon
Combe Hay, Hants
Compton, West, Dorset
Compton-Chamberlayne, Wilt
Compton Nether, Dorset
Conington, Cambridge
Cookley, Suffolk
Coombe-Keynes, Dorset
Coombes, Sussex
Corton Denham, Somerset
Cossey, Norfolk
Coton, Cambridge
Cotton, Suffolk
Courteenhall, Northants
Cratfield, Suffolk
Crayke, Yorks
Craynorth. Kent
Creake, North, Norfolk
,, South, Norfolk
Cropredy, Oxon
Croxton, Cambridge
Croydon, Surrey
Curry, North, Somerset
Dartington, Devon
Dean, West, Wilts
Depden, Suffolk
Derby, St. Alkmund
Dereham, East, Norfolk
Dewsbury, Yorks
Didbrooke, Glouc.
Digswell, Herts
Ditton, Fen, Cambridge
Doddenham, Worc.
Dodington, Somerset
Dorking, Surrey
Dorney, Bucks
Down, Kent
,, East, Devon
Drayton-Beauchamp, Bucks
Dun Chideock, Devon
Dunchurch, Warwick
Dunmow, Great, Essex
Dunsby, Lincoln
Dunton, Essex
Durham, St. Oswald
Dymock, Glouc.
Easebourne, Sussex
Easter Good, E-sex
Eastleach-Martin, Glouc.
Eastwell, Kent

Eaton, Church, Stafford
Edenbridge, Kent
Edingley, Notts
Edwalton, Notts
Egleton, Rutland
Ellingham, Norfolk
Elmdon, Warwick
Elmham, North, Norfolk
Elmsted, Kent
Evesham, All Saints, Worcs.
Exeter, St. Petroch
  ,,   St. Mary-Arches
Eydon, Northants
Eye, Suffolk
Eyke, Suffolk
Eynesford, Kent
Eyworth, Beds
Falkenham, Suffolk
Farlington, Hants
Farnworth, Lanc.
Farthingstone, Northants
Feckenham, Worc.
Ferriby, South, Linc.
Field-Dalling, Norfolk
Fillongley, Warw.
Finedon, Northants
Folke, Dorset
Foulden, Norfolk
Fownhope, Hereford
Framfield, Sussex
Frampton, Linc.
Fransham, Little, Norfolk
Freston, Suffolk
Frostenden, Suffolk
Frowlesworth, Leic.
Fryston-Monk, Yorks
Fulbourne, Cambs
Fyfield, Essex
Garveston, Norfolk
Georgeham, Devon
Gerrans, St., Cornwall
Gonalston, Notts
Goodleigh, Devon
Gosfield, Essex
Granborough, Bucks.
Gransden, Great, Hunts
Gressenhall, Norfolk
Grimsby, Great, Linc.
Gwaenysgor, Flint.
Hackeston, Linc.
Hackford, Suffolk
Hagley, Worc.
Hale-Magna, Linc.
Halifax, Yorks
Hallam, West, Derby
Hallingbury, Great, Essex
Hallow, Worc.
Halton, West, Linc.

Hampstead Norreys, Berks
Hanley Castle, Worc.
Hannington, Northants
Harborne, Staffs
Harefield, Midd.
Harpole, Northants
Harrietsham, Kent
Hartford, Hunts
Hartlip, Kent
Harworth, Notts
Haseley, Great, Oxon
Hatford, Berks
Hatton, Warwick
Heckfield, Hants
Heddington, Wilts
Heigham, Potter, Norfolk
Henbury, Glouc.
Hendred, East, Berks
Hessett, Suffolk
Hexton, Herts
Heydon, Essex
  ,,   Norfolk
Higham, Suffolk
Highworth, Wilts
Hinton, Cherry, Cambs
Hinxton, Cambs
Holme Hale, Norfolk
Holt, Worc.
Holton, St. Peter, Suffolk
Hooton Pagnell, Yorks
Hopton Castle, Salop
Horley, Oxon
Hormead, Great, Herts
Houghton Regis, Beds
Hove, Sussex
Hundon, Suffolk
Hunstanton, Norfolk
Hurstmonceux, Sussex
Ickenham, Midd.
Ilketshall, St. John, Suffolk
  ,,   St. Margaret, Suffolk
Ingham, Suffolk
Ipswich, St. Margaret
  ,,   St. Mary-le-Tower
Irstead, Norfolk
Just, St., in-Roseland, Cornwall
Kelsale, Suffolk
Kelshall, Herts
Kelston, Som.
Kenn, Devon
Kenton, Suffolk
Keswick, Norfolk
Kilve, Som.
Kilvington, Notts
Kineton, Warw.
Kingsclere, Hant
Kingsey, Bucks
Kingsland, Hereford

Kingsnorth, Kent
Kirby Bedon, Norfolk
Kirby Cane, Norfolk
Kirkby Lonsdale, Westm.
Kirton, Notts
Kislingbury, Northants
Knowstone, Devon
Knoyle, East, Wilts
Laceby, Linc.
Laleham, Midd.
Lamerton, Devon
Lammas, Norfolk
Landbeach, Cambs
Laneham, Notts
Langford, Oxon
Langford-Budville, Som.
Lapley, Staffs
Laver, Little, Essex
Lazonby, Cumb.
Ledbury, Hereford
Leigh, Worc.
Leiston, Suffolk
Lench, Rous, Worc.
Leverton, Linc.
Lexham, East, Norfolk
Lighthorne, Warw.
Lincoln, St. Margaret
,,   St. Peter-at-Gowts
Littleham (Bideford), Devon
Littleton, South, Worc.
Livermere, Suffolk
London, All Hallows, Honey Lane
,,   St. Antholin,
,,   St. Benet Finck
,,   Christ Church
,,   St. Dionis, Backchurch
,,   St. Lawrence, Jewry
,,   ,,   Pountney
,,   St. Leonard, Eastcheap
,,   St. Margaret, Westminster
,,   St. Mary, Aldermanbury
,,   ,,   Bathaw
,,   ,,   le Bow
,,   ,,   Woolnoth
,,   St. Matthew, Friday Street
,,   St. Michael, Bassishaw
,,   ,,   Crooked Lane
,,   St. Mildred, Poultry
,,   St. Nicholas, Cole Abbey
,,   St. Pancras, Soper Lane
,,   St. Peter, Cornhill
,,   St. Stephen, Coleman Street
Longdon, Worc.
Longford, Derby
Lorton, Cumb.
Loughborough, Leic.
Louth, Linc.
Ludgershall, Buck.

Lugwardine, Hereford
Lyng, Norfolk
Maismore, Glouc.
Manningford Abbas, Wilts
Marbury, Chester
Maresfield, Sussex
Marsham, Norfolk
Marston, Butlers, Warw.
Martin-Hussingtree, Worc.
Maxey, Northants
Melton, High, Yorks
Meon, West, Hants
Merrow, Surrey
Merstham, Surrey
Messing, Essex
Metheringham, Linc.
Micheldever, Hunts
Milton-Ernest, Beds
,,   (Sittingbourne), Kent
Milverton, Som.
Molland, Devon
Moreton-Morrell, Warw.
Morval, Cornwall
Navestock, Essex
Newbottle, Northants
Newbury, Berks
Newington, South, Oxon
Newton, St. Loe, Som.
Norbury, Staffs
Normanton, Yorks
Norrington, Kent
Northam, Devon
Norton, Worc.
Norton-juxta-Kempsey, Worc.
Norwich, St. Clement
,,   St. George Colegate
,,   St. George Tombland
,,   St. Giles
,,   St. Martin-at-Palace
,,   St. Michael-at-Plea
,,   St. Peter Mancroft
,,   ,,   Mountergate
,,   St. Stephen
Nympton, Kings, Devon
Oakley, Suffolk
Ockendon, South, Essex
Odiham, Hants
Offenham, Worc.
Offham, Kent
Ogbourne, St. George, Wilts
Ongar, High, Essex
Orchard-Fortman, Som.
Ordsall, Notts
Orford, Suffolk
Oswaldkirk, Yorks
Otham, Kent
Oxburgh, Norfolk
Oxwick, Norfolk

Packington, Great, Warw.
Padbury, Bucks
Parham, Suffolk
    ,,   Sussex
Paston, Norfolk
Pauntley, Glouc.
Peasemore, Berks
Pennard, West, Som.
Perrot, South, Dorset
Peterstow, Hereford
Pickworth, Linc.
Piddletown, Dorset
Pirton, Worc.
Pitcomb, Som.
Plymtree, Devon
Polstead, Suffolk
Pontesbright, Essex
Pontesbury, Salop
Poole, Dorset
Poughill, Cornwall
Preston, Sussex
Priors Dean, Hants
Privett, Hants
Pulham, St. Mary Magdalen, Norfolk
Pyon, Kings, Hereford
Reading, St. Mary
Rede, Suffolk
Redgrave, Suffolk
Reepham, Norfolk
Ridware-Mavesyn, Staffs
Rimpton, Som.
Ripe, Sussex
Risington, Great, Glouc.
Rockland, St. Peter, Norfolk
Roding, High, Essex
    ,,   Margaret, Essex
Rodmersham, Kent
Romney, Old, Kent
Ropley, Hants
Rossington, Yorks
Rothwell, York
Ruckinge, Kent
Rushbury, Salop
Rye, Sussex
Ryton-on-Dunsmore, Warw.
Saddington, Leic.
Sancton, Yorks
Sandford-Orcas, Dorset
Sandhurst, Glouc.
Sandwich, St. Mary, Kent
    ,,   St. Peter, Kent
Sandy, Beds
Saxelby, Leic.
Saxmundham, Suffolk
Saxton, Yorks
Scarning, Norfolk
Scraptoft, Leic.
Seaton Rutland, Rutland

Semer, Suffolk
Sevenhampton, Wilts
Shadingfield, Suffolk
Shadoxhurst, Kent
Shalstone, Bucks
Sheepshed, Leic.
Shelsley-Beauchamp, Worc.
Sherborne, Dorset
Sherwell, Devon
Shimpling, Norfolk
Shimplingthorne, Suffolk
Shipton, Salop
Shipton-under-Wychwood, Oxon
Shobrooke, Devon
Shocklach, Chester
Shotesham, All Saints, Norfolk
Shustoke, Warw.
Skelton-by-York, York
Slaughter, Upper, Glouc.
Solihull, Warw.
Somerton, Suffolk
Southease, Sussex
South Hill, Cornwall
Southill, Beds
Southolt, Suffolk
Sowe, Warw.
Spalding, Linc.
Spexhall, Suffolk
Spratton, Northants
Stanford Dingley, Berks
Stanford Rivers, Essex
Stanground, Hunts
Stansfield, Suffolk
Stedham, Sussex
Stevenage, Herts
Stisted, Essex
Stockland Bristol, Som.
Stoke, Norfolk
Stoke Ash, Suffolk
Stoke-by-Clare, Suffolk
Stoke Climsland, Cornwall
Stoke, East, Notts
Stoke Edith, Hereford
Stoke Fleming, Devon
Stoke Goldington, Bucks
Stoke Hammond, Bucks
Stoke Severn, Worc.
Stoke-in-Teignhead, Devon
Stone, Bucks
Stonton Wyville, Leic.
Stoughton, Leic.
Stourmouth, Kent
Stradbroke, Suffolk
Streatham, Surrey
Stretton-on-the-Foss, Warw.
Sturry, Kent
Sutterton, Linc.
Sutton, Beds

Sutton-by-Dover, Kent
Sutton, Long, St. Nicholas, Linc.
Sutton-on-Lound, Notts
Swannington, Norfolk
Swanton Abbot, Norfolk
Swardeston, Norfolk
Tawstock, Devon
Tawton, North, Devon
Taynton, Glouc.
,,   Oxon
Tendring, Essex
Terling, Essex
Terrington St. John, Norfolk
Teston, Kent
Thelnetham, Suffolk
Thelveton, Norfolk
Therfield, Herts
Thompson, Norfolk
Thornbury, Glouc.
,,   Hereford
Thorndon, Suffolk
Thorpe, Derby
Thorpe Constantine, Staffs
Thorpe Market, Norfolk
Thorpe Morieux, Suffolk
Thriplow, Cambs
Thurgarton, Norfolk
Thurnby, Leic.
Thuxton, Norfolk
Thwaite, St. Mary, Norfolk
Tickenham, Som.
Tickhill, Yorks
Tilney, All Saints, Norfolk
Tintagel, Cornwall
Tisted, East, Hants
,,   West, Hants
Tittleshall, Norfolk
Tiverton-on-Avon, Som.
Toft Monks, Norfolk
Trimley St. Martin, Suffolk
Trowbridge, Wilts
Trusley, Derby
Tunstall, Kent
Twickenham, Midd.
Uckfield, Sussex
Uffculme, Devon
Ugborough, Devon
Upleadon, Glouc.
Upton, Bucks
Urchfont, Wilts
Uxbridge, Midd.
Veep, St., Cornwall
Waddesdon, Bucks
Wallop, Over, Hants
Walsgrave-on-Sowe, Warw.
Waltham, Kent

Warborough, Oxon
Wargrave, Berks
Warmborough, South, Hants
Warmingham, Chester
Wartling, Sussex
Warwick, St. Nicholas
Wasperton, Warwick
Wattisham, Suffolk
Wensley, York
Wesbury-on-Severn, Glouc.
Westerfield, Suffolk
Westhorpe, Suffolk
Weston, Som.
,,   Suffolk
Weston Turville, Bucks
Wetherden, Suffolk
Whalley, Lanc.
Wharram-le-Street, Yorks
Whatton-in-the-Vale, Notts
Wheatacre Burgh, Norfolk
Wheatenhurst, Glouc.
Whittington, Lanc.
,,   Staffs
Wickford, Essex
Wickhamford, Worc.
Wield, Hants
Wilbraham, Little, Cambs
Wilby, Suffolk
Willesborough, Kent
Willoughby, Linc.
Wilmington, Sussex
Wimbledon, Surrey
Wingfield, Suffolk
Winwick, Hants
Wiston, Suffolk
Witley, Great, Worc.
Witnesham, Suffolk
Wittenham, Little, Berks
Woodchurch, Kent
Woodford, Wilts
Woodton, Norfolk
Woolston, Great, Bucks
Worcester, St. Helen
,,   St. Martin
,,   St. Swithin
Worlingham, Suffolk
Worminghall, Bucks
Wortham, Suffolk
Worthy, Kings, Hants
Wouldham, Kent
Wrington, Som.
Wyberton, Linc.
Wye, Kent
Wymondham, Leic.
York, St. Olave, Marygate

APPENDIX III

LIST OF PARISH REGISTERS BEGINNING IN 1539

Acton, Midds.
   ,,   Beauchamp, Worc.
Adisham, Kent
Adwell, Oxon
Aldborough, Norfolk
Aldingham, Lancs
Alveston, Warwick
Areley Kings, Worc.
Arlingham, Glouc.
Astley, Worc.
Aston-sub-Edge, Glouc.
Balcombe, Sussex
Bardfield, Little, Essex
Barnston, Essex
Battersea, Surrey
Bealings, Great, Suffolk
Beer Ferrers, Devon
Beetley, Norfolk
Belstead, Suffolk
Benger, Herts
Bentley, Hants
   ,,   Suffolk
Besford, Worc.
Beyton, Suffolk
Bicester, Oxon
Binton, Warwick
Birchington, Kent
Birts-Morton, Worcs.
Blisland, Cornwall
Boulge, Suffolk
Bow, Midds.
Boyton, Suffolk
Bradfield, Berks.
Bramfield, Suffolk
Branscombe, Devon
Broadway, Worc.
Buckland, Glouc.
Budbrook, Warwick
Burton-on-Trent, Staffs
Carbrooks, Norfolk
Caston, Norfolk
Cavenham, Suffolk
Chadwell, Essex
Chalfont St. Peter, Bucks
Chalgrave, Beds
Charlecote, Warwick
Chicheley, Bucks
Clifton, North, Notts
Clyst St. Lawrence, Devon
Coddenham, Suffolk

Columb, St. Major, Cornwall
Covington, Hunts
Cropwell Bishop, Notts
Crowle, Worcs.
Darlaston, Staffs
Darsham, Suffolk
Debach, Suffolk
Denham, Suffolk
Dominic, St., Cornwall
Donington Castle, Leic.
Durham, Great, Norfolk
Eaglescliffe, Durham
Easton-Maudit, Northants
Edensor, Derby
Edgecott, Bucks
Elm, Cambs.
Elmley-Lovett, Worc.
Emmington, Oxford
Epping, Essex
Exhall, Warwick
Eynesbury, Hunts
Farnham, Surrey
Fenton, Linc.
Fiskerton, Linc.
Fobbing, Essex
Fornham, St. Martin, Suffolk
Gazely, Suffolk
Grantchester, Cambs
Greenford, Midd.
Hampton, Great, Worc.
   ,,   Little, Worc.
Harwich, Essex
Hayes, Kent
Headley, Hants
Hedgerley, Bucks
Hemington, Som.
Hempston, Little, Devon
Henham, Essex
Henstead, Suffolk
Heveningham, Suffolk
Heyford, Lower, Oxon
Holland, Great, Essex
Huggate, Yorks
Hulcote, Bucks
Huntingfield, Suffolk
Ilford, Little, Essex
Illogan, Cornwall
Ingleby-Greenhow, Yorks
Ipswich, St. Lawrence
   ,,   St. Nicholas

Kensington, Midd.
Keyne, St., Cornwall
Kidderminster, Worc.
Kilkhampton, Cornwall
Kingsthorpe, Northants
Kingston Bagpuize, Berks
Kippax, Yorks
Kirkham, Lanc.
Knightswick, Worc.
Lambeth, Surrey
Ledsham, Yorks
Lezant, Cornwall
Limpsfield, Surrey
Linstead Parva, Suffolk
Liskeard, Cornwall
Littleborough, Notts
London, All Hallows, Bread St.
   ,,   Clement, St., Eastcheap
   ,,   Martin, St., Ironmonger Lane
   ,,   Martin, St., Ludgate
   ,,   Nicholas, St., Acons
Londonthorpe, Linc.
Lowther, Weston
Madingley, Cambs
Marston, South, Wilts
Marton-in-the-West, York
Mashbury, Essex
Milborne Port, Som.
Milston, Wilts
Morcott, Rutland
Morland, Weston
Morley, St. Botolph, Norfolk
Moulton, Little, Norfolk
Nantwich, Cheshire
Northfleet, Kent
Northwood, I. of W.
Norton, Suffolk
Norton, Cold, Essex
Norwich, St. Simon and Jude
Nunnington, York
Ockley, Surrey
Old, Northants
Orton Waterville, Hunts
Pedmore, Worc.
Pelham, Brent, Herts
Pentlow, Essex
Pettistree, Suffolk
Piddle Hinton, Dorset
Pillerton-Hersey, Warwick
Pulham, St. Mary, Norfolk
Rainham, West, Norfolk
Ravensthorpe, Northants
Rawreth, Essex

Redmarley-d'Abitot, Worc.
Reed, Herts
Ridgmont, Beds
Ringshall, Suffolk
Romansleigh, Devon
Rotherfield, Sussex
Rowley, Regis, Staffs
Runham, Norfolk
Ryarsh, Kent
Seale, Surrey
Shenfield, Essex
Soberton, Hants
Southam, Warwick
Spelsbury, Oxon
Spetchley, Worc.
Stockton-on-Teme, Worc.
Stowting, Kent
Strathfieldsaye, Hants
Sutton Courtney, Berks
Tangmere, Sussex
Tannington, Suffolk
Tellisford, Som.
Teynham, Kent
Thorley, Herts
Thornton Dale, York
Thrigley, Norfolk
Toft, Cambs
Tunstall, Suffolk
Waldingfield, Great, Suffolk
Walsham le Willows, Suffolk
Warley, Great, Essex
   ,,   Little, Essex
Warsop, Notts
Watford, Herts
Watton, Norfolk
Weald, South, Essex
Wendling, Norfolk
Weston, Herts
Whiteacre, Nether Warwick
Whittington, Glouc.
Widmerpool, Notts
Windecombe, Glouc.
Wingerworth, Derby
Witchingham, Great, Norfolk
Wolverley, Worc.
Wonersh, Surrey
Wood-Eaton, Oxon
Woolverstone, Suffolk
Wootton, North, Dorset
Yapton, Sussex
Yardley, Worcester
York, St. Martin, Micklegate

APPENDIX IV

LIST OF PRINTED PARISH REGISTERS

(The instances of Marriage entries only are not included)

Parish.	Years Included.	By whom Printed.	Date of Issue.
Abington Pigotts, Cambs .	1653–1812	W. G. F. Pigott .	1890
Adderley, Salop . . .	1692–1812	Sal. P.R.S. .	1904
Addington, Surrey .	1559–1812	Surr. P.R.S. . .	1907
Adel, Yorks	1606–1812	Thoresby Soc., vol. v.	1895
Albans, St., Abbey, Herts	1558–1689	W. Brigg .	1897
Alberbury, Salop . .	1564–1812	Sal. P.R.S. .	1902
Albrighton, nr. Shrewsbury	1555–1812	,, ,, .	1901
,, nr. W'hampton .	1649–1812	,, ,, . .	1900
Aldenham, Herts . .	1559–1659	K. F. Gibbs .	1902
Aldingham, Lancs . . .	1539–1812	Lancs. P.R.S. .	1907
Allerton Mauleverer, Yorks .	1557–1812	Yorks P.R.S. . .	1908
Almer, Dorset . .	1538–1812	Par. Reg. Soc. . .	1907
Alnham, Northumb. .	1688–1812	North. & Dur. P.R.S.	1907
Alstonfield, Staffs. .	1538–1812	Staffs P.R.S. .	1902
Alston Moor, Camh . .	1700	Robert Blair . .	...
Asby, Westm. . . .	1657–1798		1894
Ashe, Hants . . .	1606–1807	F. W. Thoyts .	1888
Askham, Westm. . . .	1568–1812	M. E. Noble .	1904
Askham Richard, Yorks . .	1579–1812	Yorks P.R.S. .	1908
Bampton, Westm. . . .	1637–1812	M. E. Noble .	1897
Banstead, Surrey . . .	1547–1789	Par. Reg. Soc. .	1896
Bardwell, Suffolk . .	1538–1650	F. E. Warren .	1893
Barlaston, Staffs . .	1573–1812	Staffs P.R.S. .	1905
Barnstaple, Devon . . .	1538–1812	Tho. Wainwright .	1903
Barton-under-Needwood, Staffs	1571–1812	Staffs P.R.S. .	1902–3
Barwick-in-Elmett, Yorks .	1653–1812	G. D. Lumb .	1908
Baswick, Staffs . . .	1601–1812	,, ,, .	1903
Bath, Abbey	1659–1800	Harleian Reg. Soc. .	1900–1
Battlefield, Salop . . .	1663–1812	Par. Reg. Soc. .	1899
Beaumont, Essex . .	1565–1678	F. A. Crisp .	1897
Bebington, Chester . .	1558–1701	F. Saunders .	1897
Bedstone, Salop . .	1719–1812	Sal. P.R.S. .	1903
Beer-Hacket, Dorset . .	1549–1812	Par. Reg. Soc. .	1896
Bekesborne, Kent . .	1558–1812	C. H. Wilkie .	1896
Berkeley, Glouc. . .	1653–1677	F. A. Crisp .	1897
Bermondsey, Surrey .	1548–1608	*The Genealogist* .	vols. vi.–ix.
Berwick-on-Tweed, Northum. .	1574–1699	Northm. & Dur. P.R.S.	1905
Bidston, Cheshire . . .	1581–1700	W. F. Irvine .	1893
Billingsley, Salop . . .	1625–1812	Sal. P.R.S. .	1903
Bingley, Yorks . . .	1577–1686	Yorks P.R.S. .	1901
Bircham Newton, Yorks .	1562–1743	Rich. Howlett .	1888
Birchington, Kent . . .	1539–1675	F. A. Crisp . .	1899

Parish.	Years Included.	By whom Printed.	Date of Issue.
Birkenhead, Cheshire . .	1719–1812	Lanc. & Chesh. Hist. Soc. . . .	1908
Birmingham, St. Martin . .	1554–1708	J. Hill & W. B. Bickley	1889
Bisham, Berks . . .	1560–1812	Par. Reg. Soc. . .	1898
Bishop Middleham, Durham .	1559–1812	Northm. & Dur. P.R.S.	1906
Bitterley, Salop . . .	1658–1812	Sal. P.R.S. Hereford Dioc. . . .	1902
Bitton, Gloucs. . . .	1572–1674	Par. Reg. Soc. . .	1900
Blacktoft, Yorks . .	1700–1812	Yorks P.R.S. . .	1901
Bobbingworth, Essex . .	1558–1785	F. A Crisp . .	1888
Bocking, Essex . . .	1558–1639	J. J. Godwin . .	1903
Bolton Abbey, Yorks .	1689–1812	A. P. Howes . .	1895
Bolton-by-Bolland, Yorks .	1558–1724	Yorks P.R.S. . .	1904
Boningale, Salop . .	1690–1812	Sal. P.R.S. Lich. Dioc.	1901
Bothal, Northm. . . .	1678–1812	Northm. & Dur. P.R.S.	1901
Boughton-under-Blean, Kent .	1558–1626	Par. Reg. Soc. . .	1903
Bramfield, Suffolk . . .	1539–1596	T. G. Hill . .	1894
Brampton, Norfolk . .	1600–1812	A. T. Michell . .	1897
Brantingham, Yorks . .	1653–1812	Yorks P.R.S. . .	1902
Bretforton, Worc. . .	1538–1837	W. H. Shawcross .	1908
Breward St., Cornwall .	1558–1900	T. Taylor . .	1900
Brewood, Staffs . .	1562–1812	Staffs P.R.S. . .	1906
Brindle, Lancs . .	1558–1714	Lanc. P.R.S. . .	1901
Broad-Chalk, Wilts . .	1538–1780	A. G. Moore . .	1880
Bromfield, Salop . . .	1559–1812	Sal. P.R.S. Hereford Dioc. . . .	1903
Broseley, Salop . . .	1570–1750	A. F. C. Longley .	1889–90
Broughton, Salop . . .	1705–1812	Sal. P.R.S. Lich. Dioc.	1900
Brundish, Suffolk . .	1562–1785	F. A. Crisp . .	1885
Bruton, Som.	1554–1680	Par. Reg. Soc. . .	1907
Buckenham, Old, Norfolk .	1565–1649	Walter Rye . .	1902
Burgh-next-Aylsham, Norfolk.	1563–1810	Norf. Archæol. . .	vol. ix.
Burnley, Lancs . . .	1562–1653	Lanc. P.R.S. . .	1899
Burnsall, Yorks . . .	1559–1812	W. J. Stavert . .	1893
Burton Fleming, Yorks . .	1538–1812	Yorks P.R.S. . .	1899
Burton Kirk, Yorks . .	1541–1711	F. A. Collins, 2 vols. . .	{ 1887, 1902 }
Burton, Long, Dorset . .	1580–1812	C. H. Mayo . .	1894
Bury, Lancs	1590–1646	Lanc. P.R.S. . .	1898
Buxhall, Suffolk . . .	1558–1699	Hist. of Buxhall . .	1902
Calverley, York . . .	1574–1720	S. Margerison, 2 vols. .	{ 1880, 1887 }
Cambridge, St. Michael .	1538–1837	Camb. Antiq. Soc. xxviii. . . .	1891
Canon Frome, Hereford . .	1680–1812	Par. Reg. Soc. . .	1905
Canterbury, St. Alphege .	1558–1800	J. M. Cowper . .	1889
„ Cathedral .	1564–1873	Harl. Reg. Soc. . .	1875
„ St. Dunstan . .	1559–1800	J. M. Cowper . .	1887
„ St. George . .	1538–1800	„ . .	1891
„ St. Mary Magdalen	1559–1800	„ . .	1890
„ St. Paul . .	1562–1800	„ . .	1893
„ St. Peter . .	1560–1808	„ . .	1880

18

Parish.	Years Included.	By whom Printed.	Date of Issue.
Carburton, Notts	1528–1812	G. W. Marshall	1888
Carlton, Suffolk	1538–1885	F. A. Crisp	1886
Castle Church, Staffs	1567–1812	Staffs P.R.S.	1903
Caundle, Bishop, Dorset	1570–1814	C. H. Mayo	1895
Chelmarsh, Salop	1556–1812	Sal. P.R.S.	1903
Chelsham, Surrey	1669–1812	Surrey P.R.S.	1907
Cherry Burton, Yorks	1561–1740	Yorks P.R.S.	1903
Chesham, Bucks	1538–1636	J. W. G. Pegge	1904
Chester Cathedral	1687–1812	Par. Reg. Soc.	1904
Chillesford, Suffolk	1740–1776	F. A. Crisp	1886
Chillingham, Northm.	1696	Robert Blair	...
Chipping, Lanc.	1559–1694	Lanc. P.R.S.	1903
Chipstead, Surrey	1656–1812	Surrey P.R.S.	1909
Chirbury, Salop	1629–1812	Sal. P.R.S. Heref. Dioc.	1903
Chislet, Kent	1538–1707	Robt. Hovenden	1887
Claverley, Salop	1568–1685	Sal. P.R.S. Lichf. Dioc.	...
Cleobury Mortimer, Salop	1601–1812	Sal. P.R.S. Hereford Dioc.	1904
Clerkenwell, St. James, Midds.	1551–1754	Harl. Reg. Soc.	vols. ix. and xx. 1884, 1899
Clive, Salop	1671–1812	Sal. P.R.S. Lichf. Dioc.	1902
Clunbury, Salop	1574–1812	Par. Reg. Soc.	1901
Clyst, St. George, Devon	1565–1812	,, ,,	1899
Cockenham, Lanc.	1595–1657	Lanc. P.R.S.	1904
Colchester, St. Leonard	1670	F. A. Crisp	...
Coleby, Linc.	1561–1812	Par. Reg. Soc.	1903
Colne, Lanc.	1599–1653	Lanc. P.R.S.	1904
Colton, Lanc.	1623–1812	A. A. Williams	1891
Columb St., Major, Cornw.	1539–1780	A. J. Jewers	1881
Condover, Salop	1570–1812	Sal. P.R.S. Lichf. Dioc.	1901
Coniscliffe, Durham	1590–1812	Northm. & Dur. P.R.S.	1908
Coniston, Lanc.	1599–1700	Lanc. P.R.S.	1907
Conistone, Yorks	1567–1812	W. J. Stavert	1894
Conway, Carnarvon	1541–1793	A. Hadley	1900
Cressage, Salop	1605–1812	Par. Reg. Soc.	1900
Cropthorne, Worc.	1557–1717	F. A. Crisp	1896
Croston, Lanc.	1543–1685	Lanc. P.R.S.	1900
Culpho, Suffolk	1721–1886	F. A. Crisp	1886
Cundall, Yorks	1582–1780	H. D. Eshelby	1898
Dale Abbey, Derby	1677–1731	Derb. Arch. Journ.	1900
Dalston, Camb.	1570–1812	J. Wilson	1893
Denham (nr. Bury), Suffolk	1539–1850	S. H. A. Harvey	1904
Denton, Durham	1586–1662	J. R. Walbran	1842
Dewsbury, Yorks	1538–1653	S. J. Chadwick	1898
Didsbury, Lanc.	1561–1757	Lanc. P.R.S.	1900
Dinsdale, Low Durham	1556–1812	Soc. of Antiq. of Newcastle-upon-Tyne	...
Doddington, Linc.	1562–1812	Par. Reg. Soc.	1898

Parish.	Years Included.	By whom Printed.	Date of Issue.
Donington, Salop . . .	1556–1812	Sal. P.R.S. Lichf. Dioc.	1901
Dunham, Notts . . .	1654–1812	Thoroton Reg. Soc. .	...
Durham, St. Margaret .	1558–1812	Northm. & Dur. P.R.S.	1904
,, St. Oswald . .	1538–1751	A. W. Headlam . .	1891
,, the Cathedral .	1609–1896	Harl. Reg. Soc. . .	1897
,, St. Mary . . .	1568–1812	Northm. & Dur. P.R.S.	1908
Durnford, Wilts . .	1574–1650	Sir T. Phillipps .	1823
Eastham, Cheshire . .	1598–1700	F. Sanders . .	1891
Ebchester, Durham .	1689–1812	Northm. & Dur. P.R.S.	1900
Ecclesfield, Yorks . .	1558–1621	A. S. Gatty . .	1878
Eccleston, Lanc. . .	1603–1694	Lanc. P.R.S. . .	1903
Edburton, Sussex .	1558–1673	C. H. Wilkie .	1884
Edgton, Salop . .	1722–1812	Par. Reg. Soc. . .	1903
Edlingham, Northm. .	1658–1812	Northm. & Dur. P.R.S.	1903
Edstaston, Salop . .	1712–1812	Sal. P.R.S. . .	1908
Edwinstow, Notts .	1634–1758	G. W. Marshall . .	1891
Eglingham, Northm. .	1662–1812	Northm. & Dur. P.R.S.	1899
Elland, Yorks . .	1559–1640	J. W. Clay . .	1897
Ellough, Suffolk . .	1540–1812	F. A. Crisp . .	1886
Elmham, North, Norfolk .	1536–1631	A. G. Legge . .	1888
Elmsted, Kent . . .	1552–1812	C. H. Wilkie . .	1891
Elsdon, Northumb. . .	1672–1812	Soc. of Antiq. Newcastle-on-Tyne	1903
Esh, Durham . . .	1567–1812	,,	1896
Exeter, the Cathedral .	1594–1813	Dev. & Corn. Rec. Soc.	{ 1905– 1907
Farnham, Yorks .	1569–1812	Par. Reg. Soc. . .	1905
Felkirk ,, .	1701–1812	A. N. J. Royds . .	1904
Fewston ,, . .	1593–1812	T. Parkinson . .	1899
Fillongley, Warw. . .	1538–1653	...	1893
Fitz, Salop . . .	1559–1812	Sal. P.R.S. .	1903
Ford ,, . . .	1589–1812	,, ,, . .	1900
Fownhope, Hereford .	1538–1673	F. A. Crisp . .	1899
Frodesley, Salop . .	1547–1812	Sal. P.R.S. . .	1903
Frodsham, Cheshire .	1558–1812	Edmund Jermyn . .	1908
Frostenden, Suffolk .	1538–1791	F. A. Crisp . .	1887
Fryston-Monk, Yorks .	1538–1678	Par. Reg. Soc. . .	1896
Fyfield, Essex . . .	1538–1700	F. A. Crisp . .	1896
Gargrave, Yorks . .	1558–1812	Yorks P.R.S. . .	1907
Garrigill, Cumb. . .	1699–1730	C. Caine . .	1901
Glasbury, Brecon . .	1660–1836	Par. Reg. Soc. . .	1904
Godalming, Surrey . .	1582–1688	Surrey, P.R.S. . .	1905
Greensted, Essex . .	1558–1812	F. A. Crisp . .	1892
Greet, Salop . . .	1728–1812	Sal. P.R.S. . .	1905
Grimsby, Great, Linc. .	1538–1812	G. S. Stephenson .	1889
Grimshill, Salop . .	1592–1812	Sal. P.R.S. . .	1902
Grinton, Yorks . .	1640–1807	Yorks P.R.S. . .	1905
Gulval, Cornwall . .	1598–1812	G. B. Miller . .	1893
Habberley, Salop . .	1670–1822	Sal. P.R.S. . .	1906

Parish.	Years Included.	By whom Printed.	Date of Issue.
Hackney, York . . .	1557–1783	Yorks P.R.S. . .	1906
Hadham, Little, Herts . .	1559–1812	W. Minet . .	1907
Halifax, York . . .	1538–1641	W. J. Walker . .	1883
Hallam, West, Derby	1538–1691	Derb. Arch. Soc. Journ.	1887
Halston, Salop . . .	1686–1812	Sal. P.R.S. . .	1899
Hampden, Great, Bucks.	1557–1812	E. A. Ebblewhite	1888
Hampsthwaite, Yorks .	1603–1807	Yorks P.R.S. .	1902
Hamstall-Ridware, Staffs .	1598–1812	Staffs ,,	1904
Hanham Abbots, Glouc.	1584–1681	Par. Reg. Soc. .	1908
Hanwood, Salop .	1559–1763	Sal. P.R.S. .	1900
Harbledown, Kent .	1557–1800	J. M. Cowper .	1907
Harewood, Hereford .	1671–1812	J. H. Parry .	1900
Harley, Salop .	1598–1812	Sal. P.R.S. .	1902
Harrow, Middl.	1558–1653	W. O. Hewlett	1900
Hartshead, Yorks .	1612–1812	York P.R.S. .	1903
Haslemere, Surrey .	1594–1812	Par. Reg. Soc. . .	1906
Haughton, Staffs .	1570–1812	Staffs P.R.S. . .	1902
Haughton-le-Skerne, Durham.	1569	Robert Blair . .	...
Hawkshead, Lanc. .	1568–1704	H. S. Cowper .	1890
Hawnby, Yorks .	1653–1722	E. E. Thoyts . .	1890
Hawnes, Beds .	1596–1812	W. Briggs . .	1891
Haydon, Linc. .	1559–1649	Par. Reg. Soc. . .	1897
Headon, Notts . .	1566–1812	,, ,, . .	1902
Hebburn, Northm. . .	1680–1812	Northm. & Dur. P.R.S.	1901
Heswall, Cheshire .	1559–1729	T. H. Way .	1897
Holbeach, Linc. .	1606–1641	G. G. W. Macdonald .	1892
Holnest, Dorset .	1589–1812	C. H. Mayo . .	1894
Hopton Castle, Salop .	1538–1812	Par. Reg. Soc. . .	1901
Horbling, Linc	1653–1837	H. Peet . .	1895
Horbury, Yorks .	1598–1812	Yorks P.R.S. . .	1900
Hordley, Salop	1686–1812	Sal. P.R.S. . .	1908
Horncastle, Linc. . .	1558–1850	J. C. Hudson . .	1900
Horningsheath, Suffolk .	1559–1639	S. H. A. Harvey	1892
Howden, Yorks .	1593–1702	Yorks P.R.S. .	1904–5
Huggate ,,	1539–1812	Par. Reg. Soc. . .	1901
Hughley, Salop	1576–1812	,, ,, . .	1901
Ickworth, Suffolk . . .	1566–1890	S. H. A. Harvey .	1894
Ingleby-Greenhow, Yorks	1539–1800	J. Howell . . .	1889
Ingram, Northm. . .	1682–1812	Northm. & Dur. P.R.S.	1903
Ipswich, St. Nicholas .	1539–1710	Par. Reg. Soc. . .	1897
,, St. Peter . .	1662–1700	F. A. Crisp . .	1897
Irby-upon-Humber, Linc. .	1558–1785	,, ,, . .	1890
Kegidog, Denbigh .	1694–1749	,, ,, .	1890
Kelsale, Suffolk . .	1538–1812	,, ,, .	1887
Kempsford, Glouc. . .	1653–1700	,, ,, . .	1887
Kenley, Salop .	1682–1812	Sal. P.R.S. . .	1902
Kensington, Middl. .	1539–1673	Harl. Reg. Soc. . .	1890
Kingston, Kent . .	1558–1837	C. H. Wilkie . .	1893
Kinnerley, Salop . .	1667–1812	Sal. P.R.S. . .	1907
Kippax, Yorks .	1539–1812	Yorks P.R.S. . .	1901
Kirkburton, Yorks . . .	1541–1711	F. A. Collins . .	1887

Parish.	Years Included.	By whom Printed.	Date of Issue.
Kirk Ella, Yorks . . .	1558–1841	Par. Reg. Soc. . .	1897
Kirklington ,, . .	1568–1812	Yorks P.R.S. . .	1909
Kirkoswald, Cumb. . .	1577–1812	Rev. Canon Thornleigh	1901
Knaresdale, Northm. . .	1695	Robert Blair .	...
Knightwick, Worc. . .	1538–1812	J. B. Wilson . .	1891
Knoddishall, Suff. . .	1566–1705	Arthur T. Winn .	1907
Lambourne, Essex . . .	1582–1709	F. A. Crisp . .	1890
Ledbury, Hereford . .	1556–1676	Par. Reg. Soc. . .	1899
Ledsham, Yorks . .	1539, 1812	York P.R.S. . .	1906
Lee, Kent . . .	1579–1784	L. L. Duncan . .	1888
Leebotwood, Salop .	1547–1812	Sal. P.R.S. .	1905
Leeds, St. Peter . .	1572–1722	Thoresby Soc. .	1889
Leigh, Lanc. . .	1559–1624	J. H. Hanning . .	1882
Lesbury, Northm. . . .	1689–1812	Northm. & Dur. P.R.S.	1908
Letheringham, Suffolk . .	1588–1812	P. C. Rushen . .	1901
Lewisham, Kent . .	1558–1750	L. L. Duncan .	1891
Leyland, Lanc. . .	1656–1710	Manch. Rec. Soc.	1890
Liverpool, Lanc. . . .	1660–1673	Henry Peet . .	1873
Llandinabo, Heref. . .	1596–1812	J. H. Parry . .	1900
Llansannan, Denbigh . .	1666–1812	R. Ellis . .	1900
Llantrithyd, Glamorgan . .	1571–1810	H. S. Hughes . .	1888
London, All Hallows, London Wall . . .	1559–1675	R. Hovenden . .	1878
,, St. Antholin . .	1538–1734	Harl. Reg. Soc. . .	1883
,, St. Botolph, Bishops-gate . . .	1558–1753	A. W. C. Hallen .	{ 1886, 1895
,, Charter House Chapel	1671–1839	Harl. Reg. Soc. .	1892
,, Christ Church, New-gate Street . .	1538–1754	,, ,, .	1895
,, Christopher, St., Le Stocks . . .	1538–1781	E. Freshfield .	1882
,, Dionis, St., Backchurch	1538–1754	Harl. Reg. Soc. . .	1886
,, Edmund, St. . .	1670–1812	W. Brigg . . .	1892
,, Helen, St., Bishops-gate . . .	1575–1837	Harl. Reg. Soc. . .	1904
,, Olave, St., Hart St. .	1563	A. Povah's *Annals of St. Olave* . .	1894
,, Lincoln's Inn Chapel	1695–1852	*Records of Linc. Inn*, vol. ii. . . .	1896
,, Martin, St., In-the-Fields . . .	1550–1619	Harl. Reg. Soc. . .	1899
,, Martin, St., Outwich	1670–1873	,, ,, . .	1905
,, Mary, St., Aldermary	1558–1754	,, ,, .	1880
,, Paul, St., Covent Garden . . .	1653–1837	,, ,, .	1906–8
,, Paul, St., Cathedral .	1697–1896	,, ,, .	1899
,, Peter, St., Cornhill	1538–1774	,, ,, .	1877–9
,, Temple Church .	1628–1853	Burial Register . .	1905
,, Thomas, St., The Apostle . . .	1538–1754	Harl. Reg. Soc. . .	1881
,, Vedast, St., Foster Lane . . .	1558–1837	,, ,, . .	1902–3

Parish.	Years Included.	By whom Printed.	Date of Issue.
London, Westminster Abbey .	1606–1875	Harl. Reg. Soc. .	1875
Longdon-on-Tern, Salop. .	1692–1812	Sal. P.R.S. .	1902
Longnor ,, .	1586–1812	,, ,, .	1905
Lowestoft, Suffolk . . .	1650–1750	F. A. Crisp .	1901
Luffenham, North, Rutland .	1572–1812	Par. Reg. Soc. .	1906
Lydham, Salop . . .	1596–1812	Sal. P.R.S. .	1903
Lydlinch, Dorset . .	1559–1812	Par. Reg. Soc. .	1899
Macclesfield, Cheshire . .	1572–1812	Macc. Par. Mag.	1886
Madron, Cornwall . .	1577–1726	G. B. Millett .	1877
Manfield, Yorks . .	1594–1812	W. J. Stavert . .	1898
Marlow, Great, Bucks . .	1592–1611	Bucks P.R.S. . .	1904
Marsham, Norfolk . .	1538–1836	A. T. Michell .	1889
Marshfield, Glouc. . . .	1558–1693	F. A. Crisp .	1893
Marske-by-the-Sea, Yorks	1569–1812	Yorks P.R.S. . .	1903
Maxey, Northants . . .	1538–1713	W. D. Sweeting . .	1892
Melverley, Salop . .	1723–1812	Par. Reg. Soc. . .	1899
Merstham, Surrey . .	1538–1812	,, ,, .	1902
Methley, Yorks . .	1560–1812	Thoresby Soc. vol. xli.	1903
Middleton St. George, Durham	1616–1812	Northm. & Dur. P.R.S.	1906
Middleton, Lanc. . .	1594–1663	Lanc. P.R.S. .	1902
Middleton Scriven, Salop	1728–1812	Sal. P.R.S. .	1906
Milwich, Staffs. . . .	1573–1711	Staffs P.R.S. . .	1904
Monk-Hopton, Salop .	1698–1812	Sal. P.R.S. . .	1903
Montford, Salop . . .	1559–1812	,, ,,	1906
Morden, Surrey . .	1634–1812	Par. Reg. Soc. .	1901
More, Salop . . .	1569–1812	Sal. P.R.S. .	1900
Moreton, Essex . .	1558–1759	F. A. Crisp .	1890
Moreton-Corbet, Salop . .	1580–1812	Par. Reg. Soc. .	1901
Moreton-Say ,, . .	1690–1812	Sal. P.R.S. .	1907
Moze, Essex . .	1551–1678	F. A. Crisp .	1899
Munsley, Hereford . .	1662–1812	Par. Reg. Soc. .	1903
Muston, Leic. . .	1561–1730	T. M. Blagg .	1908
Neenton, Salop . .	1538–1812	Sal. P.R.S. . .	1903
Newchurch Kenyon, Leic. .	1599–1812	Par. Reg. Soc. . .	1905
Newenden, Kent . . .	1559–1812	,, ,, .	1897
Norwich, St. George Tombland	1538–1707	G. B. Jay . .	1891
,, St. Michael at Plea .	1538–1695	T. R. Tallack . .	1892
Oldham, Lanc. . .	1558–1661	Giles Shaw .	1889
Ollerton, Notts . . .	1592–1812	G. W. Marshall . .	1896
Olney, Bucks . . .	1665–1812	Bucks P.R.S. . .	1907–8
Ongar, Chipping, Essex .	1558–1750	F. A. Crisp .	1886
Ormskirk, Lanc. . . .	1557–1626	Lanc. P.R.S. .	1902
Orpington, Kent . .	1560–1754	H. C. Kinley .	1895
Oswestry, Salop . .	1558–1630	Sal. P.R.S. . .	1904–6
Otley, Yorks . .	1562–1812	Yorks P.R.S. . .	1908
Padiham, Lanc. . .	1573–1650	Lanc. P.R.S. .	1903
Pakenham, Suffolk . .	1564–1766	F. A. Crisp .	1888
Pakington, York . .	1570–1731	Yorks P.R.S. . .	1900
Parkham, Devon . .	1537–1812	Dev. & Corn. Rec. Soc.	1906

Parish.	Years Included.	By whom Printed.	Date of Issue.
Peak Forest, Derby . .	1678–1812	G. W. Marshall . .	1901
Pencoyd, Hereford . . .	1564–1812	G. J. H. Parry . .	1900
Pennington, Lanc. . . .	1612–1702	Lanc. P.R.S. . .	1907
Penrith, Cumb. . . .	1556–1601	G. Watson . . .	1893
Perlethorpe, Notts . . .	1528–1812	G. W. Marshall . .	1887
Peterston - super - Ely, Gla-morgan	1749–1812	A. F. C. C. Langley .	1888
Pickhill, Yorks . . .	1567–1812	Yorks P.R.S. . .	1904
Pitchford, Salop . . .	1558–1812	Par. Reg. Soc. . .	1900
Plympton, St. Mary, Devon .	1603–1683	Par. Mag. . .	1891,etc.
,, St. Maurice ,, .	1616–1812	,, ,, . . .	1888,etc.
Pontesbury, Salop . .	1538–1812	Sal. P.R.S. . .	1909
Poulton-le-Fylde, Lanc. .	1591–1677	Lanc. P.R.S. . .	1904
Prestbury, Cheshire . .	1560–1636	Lanc. & Chesh. Rec. Soc., vol. v. . .	1881
Priors Dean, Hants . .	1538–1812	T. Hervey . .	1886
Ratlinghope, Salop. . .	1755–1812	Sal. P.R.S. . .	1909
Rattlesden, Suffolk. .	1558–1758	J. R. Olorenshaw .	1900
Ravenstonedale, Westm..	1571–1812	R. W. Metcalfe . .	1893–4
Reading, St. Mary . .	1538–1812	G. P. Crawford . .	1892
Redruth, Cornwall . .	1560–1716	F. C. Peter . .	1894
Richmond, Surrey . .	1583–1720	Surrey P.R.S. . .	1905
Ridware, Pipe, Staffs .	1561–1812	Staffs P.R.S . .	1905
Rilston, Yorks . . .	1559–1812	C. H. Lowe . .	1895–6
Rocester, Staffs . . .	1566–1705	Staffs P.R.S. . .	1906
Rochdale, Lanc. . .	1582–1641	H. Fishwick . .	1888–9
Rochester, Cathedral . .	1657–1837	Tho. Shindler . .	1892
Roos, Yorks . . .	1571–1812	R. B. Machell . .	1888
Rothbury, Northm. . .	1658–1812	Par. Magazine . .	...
Rotherham ,, . .	1542–1812	John Guest . . .	1879
Rothwell, Yorks . .	1538–1639	Yorks P.R.S. . .	1906
Ronington, Warw. . .	1612–1812	Par. Reg. Soc. . .	1899
Rushall, Norfolk . .	1686–1812	Records of Rushall .	1892
Rushbrook, Suffolk . .	1567–1850	S. H. A. Hervey .	1903
Ryton, Durham . .	1581–1812	Northm. & Dur. P.R.S.	1902
Saddleworth, Yorks . .	1613–1800	J. Radcliffe . .	1888–91
Sanderstead, Surrey . .	1564–1812	Surrey P.R.S. . .	1908
Sarnesfield, Hereford .	1660–1897	Par. Reg. Soc. . .	1898
Scorborough, Yorks . .	1653–1800	Yorks P.R.S. . .	1901
Selattyn, Salop . . .	1557–1812	Par. Reg. Soc. . .	1906
Shackerstone, Leic. . .	1558–1630	Leic. Arch. Soc. Trans. vol. xv. . .	...
Sheinton, Salop . .	1658–1812	Sal. P.R.S. . .	1902
Shelton, Notts . . .	1595–1812	T. M. Blagg . .	1900
Sheriff Hales, Salop . .	1557–1812	Sal. P.R.S. . .	1908
Shipton ,, . .	1538–1812	Par. Reg. Soc. . .	1899
Shrawardine ,, . .	1645–1812	Shrops. Arch. Soc. vol. vii. . . .	1895
Sibdon Carwood, Salop .· .	1583–1812	Par. Reg. Soc. . .	1899
Sidbury, Salop . . .	1560–1812	Sal. P.R.S. . .	1901
Simonburn, Northm. . .	1681	Robert Blair .	...

Parish.	Years Included.	By whom Printed.	Date of Issue.
Siston, Glouc. . . .	1576–1641	H. B. M'Call . .	1901
Skipton, Yorks . . .	1592–1812	W. J. Stavert . .	1894–6
Smethcote, Salop . . .	1609–1812	Par. Reg. Soc. . .	1899
Solihull, Warwick . . .	1538–1688	,, ,, . .	1904
Somerby (Grantham), Linc. .	1601–1713	Leic. Arch. Soc. .	vol. v.
Southam, Warw. . . .	1539–1657	History of Southam. .	1894
Staines, Middl. . . .	1644–1694	F. A. Crisp . .	1887
Standon, Staffs . .	1558–1812	Staffs P.R.S. . .	1902
Stanton-Lacy, Salop .	1561–1812	Sal. P.R.S. . .	1904
Stapleford-Tawney, Essex .	1558–1752	F. A. Crisp . .	1892
Stapleton, Salop . . .	1546–1812	Par. Reg. Soc. . .	1901
Stewkley, Bucks . .	1545–1643	R. B. Dickson . .	1897
Stifford, Essex . . .	1568–1783	F. A. Crisp . .	1885
Stirchley, Salop . .	1638–1812	Sal. P.R.S. . .	1904
Stockport, Cheshire . .	1584–1620	E. W. Batheley .	1889
Stoke, Essex . .	1563–1700	E. P. Gibson .	1881
Stoke Pogis, Bucks .	1563–1653	Bucks P.R.S. . .	1908
Stokeley, Yorks . .	1571–1750	Yorks P.R.S. . .	1901
Stourpaine, Dorset . .	1631–1799	E. A. Fry . . .	1900
Stourton, Wilts . .	1570–1800	Harl. Reg. Soc. .	vol. xii.
Stow, West, Suffolk .	1558–1856	S. H. A. Hervey .	1905
Stratford, Fenny, Bucks . .	1730–1812	Par. Reg. Soc.	1906
Stratford-on-Avon, Warw. .	1558–1812	,, ,, . .	1897–8
Street, Som.	1559–1762	A. J. Jewers . .	1898
Stretton, Wilts . . .	1608	Sir T. Phillipps . .	...
Stubton, Linc. . . .	1577–1628	F. A. Crisp . .	1883
Sturminster Marshall, Dorset .	1563–1812	Edith Hobday . .	1901
Swainswick, Som. . .	1557–1798	Annals of Swainswick.	1890
Tannington, Suffolk . .	1539–1714	F. A. Crisp . .	1884
Tarrant Hinton, Dorset .	1545–1812	Par. Reg. Soc. . .	1902
Tasley, Salop . . .	1563–1812	Sal. P.R.S. . .	1901
Tatenhill, Staffs . .	1563–1812	Staffs P.R.S. . .	1905
Tatsfield, Surrey . .	1690–1812	Surrey P.R.S. . .	1906
Terrington, Yorks . .	1599–1812	Yorks P.R.S. . .	1907
Thanet, St. Laurence, Kent. .	1560–1653	C. H. Wilkie . .	1902
Theydon Mount, Essex .	1564–1815	J. J. Howard . .	1891
Thorington, Suffolk .	1561–1881	T. S. Hill . .	1884
Thornbury, Glouc. .	1538–1700	Mrs. Baldwyn Childe .	...
Thornford, Dorset . .	1677–1812	Dorset Records . .	1903
Thornhill, York . .	1580–1812	Yorks P.R.S . .	1907
Thornton, Bucks . .	1562–1812	Bucks P.R.S. . .	1902
Tong, Salop	1629–1812	Sal. P.R.S. . .	1903
Topcliffe, Yorks . .	1654–1888	W. Smith . . .	1888
Toppesfield, Essex . .	1559–1650	H. B. Barnes . .	1905
Trentham, Staffs . .	1558–1812	Staffs P.R.S. . .	1906
Tynemouth, Northm. . .	1607–1703	R. H. Couchman .	1902
Uffington, Salop . .	1578–1812	Sal. P.R.S. . .	1901
Ulgham, Northm. . .	1602	Robert Blair . .	...
Ulverstone, Lanc. . .	1545–1812	C. W. Bardsley . .	1886
Upholland ,, .	1600–1735	Lanc. P.R.S. . .	1905
Uppington, Salop . .	1650–1812	Sal. P.R.S. . .	1903

Parish.	Years Included.	By whom Printed.	Date of Issue.
Upton, Berks	1588–1711	Par. Reg. Soc. . .	1897
,, Cheshire . . .	1600–1812	,, ,, . .	1900
Walesby, Notts . . .	1580–1797	,, ,, . .	1898
Wallasey, Cheshire . .	1574–1600	Lanc. and Ches. Hist. Soc. . . .	vol. xxxv.
Walsall, Staffs . . .	1570–1649	F. W. Willmore . .	1890
Walton, Bucks . . .	1598–1812	Bucks P.R.S. . .	1902
Walton-on-the-Hill, Lanc.	1586–1663	Lanc. P.R.S. . .	1900
Wanborough, Wilts . .	1582–1653	Sir Tho. Phillipps .	...
Wanborough, Surrey .	1561–1786	Surrey P.R.S. . .	1906
Wandsworth ,, .	1603–1787	J. T. Squire . .	1889
Warkworth, Northm. .	1677–1812	Soc. of Antiq., Newcastle . .	1897
Warlingham, Surrey .	1653–1812	Surrey P.R.S. .	1903–4
Warsop, Notts . . .	1539–1812	R. J. King . . .	1884
Warton, Lanc. . . .	1568–1669	Par. Mag. . .	1883, etc.
Wath-on-Dearne, Yorks .	1598–1779	Yorks P.R.S. . .	1902
Weald, South, Essex .	1539–1573	R. Hovenden . .	1889
Weddington, Warw. .	1663–1812	Par. Reg. Soc. . .	1904
Wedmore, Som. . . .	1561–1860	S. H. A. Hervey .	1888–90
Welford, Berks . . .	1559–1812	H. M. Batson . .	1892
Wellington, Som. . .	1683, etc.	Humphrey's *Hist. of Wellington* .	{ 1889– { 1908
Wellow, Notts . .	1703–1812	G. W. Marshall . .	1896
Wem, Salop . . .	1583–1675	Sal. P.R.S. . .	1908
Wenlock, Much, Salop .	1539–1560	C. Hartshorne . .	1861
Westbury, Salop . .	1637–1812	Sal. P.R.S. . .	1909
Whaddon, Glouc. . .	1674–1711	Glouc. iv. and v. .	vol. iv.
Whalley, Lanc. . .	1538–1601	Lanc. P.R.S. . .	1900
Whitburn, Durham . .	1579–1812	Northm. & Dur. P.R.S.	1904
Whitkirk, Yorks . .	1603–1700	Records of Whitkirk .	1892
Whittington, Lanc. . .	1538–1764	Lanc. P.R.S. . .	1899
,, Salop . .	1591–1812	Sal. P.R.S. . .	1909
Whorlton, Durham . .	1626–1812	Northm. & Dur. P.R.S.	1908
Wigan, Lanc. . . .	1580–1625	Lanc. P.R.S. . .	1899
Wigborough, Great, Essex	1560–1812	F. Stephenson . .	1905
,, Little ,, .	1586–1812	,, . .	,,
Wilton, Som. . . .	1558–1837	J. H. Spencer . .	1890
Winchester Cathedral .	1599–1812	Hants P.R.S. . .	1902
Windlesham, Surrey .	1677–1783	W. Glanville-Richards .	1881
Winstead, Yorks . .	1578–1811	Yorks P.R.S. . .	1900
Withington, Salop . .	1591–1812	Sal. P.R.S. . .	1904
Woldingham, Surrey .	1765–1812	Surrey P.R.S. . .	1906
Womeswold, Kent . .	1574–1812	C. H. Wilkie . .	1898
Woolstaston, Salop . .	1601–1712	Sal. P.R.S. . .	1899
Wootton-Leek, Warw. .	1685–1742	Sir T. Phillipps . .	...
Wootton, North Dorset .	1539–1786	C. H. Mayo . .	1877
Worcester, St. Alban's .	1638–1812	Par. Reg. Soc. . .	1896
,, St. Helen .	1538–1812	J. B. Wilson . .	1900
,, St. Peter the Great .	1580–1850	S. H. A. Hervey .	1903
Worksop, Notts . . .	1558–1771	G. W. Marshall . .	1894
Worthen, Salop . .	1558–1812	Sal. P.R.S. . .	1909

Parish.	Years Included.	By whom Printed.	Date of Issue.
Woughton-on-the-Green, Bucks	1558–1718	Bucks P.R.S. .	{ vols. v. and viii.
Wrockwardine, Salop . .	1591–1791	Sal. P.R.S., . .	vol. viii.
Wroxall, Warw. . . .	1586–1612	Records of Wroxall .	1903
York, the Minster . . .	1634–1836	York Arch. Soc. . .	{ vols. i., ii.,iii.,vi.
,, St. Martin's, Coney St..	1557–1812	Yorks P.R.S. .	1909
,, ,, Micklegate	1539–1653	E. Bulmer . . .	1893
,, S. Michael le Belfry .	1565–1778	Yorks P.R.S. .	{ 1899, 1901
,, Holy Trinity, Micklegate	1586–1653	W. H. F. Bateman .	1893

INDEX

Printed by
MORRISON & GIBB LIMITED
Edinburgh

THE
ANTIQUARY'S BOOKS

Edited by J. CHARLES COX, LL.D., F.S.A.

Demy 8vo.   7s. 6d. net each

MESSRS. METHUEN are publishing a series of volumes dealing with various branches of English Antiquities.

It is confidently hoped that these books will prove to be comprehensive and popular, as well as accurate and scholarly; so that they may be of service to the general reader, and at the same time helpful and trust-worthy books of reference to the antiquary or student. The writers will make every endeavour to avail them-selves of the most recent research.

The series is edited by the well-known antiquary, The Rev. J. Charles Cox, LL.D., F.S.A., Honorary Member of the Royal Archæological Institute, Corre-sponding Member of the British Archæological Associa-tion, and Council Member of the Canterbury and York Record Society, and of the British Numismatic Society. Each book is entrusted to an expert in the selected subject, and the publishers are fortunate in having secured the services of distinguished writers.

A special feature is made of the illustrations, which vary, according to the requirements of the subjects, from 50 to 150. Some are in colour. The type is large and clear, the length of each volume is about 320 pages.

METHUEN & CO., 36, ESSEX STREET, LONDON, W.C.

ENGLISH MONASTIC LIFE

By ABBOT GASQUET, O.S.B., D.D., Ph.D., D.Litt.

Third Edition. With 42 Illustrations, 5 Maps, and 3 Plans

Preface—List of Manuscripts and Printed Books—The Monastic Life—The Material Parts of a Monastery—The Monastery and its Rulers—The Obedientiaries—The Daily Life in a Monastery—The Nuns of Mediæval England—External Relations of the Monastic Orders—The Paid Servants of the Monastery—The Various Religious Orders—List of English Religious Houses—Index.

"This delightful book, so full of quaint learning, is like a painted window, through which, if one looks, one may see the old world of the Middle Ages as that world must have shown itself to a monk."—*Daily News.*

"Curiously interesting and highly instructive."—*Punch.*

"An extremely interesting summary of the laws which governed the religious and domestic life in the great monasteries."—*Yorkshire Post.*

REMAINS OF THE PREHISTORIC AGE IN ENGLAND

By BERTRAM C. A WINDLE, Sc.D., F.R.S., F.S.A.

With 94 Illustrations by Edith Mary Windle

Preface—Introductory, Divisions of the Prehistoric Period—Stone Implements, Method of Manufacture — Stone Implements, Eoliths, Palæoliths, Neolithic Types, Overlap with Metal—The Metallic Age, Copper, Bronze—Bone Implements, Engravings, Carvings, and Art of Primitive Man, Ornaments—Places of Burial, Barrows Long and Round—Megalithic Remains, Dolmens, Cists, Circles, Alignments, Menihirion—Earthworks, Camps, Dykes—Early Places of Habitation, Pit-dwellings, Hut-circles, Souterrains, Dene-holes, Beehive Houses, Pile-dwellings, Crannoges, Terramare—The Late Celtic or Early Iron Age—Physical Remains of Prehistoric Man—Appendix—Index.

"It gives a tabulated list of such remains ; divided into counties, and subdivided into earthworks, barrows, camps, dykes, megalithic monuments, and so on, with detailed explanations ; to these are added a list of museums in which specimens of prehistoric remains are preserved. Confining himself almost entirely to accepted facts in the science of archæology, the Professor devotes no more space to what he describes as theory spinning about the dates of various epochs than is necessary to present the subject with completeness, especially on its geological side. Mrs. Windle's excellent illustrations throughout the volume add greatly to its value."—*Yorkshire Post.*

THE OLD SERVICE-BOOKS OF THE ENGLISH CHURCH

By CHRISTOPHER WORDSWORTH, M.A., AND HENRY LITTLEHALES

With 38 Plates, 4 of which are in Colour

Preface—Introduction—On Mediæval Service-Books—The Various Books : Books for "Divine Service" in Choir, etc.—The Processional—Books for the Altar Service of the Mass—Books for the "Occasional Offices"—Episcopal Service-Books—The Books for Directing Public Services—Of Books used by Lay-Folk—Miscellaneous Subjects—Appendix—Index.

"It is infinitely more than a fascinating book on the treasures of past ages. It is the history of the making of a great and living book. The illustrations are most beautifully reproduced."—*St. James's Gazette.*

"Scholars will find that its pages are thoroughly trustworthy. The introduction yields a great deal of unusual knowledge pertaining to the subject. The illustrations are exceptionally numerous and creditable in execution for a book of moderate price, and are reproductions in facsimile from English originals. All save two are, we believe, given here for the first time."—*Athenæum.*

CELTIC ART IN PAGAN AND CHRISTIAN TIMES

By J. ROMILLY ALLEN, F.S.A.

With 44 Plates and 81 Illustrations in the text

Preface—The Continental Celts and How they came to Britain—Pagan Celtic Art in the Bronze Age—Pagan Celtic Art in the Early Iron Age—Celtic Art of the Christian Period—Index.

"Unquestionably the greatest living authority on the Celtic Archæology of Great Britain and Ireland, he writes as only a master of his subject can. An admirable piece of work."—*St. James's Gazette.*

"The letterpress and pictures are remarkably good throughout : both author and publishers are to be congratulated on the issue of so attractive and useful a book."—*Athenæum.*

SHRINES OF BRITISH SAINTS

By J. CHARLES WALL

With 28 Plates and 50 Illustrations in the text

Introduction—General Remarks on Shrines—St. Alban and St. Amphibalus—Shrines of Virgins and Matrons—Shrines of Prelates and Priests—Shrines of Royal Saints—Sacrilege—Index.

"The present volume may be said to be of a slightly more popular character than that on 'Old Service Books,' but the same wide research and careful compilation of facts have been employed, and the result will be, to the general reader, equally informatory and interesting."—*Academy.*

"The shrines have for the most part passed away. What they were like may be learned from this volume."—*Manchester Guardian.*

"This is a good subject and one that is well handled by Mr. Wall."—*Athenæum.*

ARCHÆOLOGY AND FALSE ANTIQUITIES

By ROBERT MUNRO, M.A., M.D., LL.D., F.R.S.E., F.S.A., Scot.

With 18 Plates, a Plan, and 63 Illustrations in the text

Preface—Prolegomena—Forged or False Antiquities in Various Parts of the European Continent—Tertiary Man in California—The Forgery of Antiquities in the British Isles—The Clyde Controversy—The Archæological Discoveries at Dunbuie, Dumbuck, and Langbank, independent of the Disputed Objects—A Critical Examination of the Disputed Objects from Dunbuie, Dumbuck, and Langbank—General and Concluding Remarks—Index.

"The author passes in review the more conspicuous instances of sham antiquities that have come to light since the beginning of the second half of the last century in Europe and in America."—*Westminster Gazette.*

"He provides us with an account of all the most famous attempts made by sinful men to impede the progress of archæology by producing forged antiquities ; and he points out a number of examples of the way in which Nature herself has done the felony, placing beneath the hand of the enthusiastic hunter of remains objects which look as if they belonged to the Stone Age, but which really belonged to the gentleman next door before he threw them away and made them *res nullius.*"—*Outlook.*

THE MANOR AND MANORIAL RECORDS
By NATHANIEL J. HONE
With 54 Illustrations

Preface—The Manor—Manorial Records—Lists of Court Rolls in Various Depositories—Miscellanea—Index.

"This book fills a hitherto empty niche in the library of popular literature. Hitherto those who desired to obtain some grasp of the origin of manors or of their administration had to consult the somewhat conflicting and often highly technical works. Mr. Hone has wisely decided not to take anything for granted, but to give lucid expositions of everything that concerns manors and manorial records."—*Guardian.*

"We could linger for a long while over the details given in this delightful volume, and in trying to picture a state of things that has passed away. It should be added that the illustrations are well chosen and instructive."—*Country Life.*

"Mr. Hone presents a most interesting subject in a manner alike satisfying to the student and the general reader."—*Field.*

ENGLISH SEALS
By J. HARVEY BLOOM, M.A., Rector of Whitchurch
With 93 Illustrations

Introductory—The Story of the Great Seal—Royal Seals of Dignity, commonly called Great Seals—Privy Seals of Sovereigns and those of Royal Courts—Seals of the Archbishops and Bishops—Equestrian and Figure-Seals of the Barons of the Realm and their Ladies—Seals of the Clergy beneath Episcopal Rank—Seals of Knights and Squires—Seals of Private Gentlemen and of Merchants—Seals of Religious Houses—Seals of Cathedrals and their Chapters—Seals of Secular Corporations—Seals of Universities and other Educational Corporations—Inscriptions upon the Great Seals of England—Charges borne in the Arms of English Dioceses and Deaneries—Arms of England—Glossary of Terms—Index.

"The book forms a valuable addition to the scholarly series in which it appears. It is admirably illustrated."—*Scotsman.*

"A careful and methodical survey of this interesting subject, the necessary illustrations being numerous and well done."—*Outlook.*

"Presents many aspects of interest, appealing to artists and heraldic students, to lovers of history and of antiquities."—*Westminster Gazette.*

"Nothing has yet been attempted on so complete a scale, and the treatise will take rank as a standard work on the subject."—*Glasgow Herald.*

THE ROYAL FORESTS OF ENGLAND
By J. CHARLES COX, LL.D., F.S.A.
With 25 Plates and 23 Illustrations in the text

Early Forests—The Forest Courts—The Forest Officers—The Beasts of the Forest—The Forest Agistments—Hounds and Hunting—The Trees of the Forest—The Forests of Northumberland, Cumberland, Westmoreland, and Durham—The Forests of Lancashire—The Forests of Yorkshire, Pickering and Galtres—The Forests of Cheshire—The Forests of Staffordshire—The Forests of the High

Peak—Duffield Frith—Sherwood Forest—The Forests of Shropshire, Worcester, Warwick, and Hereford—The Forests of Leicestershire and Rutland—The Forest of Rockingham—The Forest of Oxfordshire—The Forests of Berkshire, Bucking-hamshire, and Huntingdonshire—The Forest of Dean—The Forest of Essex—The Forest of Windsor—The Forests of Sussex—The Forests of Hampshire—The Forests of Wilts—The Forests of Dorsetshire—The Forests of Somer-setshire—The Forest of Dartmoor.

" A vast amount of general information is contained in this most interesting book."
—*Daily Chronicle.*
" The subject is treated with remarkable knowledge and minuteness, and a great addition to the book are the remarkable illustrations."—*Evening Standard.*
" The volume is a storehouse of learning. The harvest of original research. Nothing like it has been published before."—*Liverpool Post.*

THE BELLS OF ENGLAND
By CANON J. J. RAVEN, D.D., F.S.A., of Emmanuel College, Cambridge
Second Edition   With 60 Illustrations

Early History—The British Period — The Saxon Period — The Norman Period—The Thirteenth Century—Times of Development—Provincial Founders, Mediæval Uses—The Cire Perdue, Hexameters, Ornamentation—Migration of Founders, Power of Bells over Storms, etc.—The Passing Bell, Angelic Dedi-cations—The Beginning of the Black-letter Period—Early Foundries, London and the South-West—From the South Coast Eastward—The Midlands and the North—The Tudor Period—Later Founders—Change-ringing—Signa—Carillons, Hand-bells, and Tintinnabula—Legends, Traditions, Memories—Bell Poetry—Usages, Law, Conclusion.

" The history of English bells, of their founding and hanging, of their inscriptions and dedications, of their peals and chimes and carillons, of bell legends, of bell poetry and bell law, is told with a vast amount of detailed information, curious and quaint."—*Tribune.*
" The illustrations, as usual in this series, are of great interest."—*Country Life.*

THE DOMESDAY INQUEST
By ADOLPHUS BALLARD, B.A., LL.B., Town Clerk of Woodstock
With 27 Illustrations

Introductory—The Hide and the Teamland—The Vill and the Manor—The Hundred and the Shire—Sake and Soke—The Magnates—The Humbler Folk —The Appurtenances of the Manor—The Church—The Welshmen—The Stock, Eleventh Century Farming—The Encroachments—Values and Renders—The Incidence of the Geld—A Typical Village—Possessions of Certain Land-owners—Church Lands—Abstract of Population—Transcription and Extension of Frontispiece—Index.

" In point of scholarship and lucidity of style this volume should take a high place in the literature of the Domesday Survey."—*Daily Mail.*
" Replete with information compiled in the most clear and attractive fashion."—*Liverpool Post.*
" The author holds the balance freely between rival theories."—*Birmingham Post.*
" Most valuable and interesting."—*Liverpool Mercury.*
" A brilliant and lucid exposition of the facts."—*Standard.*
" A vigorous and independent commentary."—*Tribune.*

PARISH LIFE IN MEDIÆVAL ENGLAND

By ABBOT GASQUET, O.S.B., D.D., PH.D., D.LITT.

Second Edition   With 39 Illustrations

List of Manuscript and Printed Authorities—The Parish—The Parish Church —The Parish Clergy—The Parish Officials—Parochial Finance—The Parish Church Services—Church Festivals—The Sacraments—The Parish Pulpit— Parish Amusements—Guilds and Fraternities—Index.

" A rich mine of well-presented information."—*World.*
" A captivating subject very ably handled."—*Illustrated London News.*
" A worthy sequel to the Abbot's scholarly work on monastic life."—*Liverpool Post.*
" Essentially scholarly in spirit and treatment."—*Tribune.*

THE BRASSES OF ENGLAND

By HERBERT W. MACKLIN, M.A., St. John's College, Cambridge. President of the Monumental Brass Society

Second Edition   With 85 Illustrations

Introductory—Brasses in the Reigns of the Two First Edwards, 1272–1327 —The Golden Age of Plantagenet Rule, 1327–1399—Architectural Ornament —Foreign Workmanship—The Mediæval Clergy of England—The Lancastrian Period, 1400–1453—The Wars of the Roses, 1453–1485—Brasses in the Tudor Period, 1485–1547—Spoliation of the Monasteries—The Elizabethan Revival, 1558–1625—Brasses and Despoiled Slabs—Index of Places—General Index.

"There is no volume which covers the ground so fully as this study."—*Birmingham Post.*
" Mr. Macklin writes with enviable lucidity."—*Standard.*
"Reveals the value of English brasses as historical documents."—*Westminster Gazette.*
" The illustrations are plentiful and excellent."—*Spectator.*

ENGLISH CHURCH FURNITURE

By J. CHARLES COX, LL.D., F.S.A., and A. HARVEY, M.B.

Second Edition   With 121 Illustrations

Altars, Altar Slabs, Altar Rails, Altar Screens or Reredoses—Church Plate, Chalice and Paten, Pyx, Cruets and Flagons, Spoons, Pax, Censers, Chrismatories, Altar and Processional Crosses, Croziers and Mitres, Alms Dishes, Heraldic Church Plate, Cuirbouilli Cases, Pewter—Piscina, Sedilia, Easter Sepulchre, Lectern—Screens and Rood-lofts—Pulpits and Hour Glasses — Fonts, Font Covers, Holy-water Stoups—Alms Boxes, Offertory Boxes, and Collecting Boxes —Thrones and Chairs, Stalls and Misericords, Seats and Benches, Pews, Galleries, Church Chests—Almeries or Cupboards, Cope Chests, Banner-stave Lockers— The Lights of a Church—Church Libraries and Chained Books—Church Embroidery—Royal Arms—Ten Commandments—General Index.

" A mine of carefully ordered information, for the accuracy of which Dr. Cox's name on the title-page is a sufficient guarantee."—*Athenæum.*